THE
LUTHERANS

THE
LUTHERANS

STUDENT EDITION

L. DeANE LAGERQUIST

Westport, Connecticut
London

The Library of Congress has cataloged the hardcover edition as follows:

Lagerquist, L. DeAne.
   The Lutherans / L. DeAne Lagerquist.
      p.   cm.—(Denominations in America, ISSN 0193–6883 ; no. 9)
   Includes bibliographical references and index.
   ISBN 0–313–27549–1 (alk. paper)
     1. Lutheran Church—United States. I. Title. II. Series.
  BX8041.L34 1999
  284.1'73—dc21   99–22099

British Library Cataloguing in Publication Data is available.

An expanded hardcover edition of *The Lutherans* is available from
Greenwood Press, an imprint of Greenwood Publishing Group, Inc.
(Denominations in America, Number 9; ISBN 0–313–27549–1).

Library of Congress Catalog Card Number: 99–22099
ISBN: 0–275–96393–4 (pbk.)

First published in 1999

Praeger Publishers, 88 Post Road West, Westport, CT 06881
An imprint of Greenwood Publishing Group, Inc.
www.praeger.com

Printed in the United States of America

The paper used in this book complies with the
Permanent Paper Standard issued by the National
Information Standards Organization (Z39.48–1984).

10 9 8 7 6 5 4 3 2 1

"for all the saints . . . "
with gratitude for the lives of
Gerhard Belgum and
Paul Sonnack

CONTENTS

FOREWORD

The Praeger series of denominational studies follows a distinguished precedent. These current volumes improve on earlier works by including more churches than before and by looking at all of them in a wider cultural context. The prototype of this series appeared a century ago. Between 1893 and 1897, twenty-four scholars collaborated in publishing thirteen volumes known popularly as the American Church History Series. These scholars found twenty religious groups to be worthy of separate treatment, either as major sections of a volume or as whole books in themselves. Scholars in this current series have found that outline to be unrealistic, with regional subgroups no longer warranting separate status and others having declined to marginality. Twenty organizations in the earlier series survive as nine in this series, and two churches and an inter-denominational bureau have been omitted. The old series also excluded some important churches of that time; others have gained great strength since then. So today, a new list of denominations, rectifying imbalance and recognizing modern significance, features many groups not included a century ago. The solid core of the old series remains in this new one, and in the present case a wider range of topics makes the study of denominational life in America more inclusive.

Some recent denominational histories have improved with greater attention to primary sources and more rigorous scholarly standards. But they have too frequently pursued themes for internal consumption alone. Volumes in the Praeger series strive to surmount such parochialism while remaining grounded in the specific materials of concrete ecclesiastical traditions. They avoid placing a single denomination above others in its distinctive truth claims, ethical norms, and liturgical patterns. Instead, they set the history of each church in the larger religious and social context that shaped the emergence of notable denominational features. In this way the authors in this series help us understand the interaction that has occurred between different churches and the broader aspects of American culture.

Each of the historical studies in this current series has a strong biographical focus, using the real-life experiences of men and women in church life to highlight significant elements of an unfolding sequence. The first part(s) of every volume singles out important watershed issues that affected a denomination's outlook and discusses the roles of those who influenced the flow of events. The last part consists of biographical sketches, featuring those persons and many others who contributed to the vitality of their religious heritage. This format enables authors to emphasize the distinctive features of their chosen subject and at the same time to recognize the sharp particularities of individual attributes in the cumulative richness that their denomination possesses.

The author of this volume has been associated with Lutheran institutions for more than two decades, both during the course of her formal training and in her current professoriate at St. Olaf College. She brings many new strengths to a perception of Lutheran experience as it has unfolded in the United States. This denomination has traditionally been defined by the leadership of male clergy and theology, particularly as expressed in the Augsburg Confession and the Book of Concord. Lagerquist pays due attention to these elements, locating precedents for thought and polity in Europe before bringing them to this country. Then in full historical narrative she depicts the colonial experience of American Lutheran beginnings and expands on them through the nineteenth century. Familiar categories receive full treatment here.

But that is hardly enough these days, and Lagerquist distinguishes her contribution by highlighting new categories. She is especially interested in the question of gender as related to leadership roles, and she repeatedly enriches our reading by mentioning the myriad ways in which women have served as the backbone of Lutheran enterprises. A concomitant of that interest is a focus on laity in general as complement to, not as substitute for, ordained clergy. The topic of ethnic identity has usually been basic to Lutheran studies, and here too Lagerquist notes the centrality of German and Scandinavian peoples who populate the denomination's many varieties. But she moves beyond the old limits to include other groups, including African Americans, and depicts the growth of churches as they expanded from Pennsylvania throughout states in the upper Midwest. Lagerquist notes the worth of traditional emphases on the Bible and magisterial sacraments. But readers benefit even more through her supplemental discussions of worship patterns and education that emerged in the American heartland. The people express modern versions of a tradition that began in Europe, one that has culminated in these times as the Evangelical Lutheran Church in America. This important volume provides us with a microcosm of what has transpired in every denomination on this continent.

HENRY WARNER BOWDEN

PREFACE

This book has come to life slowly, over half a dozen years and through an equal number of moves in household and office. As I have been at work, I have received assistance of various sorts from a myriad of people, some knowing and some unknowing. The project has benefited from this aid, as have I. Readers will share my gratitude for the improvements that resulted and may wish that I had listened more to the counsel of others to correct the faults that remain. No work of human hands is perfect; this one has limitations and flaws. I hope that it brings its readers both understanding of the lives of the people portrayed here and deeper insight into the dynamics that are common in human efforts to live faithfully.

Financial support for this work came from St. Olaf College, notably, in the form of a sabbatical in 1994–1995; from the Louisville Institute for a research leave in 1992; and from the Evangelical Lutheran Church in America by way of the J.C.K. Preus Leadership Award. Technical support from librarians and archivists at St. Olaf, Luther Seminary, Pacific Lutheran Theological Seminary, Lutheran Theological Seminary at Chicago, Lutheran Theological Seminary Philadelphia, and the Evangelical Lutheran Church in America (ELCA) has been crucial to my progress. Bryn Geffert at St. Olaf gave me the astonishing tool of a new electronic index just when I most needed it. Several St. Olaf students worked diligently at the details of biographies and references. Anna Marie Johnson, in particular, helped to put the notes right.

Along the way opportunities to present work related to this book have allowed pursuit of particular issues and provided useful response: at Carthage College, "A Question of Belonging"; at the Lutheran Deaconess Conference, " 'Peculiar Identity': The Beguines, the Lutheran Deaconess Association, and the All-American Girls' Professional Baseball League''; at Lutheran Theological Seminary, "Revisiting the Founding of Philadelphia Seminary" (published in *Lutheran Quarterly*); at the Lutheran Historical Conference, "The Henkels: A

Family and a Church through Six Generations''; at the American Society of
Church History, "The Problems of Denominational History." At the outset I
was also privileged to be simultaneously engaged in two projects related to
multicultural issues in the ELCA and found that activity informing my research
questions.

The opportunity to make this study came to me through the kindness of
Christa Ressmeyer Klein. This is not the book she would have written, but it is
informed by her fine scholarship. I have also been instructed by the work of
members of the Lutheran Historical Conference, in particular, by conversations
with Susan Wilds McArver. Other members suggested names of figures to be
included in the biographical dictionary. Not all of anyone's list (even mine)
made it in, but everyone's nominations were useful. Michael Aune, Bruce Ben-
son, Peter Dahlen, and Mark Granquist each read substantial sections of the
manuscript. Their responses and encouragement shaped the work in progress.

The two American Lutherans with whom I live, my husband, Richard Dunning, and our son, Thomas Bjorn Lagerquist Dunning, have also lived with this
book. Thomas was born early in the project, and it took so long in part because
he didn't know I was writing a book. Wrick, on the other hand, has been very
aware and characteristically patient about it. I'm grateful to him for his support
and I hope that both he and Thomas will find here something of their own story.

INTRODUCTION

Denominational history has a risky potential to become merely an exercise in group autobiography or a saga of family history. The historian who is herself a member of the denomination (as I am) and who imagines her audience to share that membership is tempted to write as an insider for insiders, focusing on the familiar and happy moments while passing by the troublesome ones and giving at least passing reference to each and every cousin and in-law. Lutherans have not been immune from this inclination toward private accounts of their past. Taking others of their own kind as the primary audience has directed both the approach and the content of much of Lutheran historical work, as in other denominations. Lutheran theological concern for the church as the location of preaching and administration of the sacraments, both carried out by clergy, has augmented many historians' prior tendency to focus upon the official actions, major debates, and public leaders of any group. American Lutherans' perennial wrestling with policy and organizational matters has similarly generated lengthy and detailed descriptions of the frequent shifts in synods and other forms of governance and left little space for the lives and ministry carried out inside those structures.

Although the author of this volume is a Lutheran, I do not anticipate that its readers will be. I do not expect that most of them will come here for definitive accounts of internecine disputes or for exhaustive treatments of developments within specific subgroups of American Lutheranism. Rather, I imagine the readers of this history to resemble in many ways my students at St. Olaf College (or earlier at Valparaiso University) in a course on American Lutheranism. While some are Lutherans, they often know little about the history of Lutherans; and many who are not Lutheran know only what they have intuited from attending a college affiliated with a Lutheran church. These students have significantly informed my approach to this topic, my selection of material, and my presentation of it here. I have been informed by the questions they asked and by asking myself why a particular piece of information or interpretation would matter to them.

While I affirm the centrality of Word and sacrament to the life of the church, I also know that those practices are embedded in the larger social worlds occupied by those who hear the gospel preached and receive the sacraments. I have attempted to portray Lutheranism in the United States by attending to Lutheran people, to keep the members and their practice in the foreground with matters of structure and often of theological debate in the background. Those readers who long for more details or greater engagement in the issues will need to consult other works. Here they encounter descriptions of patterns and representative or significant examples. There is no intention to be exhaustive, though there is effort to be evenhanded. This is the case in the narrative as well as in the biographical entries. In my commitment to attend to laypeople, to women, and to people of color, other individuals and concerns have moved from center stage, and some have disappeared altogether from these pages. I have attempted to include some figure from most major synods and to strike a balance with regard to chronology and regions. I have taken the formation of the Evangelical Lutheran Church in America as the end point, not because it is the end of the story, but because it provides a clear place for a pause as the story continues.

No doubt some readers will object that I have not achieved all that I set out to do, that I have not made good on my convictions in one way or another, and I will have to plead guilty as charged. There are aspects of Lutheran life in the United States that I hoped to explore but was prevented from doing so for want of time or sources. What does appear here bears the marks of my own experience of American Lutheranism as a white laywoman, of a certain age, who has lived in the upper-Midwest and in southern California, and who has been nurtured in specific congregations and educated at specific schools.

Nonetheless, I hope that this book will introduce American Lutherans to readers who do not know us in a way that gives them access to our critical concerns, characteristics, and contributions and that suggests points of commonality with, as well as challenge to, other traditions. I hope, further, that Lutheran readers will learn something of themselves, not only or primarily the facts of names, dates, and places but more the dynamic life of people nurtured by, and nurturing, a tradition whose founder described faith as "a very mighty, active, restless, busy thing, which at once renews believers, gives them a second birth, and introduces them to a new manner and way of life, that it is impossible for them not to do good without ceasing" (Weimar, vol. 10, III, 285).

ABBREVIATIONS USED IN THIS VOLUME

ALB   Jens Christian Roseland. *American Lutheran Biographies: or, Historical Notices of Over Three Hundred and Fifty Leading Men of the American Lutheran Church* (Milwaukee, WI: Press of A. Houtkamp and Son, 1890).

CHIQ   *Concordia Historical Institute Quarterly.*

DAB   *Dictionary of American Biography* (New York: Scribner's Sons, 1928–).

DARB   Henry Warner Bowden, *Dictionary of American Religious Biography* (Westport, CT: Greenwood Press, 1993).

DCA   *Dictionary of Christianity in America*, ed. Daniel G. Reid. (Downers Grove, IL: InterVarsity Press, 1990).

ELC   *The Encyclopedia of the Lutheran Church*, ed. Julius Bodensieck. (Minneapolis: Augsburg Publishing House, 1965).

LC   *Lutheran Cyclopedia*, ed. Erwin L. Lueker. (St. Louis: Concordia Publishing House, 1975).

LHC   *Essays and Reports—Lutheran Historical Conference.*

NCAB   *The National Cyclopaedia of American Biography* (New York: J. T. White, 1898–).

RLA   *Religious Leaders of America: A Biographical Guide to Founders and Leaders of Religious Bodies, Churches, and Spiritual Groups in North America*, ed. J. Gordon Melton. (Detroit: Gale Research, 1991).

1
TWO CONTEXTS AND
A QUESTION

In the early 1990s a character on the popular television situation comedy *Cheers* was about to be married. Woody, a bartender in that local Boston bar "where everybody knows your name," discussed with his customers and friends a complication in his plans: he and his fiancée belonged to different Lutheran churches, not different congregations but he to the Missouri Synod and she to the Evangelical Lutheran Church in America. This episode was the subject of conversation among Lutherans who had not seen it, indeed, who had never seen the show at all. Why? Because Lutherans in the United States don't expect anyone who isn't one of them to notice them, much less to know enough about them to make a joke recognizing that by the late twentieth century there were two large groups of Lutherans whose members might consider a marriage across that boundary as "mixed." Of course, what made the joke funny was the contrast between the seriousness with which Woody took the complication and the triviality of it in his friends' estimation. This incident suggests three questions that this book explores. Why don't American Lutherans expect to be noticed, much less understood? How did there get to be two kinds of American Lutherans? Why would marriage of their members be viewed as unlikely by insiders but as of little consequence to others?

In exploring these questions we also consider various ways of defining Lutheranism: what it is and who is one. Indeed, a case could be made that this two-part question of identity defines the central task that has confronted Lutherans in the United States since before there was a United States and does so even today. These identities continue to be subject to reassessment and redefinition in two contexts: the first is the religious context of Lutheranism as a historic and contemporary phenomenon as well as a European and global one; the second is the equally diverse and ever-developing national context, the United States and its society. The story of American Lutherans is a complex narrative about an ongoing struggle—or set of struggles sometimes separate and sometimes

interlocking—to construct an identity that is simultaneously genuinely Lutheran
and authentically American.

Often this struggle has taken the form of theological debate. Christa R. Klein
has persuasively suggested that Lutheranism might even be understood as a
continuity of argument.[1] Mark Noll has written about the struggle as learning
to speak Lutheranism with an American accent.[2] Though these historians and
others such as Robert Bruce Mullin cast the task of denominational identification
in terms of language—and rightly so since language has been a major factor
among Lutherans—more than words and ideas have been at stake.[3] The struggle
to construct an identity both Lutheran and American has also included financing
voluntary religious institutions from the congregation to the college; providing
qualified leadership and devising adequate organizational forms; responding to
innovations such as revivalism, Sunday school, and women's organizations; and
participating in non-Lutheran activities such as public education, social and service organizations or ecumenical worship.

Lutherans appear in general histories of American religion such as Sidney
Ahlstrom's *A Religious History of the American People* or Winthrop Hudson's
Religion in America or Mark A. Noll's *A History of Christianity in the United
States and Canada* as an exceptional case—one that neither fits the conventional
patterns for Protestant descendants of Puritans nor is so innovative nor so exotic
as others, Shakers or Mormons, for example.[4] Historians have written Lutherans'
tale into the counterpoint rather than the melody. American factors contribute
to this. The coincidence of the arrival of large numbers of non-English-speaking
Lutherans with the settlement of the Midwest, for example, resulted in both
linguistic and geographic isolation of many Lutherans. Nonetheless, factors in
the religious Lutheran identity also help to account both for their different response to the common challenges and for their rendering as challenge things
others regard as commonplace. Efforts to conserve both ethnic and religious
culture combined, in some cases, in support of parochial schools as alternatives
to the public schools. Differing legacies of piety lead some Lutherans to embrace
and others to oppose temperance and some to participate in, and others to protest, revivalism.

Let us turn now to a preliminary consideration of Lutheranism, specifically,
to the double question, What is Lutheranism, and who is one? The most
commonsense response to the second question is the institutional one. A Lutheran is a person who belongs to a Lutheran church. Unfortunately in this case
what is obvious is not always true, nor even very helpful.[5] What Nancy Ammerman has pointed out in reference to surveys about church membership applies
here. People report themselves as belonging without any behaviors of affiliation.[6]
So, too, there are people who consider themselves Lutheran but who neither
hold membership in a Lutheran congregation nor attend one. Some count themselves as Lutherans when no congregation does, on the basis of family affiliation
or a general sense of belonging to a culture rather than to an identifiable institu-

tion. An additional limitation of this commonsense definition is that it provides no basis for determining which institutions are Lutheran. Some individuals name themselves Lutheran because of their personal adherence to a set of criteria that could also be applied to institutions, though they do not themselves belong to those institutions. Similarly, there are persons belonging to Lutheran churches who might not meet those criteria. They are Lutherans in name but not in confession.

Confession is a more useful approach to these questions. It moves into the realm of theology and perhaps even piety. These two—confession as a statement of religious belief and confession of sin as a component of religious behavior—are central to Lutheranism. The very name Lutheran suggests that one should turn to Martin Luther for clues about what the thing is. This is almost as obvious and commonsensical as the institutional approach. Defining Lutherans as persons who follow Martin Luther as their teacher in matters of theology and piety would not be all wrong. There are ways in which the founder is paradigmatic of the movement. Of course, there are also ways that many contemporary Lutherans do not follow Luther; technically, only a small fraction of his work has authoritative status for Lutherans. Those are the pieces included in the Book of Concord, the 1580 collection of the Lutheran Confessions, namely, his catechisms and the Smalkald Articles.

The term "confession" takes on a technical meaning to refer specifically to the Book of Concord and those documents that set out the Lutheran theological position. The book includes the three ecumenical creeds (the Apostles, the Nicean, and the Athanasian), the Augsburg Confession made to Emperor Charles in 1530, its Apology or explanation, and two other treatises in addition to those by Luther already mentioned. These Confessions have functioned for Lutherans analogously to the U.S. Constitution and have been given central authority as the criteria for determining what and who is Lutheran. Thus, we appear to have answered the question about what constitutes authentic Lutheranness; however, the question is not so easily resolved. Among those who appeal to the Confessions there is ongoing disagreement about the relative authority of the several Confessions and about what is expected of adherents. The names chosen by two Lutheran groups in the United States for their colleges suggest distinct approaches. The Lutheran Church Missouri Synod called its colleges Concordia, recalling the whole of the Book of Concord; the Augustana Synod called its college in Rock Island, Illinois, Augustana after the Augsburg Confession. These two names suggest, on one hand, a maximum standard of authentic Lutheranness that requires complete agreement as to meaning and subscription to the entire set and, on the other, a minimalist standard that asks for common recognition of a single Confession while allowing some flexibility for interpretation. Krister Stendahl, a Swede whose tenure at Harvard Divinity School gave him opportunity for long observation of Lutherans in the United States, has characterized the latter approach as a doctrinal asceticism.[7] Nonetheless, Lutheranism in the

United States has been animated by vigorous debate about these matters, so
much so that one might follow Klein and assert that a Lutheran is one who
debates about the Confessions.

While this definition serves well and especially so for the trained theologian—
whether a pastor or a layperson, a teacher or an executive—it is not the whole
story. Other factors come into an adequate description of Lutherans and Lutheranism. Among these are particular emphases of theology and practice that derive
from Luther, from the sixteenth-century Reformation agenda, and from political
and religious developments in the intervening centuries. Therefore, before leaving behind the Lutheran context of American Lutherans' struggle to construct
their identity, we must give some attention to these factors. Without any preten-
sion of providing an exhaustive treatment, we will look at Luther's own life and
theology as well as the movement's growth and the refinement of its teachings
and practices. The criterion for inclusion in this brief discussion is its relevance
to later development in the North American context.

Martin Luther was the son of a devout copper miner whose fortunes were
increasing adequately for him to entertain aspirations for his son Martin.[8] Consequently, young Martin was sent to school in hope that he would become a
lawyer, bringing honor and greater prosperity to the family. He was a serious
enough lad, whose studies progressed and who also applied himself to spiritual
matters, though it seems unlikely that the *Anfechtung*—fear and despair—that
later assailed him was absent even in his youth. When returning to the school
after a visit home, in part to attend the funeral of a friend, Martin found himself
in a storm and was filled with fear. His plea for safety has been pointed to as
the turning point in his occupation and thus in his life. There he resolved to
become a monk. He joined an Augustinian house and applied himself to the
tasks of devotion as if his life depended on it. Unfortunately, the Catholicism
of his time promised the young German more than it could deliver. Despite his
extreme efforts in the monastic discipline, neither fasting nor confessing nor
praying nor anything he did brought him God's peace. Finally, his confessor,
Johann von Staupitz, set him to a different sort of task—studying and teaching.

Brother Martin was sent to study the Bible and then to teach at the newly
founded University of Wittenberg. There, in the midst of this work, he discovered the insight that would change his life. While studying God's Word revealed
in the Bible, Martin Luther confronted the theological truth that his salvation
was not dependent on his own work; it was a gift of God's grace given to him
through faith. This Pauline assertion was not new to Christianity, but it shed a
light on Luther's own experience as dazzling as the one that had blinded Paul
on the road to Damascus. When Luther began to see with his renewed vision,
he had many questions, among them fundamental questions about the Roman
Catholic Church and its inability to convey the gospel of freedom to him and
others like him. With the urgency of the newly converted, he asked his questions
and preached the reply he learned from his study of God's Word.

Luther himself cannot be held responsible for the whole of the Reformation, whether for good or for ill. But it can be said that without him there would be no Lutheran Church in precisely the sense that there now is. He took part in decisive actions that punctuated the division of the church and the development of Lutheran Protestant Christianity. In 1517 Johann Tetzel's coming mission to Wittenberg was announced; Tetzel was to sell indulgences whose benefit to the purchasers was reduction of the penalties for sin and whose benefits to Albrecht, archbishop of Mainz, and to the pope were more earthly and material. Luther responded by writing and posting for debate, as was university custom in that day, a series of propositions about the pope's powers and the practice of selling indulgences. Though there were still moments at which the Reformation and certainly Luther might have been turned back after this, the posting of the Ninety-five Theses stands well as a symbolic beginning of the Reformation. In the following years Luther gained a following composed of an array of people: priests and princes, scholars and the barely educated. Philip Melanchthon, his younger colleague and friend, and Katherine von Bora, his wife and a former nun, were among his close companions. Some were influenced by his ideas and many publications without joining in the movement; others were more radical than he. At the Diet of Augsburg in 1530, seven princes and representatives of two free cities presented Emperor Charles with the Augsburg Confession, detailing their beliefs. Written, in large part, by Melanchthon, the Augsburg Confession stated both the points of agreement with Rome and the point at which they disagreed and protested—hence the term Protestants.

When we turn to Luther for insight into Lutherans, however, we must acknowledge that his own writings are not well suited to the task of definition. He was prolific both as a preacher and as a writer in several genres, including letters and commentaries as well as polemical treatises. These works were often occasional, responding to specific circumstances rather than laid out in a carefully developed system. In the standard American edition, Luther's works run over fifty volumes, and this does not include all that he wrote. From the standpoint of the struggle to construct an American Lutheran identity this characteristic has had several consequences. One is the malleability of the tradition. Because his own writings are nonsystematic, Luther can be used to various ends or to support multiple positions, sometimes conflicting ones. Until this century a rather small proportion of Luther's works has been widely accessible, so his authority has rested less upon the whole corpus and more upon a few pieces. For those Lutherans from Scandinavia, more particularly from Norway, the Small Catechism as further explained by Bishop Pontoppidan had a central place. Some version of the Small Catechism has been used consistently in confirmation instruction for generations; therefore, if judged by the numbers of people who have read it and been shaped by it, this is likely Luther's single most influential writing, with the possible exception of his hymns.

This leads easily to a second characteristic of Luther that is telling for the whole: he was musical. While this is surely not a unique feature of Lutheranism or perhaps even a definitive one, it is notable. The man Luther was fond of

music, and his skill has been judged as better than average. Whether he used
tunes from drinking songs or more sedate folk sources, there is no doubt that
he recognized the value of music both to convey the gospel message and as a
vehicle of praise. Nor is there any doubt that when asked to describe Lutherans
today, many people respond immediately with a comment about Lutherans' singing: sung liturgy, congregational hymn singing, or college choirs. Translating
the words of old favorite hymns from their European originals, borrowing from
the Anglo-American tradition, and writing new words and music have been an
important part of developing an American Lutheranism.[9] So, too, devising the
right combination of text and music for liturgy has been a continual task.

Even as sketchy a biography of Luther as given here points to the centrality
of the Bible to his own religious life and to the reform he took part in. In his
days as a monk he sang and prayed the Bible; he was a university teacher of
Bible; he preached often on biblical texts; and his translation of the Bible into
German was widely read. When, at the Diet of Worms, he was faced with the
pope's authority and asked to recant his views, Luther declared that he could
do so only if convinced from the Scriptures and his conscience—thus, the Reformation slogan *sola scriptura*, asserting that the Bible is the sole authority. However, Luther was no literalist or fundamentalist in the modern sense. He did not
equate the Bible with the Word of God as if the Bible contained all that God
has to say. Rather, he pointed to Jesus as the incarnate Word and demonstrated
in his own sermons the vitality of the preached Word. Lutherans would have
many opportunities to wrestle with the Bible and its place among them, both
prior to the beginnings of the American church and in its development. Although
nineteenth-century German Lutherans made an enormous contribution to the
development of modern biblical scholarship, Lutherans in the United States man-
aged to avoid it until this century and even then escaped until the 1970s the
stormy debates that ripped through other Protestant groups much earlier. Lutherans have followed a prescribed series of biblical texts, a lectionary, as the basis
of preaching and to provide biblical education for children and adults.

A final observation about Luther returns to his experiential and realistic theology. It was experiential in the sense that the things that happened to him and
to those around him had a profound impact upon his ways of thinking about
and talking about God. Perhaps the best-known examples of this come from his
family life. Luther's marriage to Katherine von Bora seems to have been motivated by ideology as much as by affection. By marrying her he would please
his father, spite the pope, and demonstrate his conviction that clergy could
marry. Nonetheless, his written references to his life as husband and father make
clear that for Luther himself marriage was a school for character. Similarly, his
letters of spiritual counsel are filled with attention to the specific circumstances
of his correspondents. The catechetical question, What does it mean for me? is
indicative of the central expectation that religious faith has personal and experiential consequences as well as a basis in objective truths. This concern would
reemerge and be emphasized by the pietist movement.

The realism of Luther's theology is vividly expressed in the Latin phrase *simul justus et pecatar*: at the same time saint and sinner. While clinging to the truth that he was justified and made a saint by God's grace, Luther was also profoundly aware of the grip of sin—self, Satan, death—tight upon him. Like the apostle Paul, who did not do the good he intended but did the evil he willed not to do, Luther recognized the mixed character of the Christian who lives in the time between Christ's victorious work and that of his triumphant return to institute God's heavenly reign. This mixedness is characteristic of the whole church as well as of the individual Christian. The simultaneity of saintliness and sin, seemingly mutually exclusive, is also indicative of the frequent appearance of paradox in Lutheran theology.

Once begun, the reform moved with remarkable speed, and as its advocates increased in number, so did its forms. After theological insight came tangible changes in practice that affected many arenas of life from public worship to family life. The Lutheran reform, like the Calvinist, was relatively moderate in contrast to the Anabaptists or the Spiritualists. Unlike many other Protestants, Lutherans judged numerous elements of Roman Catholicism worthy of retention, or at least not so harmful as to require discarding them. Lutherans rejected monasticism as a system that gave undue status to one calling in life and encouraged everyone to think that special disciplines could alter one's relationship with God. Instead, Luther proclaimed that all believers should regard themselves as priests and their work and relationships as means of responding to God's calling them. However, the special office of the pastor was not abolished. Unlike more radical reformers who did away with sacraments, Lutherans merely reduced the number of sacraments from the Roman Catholic seven to two—baptism and the Lord's Supper, while affirming that the finite elements could be vehicles of the infinite.[10] Recognizing their educational value, Lutherans did not dismantle organs, paint over frescos, or break stained glass windows. Four elements of the sixteenth-century Lutheran agenda are of particular significance for American Lutheranism. These include worship, education, lay participation, and alliances with civil authorities.

The alterations Lutherans made in the Roman Mass were both minimal and profound. Much of the structure and even of the language was continued, but worshipers were given the opportunity to take a more active part in what was going on. Of primary importance was the switch to using the vernacular language, that is, the language people used in their everyday transactions. This allowed them to understand the words of the liturgy as well as the sermon and thus opened the door to their being transformed by those words. The sacraments and preaching were given central place in worship, each offering an opportunity for the worshiper to encounter God's grace. The visible location of both altar and pulpit signaled the importance of these two activities. In contrast to the practice of American Lutherans in the nineteenth and early twentieth centuries, early Lutherans celebrated the Lord's Supper regularly and often. The seasons of the church year continued to be observed, giving worship a familiar pattern of cyclical changes. These moderate changes in liturgical practice were not made uniformly in all Lutheran churches; there was allowance for variations in matters of indifference, *adiaphora*. Consequently, immigrant Lutherans brought with them to North America, in several languages, a variety of forms for worship that shared key elements. Efforts to devise consistent patterns or even a single uniform standard have been part of the struggle to become an American Lutheran church. Although the practices of the early nineteenth century strayed a good deal from them, the sixteenth-century patterns have been appealed to as a source for, and standard of, authentic Lutheran worship for the last century. Lutheran worship in the United States has consistently distinguished itself from the more informal practices of some other Protestant groups and has seemed to some observers to identify Lutherans as like Roman Catholics.

Lutheran involvement in education was directed toward three goals. The first, education for piety, had the most widespread effect. The motivation for this very basic education was equipping students with the tools to learn and understand the fundamental teachings of their faith. Luther appealed to the civil authorities, urging them to provide schools that would teach both boys and girls who would then be able to read the Bible and the catechism.[11] Parents were encouraged to instruct their children in the contents of these two books. A second sort of education was directed toward believers' competent and faithful response to their occupational calling. Faithful magistrates, for example, needed appropriate education to carry out the tasks of their office. So, too, did parents, shoemakers, and princes. The third sort of education provided for one specific occupation—pastors.

This Lutheran devotion to education would have several ramifications for American Lutherans. From the outset of their presence in North America, commitment to an educated clergy combined with the expectation that in all but the most extraordinary circumstances preaching and administration of the sacraments were tasks reserved to the clergy and produced a long-term shortage of pastoral leadership and restrictions of church life. The need for an educated clergy contributed to Lutheran entry into formal education, sponsoring first seminaries, then preparatory colleges for potential seminarians. The parallel concern for informed piety combined with desire to preserve imported European cultures and languages and fueled, among some Lutherans, vigorous support for parochial schools. Even when the linguistic purposes were removed, this concern continued, and confirmation instruction gave Lutheran children a basic education in the theology of their church. Colleges founded by Lutherans addressed all three concerns in various combinations and benefited from the strong commitment to education in their tradition, which began in a university.

As this brief discussion of schools suggests, the Lutheran reformers were mightily interested in active participation by the ordinary Christian believer. Two teachings are of particular relevance to this concern: vocation and the priesthood of all believers. Both reject the prior notion that certain occupations and ways of life, namely, the priesthood and monasticism, were of particular value and greater spiritual benefit than others. Rather, the notion of calling is expanded to include all believers and the whole of their lives. The objective fact of baptism has personal and subjective consequences for each believer. This interaction of the objective and the subjective elements of faith appears in various forms again and again in Lutheranism. Like a two-part epoxy that adheres only when both the resin and the curing agent are present, authentic Lutheranism needs both elements in dynamic combination. When reliance upon the objective reality of baptism as a means of God's saving grace overwhelms the need for assuming personal responsibility for one's action, the vitality of Lutheranism is lost, and Lutherans earn their reputation for quietism. On the other hand, undue concern for subjective experience is equally out of balance and can paralyze the Christian with doubts about God's forgiveness, as Luther's biography demonstrates. In the *Freedom of a Christian*, Luther wrote about the paradox of Christian life in which the believer is totally free, subject to no one, and simultaneously servant of all. He cited the analogy of a good tree that gives good fruit to illustrate his assertion that while good works do not make a person righteous, one who is made righteous by God's grace does do good works. These are the works of love that each believer carries out in response to vocation. A principal arena for that work is the family, in which the parents are charged to teach their children and bring them up in faith. For Lutherans in the United States this cluster of teachings has been significant for their response to revivalism, for their understanding of their responsibilities for social service and political activity, and for their ability to carry on corporate life without clerical leadership.

A fourth item in the reform agenda concerned the ongoing relationship between civil and churchly officials.[12] Unlike radicals such as the Mennonites, Lutherans maintained an alliance between these two sets of authorities without specifying the precise arrangements of the alliance. The central Lutheran statement of faith, the Augsburg Confession, though written by a theologian, was signed by princes and representatives of cities to be presented to the emperor. Luther himself gave extraordinary authority to princes, asking them to serve as emergency bishops in a time of extreme need. In Lutheran areas this alliance took on a character different from that in Calvinist Geneva. There the arrangement approached theocracy with some hope of establishing a Christian order. This model stands behind much of Protestant thinking in the United States, though not behind specific arrangements. In contrast Luther hoped for officials who were Christian and allowed them remarkable jurisdiction over religious matters, but he also recognized that the good rule of an unbeliever had benefits for the believing citizen and might be better than bad rule by a Christian. His distinction between the two kingdoms—the temporal realm on the left and the spiritual realm on the right—did not prevent civil intervention in churchly affairs or the reverse. It did indicate the limits of such intervention, in particular, the impossibility of earthly efforts bringing in God's heavenly reign. Even as individual Christians live out their vocation while both saints and sinners, so, too, the earthly order continues to strive for what it cannot obtain. This recognition of the limits of temporal efforts can discourage engagement in the realm of government or social action, as in the case of American Lutherans' general disinterest in the Social Gospel movement; it can also produce a tempered expectation and complex motivations such as demonstrated by Dietrich Bonhoeffer's resistance to Hitler.

The continuing history of the Lutheran movement includes Luther's own experience and theology; the practical agenda carried out by the reformers; definition of doctrinal positions, particularly as recorded in the Augsburg Confession and the other documents in the Book of Concord; the spread of the movement into Scandinavia and other areas; and several phases of development marked by distinctive emphases in theology and piety. Among these items three have ongoing ramifications for American Lutherans as they have endeavored to be both American and Lutheran. The teachings about the church laid out in the Augsburg Confession have made Lutherans unusual among Protestants in the United States, both by what is said and by what is left undefined. The minimal toleration for religious variety and the close relationship between government and church established first by the Peace of Augsburg (1555) and then by the Peace of Westphalia (1648) meant that Lutheran immigrants to the United States confronted an unfamiliar situation with regard to such practical matters as definition of membership and financial support as well as in more ideological ones. Finally, the phase of theological orthodoxy followed by one of pietist awakening each provided people and ideas to the American church, and the interaction of the two impulses continues to contribute to the vitality of American Lutheranism.

Articles 7 and 8 of the Augsburg Confession are directed to defining the church. There the church is defined by action, by the actions that make God's grace known. Specifically, these are preaching the gospel in purity and administering the sacraments in accord with the gospel. Of course, this takes place in "the assembly of believers," but in contrast to the gathered church ecclesiology of revival-influenced American churches, it is not the coming together of the congregation that makes the church. Rather, in Lutheran teaching the preaching and the sacraments make the church, drawing the people and giving them reliable access to divine forgiveness and grace. This contributes to the Lutheran insistence upon having clerical leaders who are trained to preach and administer the sacraments, and it accounts, in part, for the vigorous debates about who is equipped by training and confession to do these things in purity and in accord with the gospel. The Augsburg Confession also notes that this assembly contains, in addition to believers, "false Christians, hypocrites, and open sinners." This, too, is in contrast to perfectionist teachings that try to exclude persons whose experience, confession, or life is not in accord with the community's standards of belief and holiness. Such teachings, prevalent among some sixteenth century-Anabaptists, were a common feature of the gathered church view advocated by revivalists. The notion of the church as a mixed assembly was well suited to state or folk church arrangements. In the United States, where membership in churches is voluntary, and many options are available, its meaning was less obvious, and the notion of the congregation as a gathered community of like-minded individuals gained pragmatic currency. Neither article of the Confession prescribes a polity for organizing church life, leaving this open as a matter, if not of indifference, certainly of lesser importance and thus allowing for variety. This flexibility gave American Lutherans the task of devising a polity appropriate to the political and social circumstances in which they found themselves. The advantage of not being tied to a single pattern carried with it the inevitability of continual debate and adjustment.

As has been alluded to, one of the marked differences between the European situation from which Lutheran immigrants came and the one that greeted them was the legal relationship of church and state. The alliance that the Lutheran reformers allowed between the religious and the civic was formalized in the emergence of the nation-state. The Treaties of Augsburg and Westphalia were critical steps. The first, at the conclusion of the Smalkald War, established the principle of territorialism with regard to religious identity (*cuius regio, eius religio*). Though reducing the scale, it was essentially a continuation of the Constantinian principle that linking religion and culture in the expectation that a single religion would contribute to maintenance of a cohesive cultural identity. However, in early modern Europe the scale shrank from that of an empire to the smaller region of a free city or a country. In that territory the ruler had the authority to determine the religion for all inhabitants. Should some people decline the ruler's religion, they were free to move to another region. This was toleration of religious variety in an extremely minimal form, especially since Augsburg includes only Roman Catholics and Lutherans, and Westphalia added only Calvinists to the agreement. The consequences for Lutherans included their membership in churches that received government support and that were sometimes organized as a department of the state government. Lutherans, with minor exception, lived in areas almost homogeneously Lutheran where they had little experience of interaction with members of other churches.

When European Lutherans immigrated to North America, they found themselves in quite different circumstances. With the unenduring exception of New Sweden and the more long-lasting one of the Virgin Islands, Lutherans who traveled the Atlantic left behind government support and forfeited the official services of the state church. Once the United States established its legal separation of church and state, and all states ended religious establishment, all churches had the same legal status, though not the same cultural standing. Lutherans had the largely unfamiliar experience of being a religious minority, although those who began the congregation in the New Netherlands were a notable exception. This legal status of denominations in an arrangement of religious freedom meant that no one was compelled to be Lutheran; all membership was voluntary and in competition with the attractions of other churches or no church. An astonishingly small proportion of those who boarded ships as Lutherans affiliated with that church in the United States. All financial support for the church had to be raised by the members themselves, an arrangement that encouraged members of churches of all sorts to regard themselves as the owners. At the same time, sustaining a large enough membership to provide this support gave at least a utilitarian motive to actively recruit new members; more evangelically put, freedom of religion opened opportunity to preach the gospel widely. Every group of Lutherans who immigrated to the United States encountered these circumstances, but few can be said to have come seeking them. The two notable instances of Lutherans' coming to North America for religious reasons were the Salzburger refugees who settled in colonial Georgia and the Saxons who immigrated to Perry County, Missouri, in the mid-nineteenth century.

When the Peace of Westphalia concluded the Thirty Years' War in the mid-seventeenth century, the Lutheran Reformation was well established in several areas of as yet un-united Germany as well as in Scandinavia. The spread of this movement north was accomplished, in part, by the influence of scholars and churchmen who were themselves influenced by Luther and his colleagues. The roles of government leaders and of social and political change were of at least equal importance. In the sixteenth century Scandinavian nations were realigned into two unequally yoked pairs. Consequently, the religious developments in Norway and Finland followed those in Denmark and Sweden. Sweden's efforts to free itself from Denmark coincided with religious reform in the 1520s with leadership from Gustavus Vasa, in the first case, and brothers Olaf and Lorenz Petri, in the second. However, in Sweden the church remained somewhat more independent of the monarchy than would be the arrangement in Denmark. Popular support for reform appears to have been more widespread in Denmark, where both Frederick I and his son Christian III were in sympathy with Lutheran views. A Protestant Church Order, written by Luther's colleague Johannes Bugenhagen, was adopted in the late 1530s.

After the Formula of Concord was written (1580) and the Book of Concord collected, as the first generation of leaders died, Lutheranism entered a second phase of development. In this phase attention turned to practical institutional matters, to clarification of teachings, and to the sort of systematic thinking that Luther did not do. In the midst of efforts to organize a unified church, controversies arose on several points, such as the proper role of good works and theories accounting for the incarnation. As each was resolved, the criteria for purity of doctrine were more carefully delineated. At the same time Lutheran theologians encountered and responded to the intellectual trends of their time. These controversies and encounters led to development of Lutheran orthodoxy represented especially by people such as Martin Chemnitz, Johann Gerhard, and Abraham Calov, men of faith and intellect. Their work was characterized by great confidence in the reliability of Scripture, by precision of thought and expression, and by their return to the methods of Aristotelian philosophy. At its best, orthodoxy produced a clearer more articulate version of distinctly Lutheran teachings; in caricatured form it was spiritually arid and contentious. Although the era of orthodoxy passed, its emphases did not. They continued to define one focus in the ellipse of Lutheranism, and individual Lutherans positioned themselves in greater or lesser proximity to that focus while still inside the region.

Following orthodoxy came a third phase whose concerns define the second focus of the ellipse. This was the Pietist movement which arose, in part, as a reaction to the weaknesses of orthodoxy and, in part, as a response to the conditions and consequences of long warfare in the seventeenth century. The pietist movement called for, and worked toward, renewed animation of religion among believers and the church. These concerns were sometimes shared with persons identified with orthodoxy but shifted attention away from preoccupation with right thinking to primary concern for right feeling and right action. Like Luther himself, the pietists were attentive to the experience of faith and its meaning for the believer's own life. In large degree they affirmed the doctrines defined by the reformers' generation and by the orthodox theologians but did not focus upon them. Drawing upon the prior work of Johann Arndt, in particular, his enduring devotional volume *True Christianity* (1606), Philipp Jacob Spener outlined a plan for renewal of the church in his *Pia Desideria* (1675).[13] He also instituted practical measures to bring faith alive. Among these were small groups of laypeople who met to read the Bible together, pray together, and encourage one another's growth as Christians. These conventicles and their "reading" were distinguishing marks of the movement. Spener and his younger colleague August Hermann Francke extended their influence and the movement through the University of Halle and a cluster of charitable institutions located there. These included an orphanage, schools, hospital, and a Bible publisher. From this center emanated both renewal within the existing church and evangelization by missionaries sent throughout the world. The Danish Royal Mission to Tranquebar, India, among the earliest Protestant missions, was staffed by Germans from Halle. So, too, an influential cadre of pastors in colonial North America had connections to Halle.

Scandinavia was awash in later waves of pietism just as immigration to the United States was taking place. Many immigrant trunks contained a copy of *True Christianity* as well as a prayer book, a catechism, and a Bible. Though each wave had distinctive characteristics, most shared the concern for right feeling and right action. In some areas, such as southern Sweden, the feelings ran higher, and the expectations for action took on a particularly austere tone. In the late eighteenth century, Norway lay preacher Hans Neilsen Hauge traveled the length of the country preaching the need for a profound conviction of one's sin, a concomitant sense of God's grace, and a reformed life free from such sins as dancing, cardplaying, and drinking. He also disseminated information about agricultural technology and helped to galvanize the political self-consciousness of his followers. However, this sort of pietism was also inclined toward the extreme moralism and gloomy worldview that earned one group of Lutherans the nickname "sad Danes." Although it is not well described as anti-intellectual, this pietism did downplay the specificity of the Lutheran confessional position. This minimizing of doctrine combined with the accent on the affective produced

affinities between pietist Lutherans and American revivalism, though the fit was
never perfect.

The Lutheran context of the struggle to construct an identity simultaneously
authentically Lutheran and American is also distinct from some other Christian
groups in that the European heritage remained a critical factor for so long.
However, this ought not to overshadow the contemporary fact that the Lutheran
movement has become global, with churches in Madagascar, Namibia, India,
New Guinea, and Japan that are a century or more old. Nor should the ongoing
importance of this European heritage be collapsed into the cultural traits of
Northern European people. While language, communication patterns, aesthetics,
and other characteristics of culture have been imported from Europe and exerted
long influence within Lutheran communities, these finite features are not equiva-
lent to the infinite ones they have carried. Certainly, those persons from other
cultures who have become Lutheran have wrestled with the persistence of characteristics foreign to them; they have also brought their own cultural traits with
them.[14] It may be the case that Lutheranism needs a culture, just as the sacraments require a visible sign, but it is not clear that there is a single Lutheran
culture, not even an American one in the United States. There is a perennial
danger that any culture used to convey the infinite is confused with, or substituted for, the central confession of God's gracious action. Surely, this is a logical
implication of the paradoxical relationship between Christ and culture that H.
Richard Niebuhr attributed to Lutherans in his typology.

The double question of Lutheran identity, which lurks behind the narrative in
this book, is also a question about the existence of a Lutheran culture. It is
informed by current discussion about the nature of denominations—as organizations, as beliefs and practices, as purposive missionary associations, as cultural
identities, or as bilingual communities—without actively engaging that discussion.[15] It is also an effort to enrich prior treatments of American Lutheran history
by adding to the doctrinal and institutional approach greater attention to the
social world in which preaching and the sacraments are embedded. Contemporary issues about the role of the laity in the church, about inclusiveness and
multiculturalism, and about women's participation and leadership direct this approach in a particular way and bring these groups into sharper focus, nearer the
center of the story, while leaving treatment of other topics more in the background with less detail. Additionally, this work is influenced by recent developments in congregational studies and endeavors to give local phenomena some
visibility.[16] Like many denominational histories this one is organized chrono-
logically. It begins with the early Lutheran arrivals and traces subsequent events
through time to the present. Within that most basic structure, however, there
must be a story, and very likely there need to be images that enhance the story
and help us to understand what happened. Since the story and images are so
important to what we understand, it may be worth considering them before
taking up the story.

American Lutheran history has often been told as the movement from many kinds of Lutherans distinguished by their countries of origin, their piety, and their American organizations to fewer and fewer sorts. This is a good American story that fits well with a concern for a new thing being forged in North America. This story can be laid out on an organizational flowchart of corporate mergers. Despite all the lines at the beginning—and especially in the late 1800s, when there were more than five dozen synods—this image and its story of institutional unification have the advantage of simplicity. They seem to have served us well. The same story might be otherwise represented. The image of a river suggests that while mergers may result in fewer organizations, they usually don't make church life less complex. Tributaries flow together into a larger river that contains all the streams; its current may vary; and its path may meander. Rain contributes to the river, indicating that not all Lutherans have always been Lutheran. A braid is another image sometimes used in conjunction with this story. Usually, the braid represents the parts being woven together to become one. However, in a fictional account of the 1960 merger of the American Lutheran Church a young girl's unwinding and loosening of the strands of her braid suggest the three churches' new unity that comes from loss of old boundaries.[17] A difficulty with this story and with these images—flowchart, river, or braid—is that all of them are toward oneness, and none are friendly toward either divisions or innovations that result in more groups or rival institutions. These are detours from the goal toward which the history is tending, the point toward which the river flows.

The church can also be represented as a person who moves through successive stages of development from its colonial infancy, to its nineteenth-century adolescent search for identity, to greater maturity and responsibility in this century. This image may fit better with a story about adaptation to new circumstances. However, the singularity of an individual life prevents easy accommodation of additional organizations or groups of people regardless of their origin. Efforts to use this image for the whole of American Lutheran history may result in portraying American Lutheranism as a profoundly disturbed person, and here the founding of new synods and institutions might be seen as an onset of multiple personality disorder.

Perhaps the image of a family is better suited to such a complex story. There are a certain literal appeal and utility to this image, as Lutheran history includes several clusters of characters from single families. The Henkel family can be used as a window on the developments of several decades; knowledge of Preus family genealogy is useful to understanding many developments in midwestern Lutheranism. In other episodes the important role played by successive generations of Schmuckers and Krauths is striking and hints at unexplored dynamics of the events, dynamics that were probably obvious to contemporary observers. In a figurative sense the image of family is appealing because it does allow for the sorts of developments that take place within a family between generations and even the differences between siblings. Though cousins are distinct individuals, the similarities within nuclear families and between all the members highlight common family origin. So, too, among Lutherans: though there are many types, there are characteristics that mark all as Lutheran rather than members in any other group. This observation is in keeping with the story about constructing an identity both Lutheran and American. The literal reality of the image holds the danger that this image may appear too inward-looking and render many readers as outsiders. Perhaps careful addition of in-laws and neighbors to the story remedies the potential problem and makes more obvious the interaction between Lutherans and other Americans.

Another rather different image can be drawn out of Henry M. Muhlenberg's phrase about the church being planted, *"Ecclesia non planta, sed plantanda."* This is a horticultural image of the American Lutheran Church as a plant, imported to a new environment, cultivated by different gardeners, and bearing fruits suitable for the inhabitants. This image is particularly well suited to a story about adaptation because it allows for change in several arenas and need not regard all division as retrograde. There are some precedents for using a horticultural image. Sidney Ahlstrom, a Lutheran and a historian of American religion, wrote in the 1950s that "Lutheranism is best understood when it is seen not as something indistinguishably blended in with the luxuriant foliage of American denominationalism but as a tradition living in a real but fruitful state of tension with American church life."[18] In the previous century, William Julius Mann often employed this sort of image. For example, in connection with the American Lutheranism controversy he observed, "The hard dogmatic knots of the old Lutheran oak were forced to give way under the Puritan plans. The body was deprived of its leaves and its heart, and empty skin was filled with whatever was most pleasing, if only the Lutheran name was retained."[19] So one might suggest that the struggle to construct an American Lutheran identity is a reappraisal of the root stock of Lutheranism, a discussion about how that plant should be pruned and cultivated in the soil and climate of North America in the hopes of cultivating a strong "new" variety. This image allows the possibility that divisions may be for the good of the plant, as they are for overgrown iris, and that variety might produce a hardier, more productive hybrid.

In this volume the image of the plant appears most often to enhance the story of Lutheranism in the United States. This story is not one that builds steadily and then comes to a satisfying resolution. Rather, the struggle to construct an identity that is two things at once is an ongoing struggle, passed on to the next generation unfinished. Though less is discussed here of the United States and its society, that context is also fluid, always changing. The political and social conditions of colonial New Amsterdam, the Ohio frontier, and post–World War II California were as different as the soils and climates of those places are today. The story of American Lutheranism is about the hard task of learning again and again to adjust when giving up would be easier. It is not the martyrdom of rigid integrity without any flexibility, nor is it the slow suicide of always giving in; rather, it is the long haul of faithfulness in the midst of imperfection, of starting over and trying again. This is the difficult task of being both/and: both Lutheran

and simultaneously American people of a certain time who speak a particular
language, and who are both men and women, lay and clergy. The image of a
plant and the story of adaptation reveal within the Lutheran churches a persistent
variety in matters profound and trivial: of theological emphasis, of styles of
piety, of language, of social custom, of attitudes toward one another, and so on.

This story about adaptation and internal variety plays out on several fronts—
worship, leadership, governance, and ministries are among them. Each of these
receives attention in the chapters that follow. We trace American Lutherans'
transition from being the recipients of European missionaries, to self-sufficiency,
to providing leadership in the global Lutheran community and anticipating a
more mutual partnership role. Part of the transition was the organization of
patterns of governance for congregations, regional synods, general bodies, and
cooperative agencies as well as for parachurch groups. With realignment of
synodical structures—which has happened regularly since the mid-nineteenth
century—polity needed to be rethought and often was redesigned. These arrangements functioned rather like a trellis or topiary form supporting and
shaping the plant, so although this process is not the central focus of this book,
it does appear. A crucial factor in becoming self-sufficient was devising ways
to provide a reliable supply of qualified leaders, both pastors and laity. This task
led to establishment and operation of educational institutions and, to a lesser
degree, cooperation between groups. Leading worship was one of the definitive
responsibilities of the pastor's office. From the earliest decades gathering to
worship also defined Lutheran communities, and when no other activities were
carried out, worship went on. Development of forms of worship appropriate to
the contemporary cultural situation and faithful to the theological heritage was
a continual process. As the Lutheran churches became more self-sufficient, they
also expanded the scope of their activities and ministries into new areas of
evangelism and social concerns. All of these developments are part of the story
of Lutherans' adaptation in the United States.

Jaroslav Pelikan has astutely remarked that in the United States Lutherans
have passed through the same phases as European Lutherans, but in reverse
order.[20] There the dynamism of the Reformation was followed by intense attention to theological orthodoxy and then by an equally intense concern for piety.
Many Lutherans who immigrated from Europe brought pietism with them, and
so it influenced the churches and all their members; beginning in the mid-
nineteenth century Lutherans in the United States turned again to the Confessions and engaged in conferences and debates about them; most recently, a
revival of interest in Luther studies may have returned American Lutherans to
the era of the Reformation. This useful and instructive scheme appears again in
this book. However, its very clarity as a chronological device may obscure the
truth that the central concerns of all three phases are continually interacting
among Lutherans, perhaps even within individual Lutherans. Sidney Ahlstrom
pointed this out by identifying three sorts of Lutherans, which he labeled the
scholastic, the pietistic, and the critical.[21] Perhaps the critical impulse holds

together scholastic concern for objective truth and pietistic attention to personal appropriation of that truth, realizing that their cross-fertilization produces a hardy and fruitful Lutheran plant.

NOTES

1. See Christa R. Klein, "Denominational History as Public History: The Lutheran Case," ed. Robert Bruce Mullin and Russell E. Richey, *Reimagining Denominationalism: Interpretive Essays* (New York: Oxford University Press, 1994), pp. 307–317.

2. Mark A. Noll, "The Lutheran Difference," *First Things*, no. 20 (February 1992): 31–40.

3. Robert Bruce Mullin, "Denominations as Bilingual Communities," *Reimagining Denominationalism: Interpretive Essays*, pp. 162–176.

4. L. DeAne Lagerquist, "Does It Take One to Know One? Lutherans and the American Religious Historical Canon," *dialog* 25 (Summer 1986): 201–206.

5. In his article "When Is a Lutheran a 'Good Lutheran'?," *Lutheran Church Quarterly* 13 (1940): 111–123, Merle W. Boyer suggests four types of Lutherans based on (1) prior, shaping affiliation; (2) present association with a congregation; (3) sympathy with Lutheran symbolic formulations; and (4) concurrence with Luther. See esp. pp. 115–121.

6. Nancy T. Ammerman, "Denominations: Who and What Are We Studying?," *Reimagining Denominationalism: Interpretive Essays*, p. 119.

7. Krister Stendahl, "What Does It Mean to Be a Reforming Church?," ed. Charles P. Lutz, *The Reforming Church: Gift and Task* (Minneapolis: Kirk House, 1995), p. 26.

8. See Roland Bainton, *Here I Stand* (New York: Abingdon-Cokesbury Press, 1950); James Kittelson, *Luther the Reformer* (Minneapolis: Augsburg Publishing House, 1986).

9. See Paul Westermeyer, "Church Music at the End of the 19th Century," *Lutheran Quarterly* 8 (Spring 1994): 29–51 and "Church Music at the End of the 20th Century," *Lutheran Quarterly* 8 (Summer 1994): 197–211.

10. Some debate remains over whether Luther considered confession and absolution a sacrament. Luther's desire that confession and absolution continue to be practiced seems clear, but it is not evident that he regarded it as "sacrament" based on his three criteria for the constitution of a sacrament: (1) institution directly by Jesus; (2) making use of a tangible material element; and (3) acting as a means of grace.

11. "To the Councilmen of All Cities in Germany That They Establish and Maintain Christian Schools," in Timothy F. Lull, ed., *Martin Luther's Basic Theological Writings* (Minneapolis: Fortress Press, 1989), pp. 704–735.

12. For an accessible and helpful treatment of this topic see Steven E. Ozment, *The Protestants: The Birth of a Revolution* (New York: Doubleday, 1992).

13. Johann Arndt, *True Christianity*, trans. and intro. Peter Erb, Library of Christian Classics (New York: Paulist Press, 1979); Philip Jacob Spener, *Pia Desideria*, trans., ed., and intro. Theodore G. Tappert (Philadelphia: Fortress Press, 1964).

14. For an instructive and fertile effort to understand how the Lutheran witness interacts with other than European cultures see Albert Pero and Ambrose Moyo, eds., *Theology and the Black Experience: The Lutheran Heritage Interpreted by African and Africa-American Theologians* (Minneapolis: Augsburg Publishing House, 1988).

15. All of these are drawn from essays contained in *Reimagining Denominationalism:*

Interpretive Essays. See, in particular, essays by Ammerman, Mullin, and Russell E. Richey, "Denominations and Denominationalism: An American Morphology," pp. 74–98.

16. In particular, see James P. Wind and James W. Lewis, eds., *American Congregations*, 2 vols. (Chicago: University of Chicago Press, 1994).

17. Eunice Victoria Scarfe, *Pillars of Salt: A Novel Told in Stories* (Typescript), pp. 14–16.

18. Sydney Ahlstrom, "The Lutheran Church and American Culture: A Tercentenary Retrospective," *Lutheran Quarterly* 9 (November 1957): 326.

19. Emma T. Mann, *Memoir of the Life and Work of William Julius Mann* (Philadelphia: Jas. B. Rogers Printing, 1893), p. 88, cited by David A. Gustafson, *Lutherans in Crisis: The Question of Identity in the American Republic* (Minneapolis: Fortress Press, 1993), p. 125.

20. Jaroslav Pelikan, "Lutheran Heritage," *Encyclopedia of American Religious Experience*, vol. 1 (New York: Charles Scribner's Sons, 1988), pp. 419–430.

21. Sydney E. Ahlstrom, "What's Lutheran about Higher Education?—A Critique," in *What's Lutheran about Higher Education? Papers and Proceedings of the 60th Annual Convention Lutheran Educational Conference of North America* (January 1974), p. 8.

2
SCATTERED BEGINNINGS

The earliest mention of Lutherans in North America results from a case of mistaken identity; in the 1560s a Spanish general, Peter Menendez, slaughtered a group of French Huguenots in Florida and then explained his action as against *Luteranos*, which they were not, rather than against Frenchmen. This would not be the last effort to distinguish nationality and religion in the project of defining Lutheran identity, nor was it the last time Lutherans would be confused with some other group. Indeed, a primary theme of this volume is precisely Lutherans' struggle to define who they are in the American context, so it ought not be surprising that a Spanish Roman Catholic would make such a mistake. Fortunately, the confusion of identity led to slaughter only this once.

In 1619 a Danish expedition searched for the Northwest Passage with a crew of Danes, Norwegians, and Swedes—or perhaps Germans. The chaplain, Rasmus Jensen, conducted Lutheran worship in the Canadian Hudson Bay. Though this episode is a more legitimate candidate for the first Lutheran presence in North America, it was a fleeting one that left few, if any, traces. However, the nationalities represented in the crew did anticipate those that would later provide the majority of immigrant Lutherans, and the activity that Jensen led pointed to the central role of worship in defining a distinctly Lutheran way of being in America. Other themes and issues that the scattered beginnings of this chapter foreshadow include the relationship between these fledgling churches and the established and more mature Lutheran churches of Europe; the need for adequate, authorized leadership and organization; and relationships between Lutherans and members of other religious groups.

Lutheran beginnings in the Western Hemisphere were scattered. The period in which Lutherans established their presence here was temporally large, scattered over more than a century stretching from the early 1600s into the mid-1700s. Lutherans also were scattered over a large geographic area from the Canadian Hudson Bay to the Caribbean Island of St. Thomas. These distances and the separate European origins of each group of Lutherans isolated congregations and pastors from each other, save for informal, personal, and episodic contacts. Finally, these beginnings are described as scattered in a way analogous to the scattering of seed—some took root, some did not. Scattered beginnings in the New Netherlands, New Sweden, the Virgin Islands, and Ebenezer, Georgia, all had their start independent of the work of Henry Melchior Muhlenberg, who stands at the center of the next chapter. Aside from Ebenezer, all were well under way by his arrival in 1742, though his influence was later important in the areas occupied by the New Netherlands and New Sweden as well. Each one foreshadows themes and issues that reappear in other places and in other times. None of them, however, are the main story in subsequent chapters.

THE NEW NETHERLANDS

The Lutherans from the Netherlands were, in some ways, better prepared for the American situation as it would develop than any other immigrant group. Unlike most European Lutherans in state churches, they lived as a minority within a religiously diverse nation, a situation replicated in the colony of the New Netherlands founded in the 1620s. There, too, the mercantile purposes of the colony made it prudent—or better, profitable—to connive or to wink at private practice of the several religions found among the settlers from various nations. Between the Peace of Westphalia in 1648 and the British takeover of the colony in the mid-1660s, a stricter interpretation of the religious establishment gave Lutherans a taste of opposition nearly as strong as they would ever encounter in the United States. The British again relaxed regulations, allowing Lutherans to organize themselves and conduct public worship. Lutherans in the New Netherlands, become New York, wrestled with a shortage of adequate clerical leadership and developed forms of governance that reflected both their minority status and the influence of other Christian groups.

Though the Netherlands is seldom regarded as a center of Lutheranism, and rightly so, there were several congregations there, including one in Amsterdam, with a membership in the thousands.[1] In the early 1600s six congregations joined together in a sort of a synod and developed one of the earliest Lutheran "free" churches, independent of national government and thus with its own churchly administration; this would be the situation of Lutherans in the United States as well.[2] They also instituted an order of worship that would guide development of worship patterns in colonial Lutheran congregations. The model was carried not only to New Amsterdam but also through the London Savoy congregation to the southern colonies and Pennsylvania. Both the order of worship and the governing organization showed the influence of the Reformed majority in the Netherlands.

The charter granted to the Dutch West India Company stipulated that only the Reformed religion, "as present[ly] preached and practiced by public authority in the United Netherlands," would be given official recognition.[3] Nonetheless, several other religious groups, including Judaism, were represented among the early residents. Among the Lutherans there was national variety: Scandinavians, Germans, Dutch, and others. A Danish farmer named Jonas Bronck, for example, gave his name to the borough of the Bronx. As in the Netherlands, so, too, in the colony, official policy and actual practice diverged, allowing more freedom in private than in public as long as church taxes were paid. However, this situation of limited, de facto toleration was tempered by requirements for official conformity, and the benefits should not be over-estimated. The irritation of requirements such as having one's child baptized in a Reformed ritual, particularly when contrasted to the situation in old Amsterdam, prompted the Lutherans in New Amsterdam to appeal to their coreligionists in Europe for their own pastor.

Lutherans organized themselves into a congregation, stretching from New Amsterdam (Manhattan) to Albany, in 1649 and sent their request for a pastor to the Consistory of the Lutheran Church in Amsterdam. Among the signers of the letter was a Hollander, Germans, Danes, Frisians, and a Norwegian. Despite this national and linguistic variety, the appeal was for a pastor who would minister in Dutch, the language of the colony. Their request was unfulfilled for several years. When various other Lutherans in North America asked for help from the churches of Europe in subsequent decades, the delayed response would be repeated again and again. The slowness of communication by sailing ship contributed to the delay, but that technical reason by itself is not an adequate explanation. More critical was the fact that, except in a few cases, the European churches did not have official responsibility for their members across the Atlantic. Clergymen who came to serve in America were undertaking a dangerous and remote calling, not a prestigious one. In this specific case the situation was complicated by the clear indication that the civil leaders of the colony would not welcome a Lutheran pastor.

Finally, John Ernst Gutwasser was ordained and sent, arriving in New Amsterdam in 1657, eight years after the open call was issued. During the delay Governor Peter Stuyvesant instituted a new regime, one less open to varieties of religious practice. For example, fines were levied against leaders and attenders of conventicles (private religious meetings in homes), and some Lutherans were even jailed. Though the directors of the Dutch West India Company advised moderating these policies, Pastor Gutwasser was forbidden to hold meetings and even barred from baptizing children. After over a year of hiding out at a farm on Long Island and unable to do the very things for which he had come, he was compelled to return to Europe. His parishioners were still without a pastor of their own confession to minister to their needs. Instead, they again resorted to attending Reformed services, though not to joining Reformed congregations.[4]

The British took over the colony in 1664, renaming it New York; they prudently resisted the temptation to try to establish their own Church of England. The privileges granted to the previously established Reformed church encouraged the Lutherans, who petitioned the new governor on their own behalf. He granted them "liberty to send for one minister or more of their religion and they may freely and publicly exercise divine worship according to their consciences."[5] This liberty opened the way for development of a fuller church life, including the public undertakings of erecting a building and securing a pastor to preach and to celebrate the sacraments, pastoral tasks central to the practice of Lutheranism. Pastor Jacob Fabritius, a refugee from Hungary driven out by the Turks, arrived in 1669. Within a month of his arrival, he made use of the Amsterdam orders for worship to conduct the first Lutheran celebration of the Lord's Supper in New York. Before many more weeks passed, he also baptized people, including an African man named Emmanuel. With pastoral leadership at hand, the large congregation divided itself into two congregations (later known as St. Matthews in Manhattan and First Lutheran in Albany), and both secured land in anticipation of building.

Unfortunately, Fabritius' ministry in New York did not fulfill its early promise. His fondness for strong drink, his habit of wearing flamboyant red clothing, and his equally colorful vocabulary brought his congregations notoriety that the long-decorous Lutherans preferred not to receive. They wrote to Amsterdam, "Thanks be to God, we now have the privilege from his Royal Majesty and the Duke of York himself of burying our own dead and doing all that goes with it, for we bought a house here, with a place for a churchyard, and had the house put in order, so that we perform our service therein until we can build a church. All we now [need] is a capable pastor."[6] Fabritius moved on to New Sweden, where he served well. His successor in New York, Bernhard Arensius, the only Dutch pastor to serve there, was the capable leader the congregations had longed for. He ministered to them faithfully and well for two decades. During his tenure the Manhattan congregation constructed a wooden building. Arensius' death left his flock without a shepherd for another eleven years. This string of events— an unacceptable pastor, followed by a fine one, then by none—is indicative of the colonial situation of a church dependent on the goodwill of those far away to supply their needs. When the pastor's office was vacant, the church was not. The lay Lutherans of New York responded as others would in similar situations and, as they were able, provided themselves with worship and education, though of necessity forgoing the sacraments.

The next pastor came to New York from the nearby colony of New Sweden, although the Lutherans of the two settlements were not officially connected. Illness had forced Anders Rudman to secure another pastor from Sweden to take over his responsibilities in New Sweden, but when he recovered somewhat, he assumed leadership among the New York congregations. There, too, he provided for a successor, this time by encouraging a member of his former congregation to accept the call. Justus Falckner was trained at the newly founded University of Halle. Like his brother Daniel, he turned to more temporal pursuits and was not ordained before immigrating. However, Rudman recognized Justus' suitability for the task at hand and persuaded him to be ordained. The ceremony took place at Gloria Dei in Philadelphia in November 1703 with participation by Jonas Auren and Eric Bjork as well as Rudman. This event signaled several key features of the church that would develop. It was multilingual, Swedes using Latin to set aside a German to serve Scandinavians, Poles, Germans, and others in Dutch. Such variety of language and culture continues to challenge contemporary Lutherans. The event was also cooperative; the needs of the New York congregations brought together for a single task those united in their adherence to a common confession of faith as articulated in the Augsburg Confession. The one ordained was the first of a long line of Halle-trained pastors—including Johann Boltzius, Henry Muhlenberg, and John Kunze—to serve the American church and cultivate in it the practical piety and concern for the quality of spiritual life characteristic of that school.

Falckner did not confine his work to the congregations in Albany and Manhattan. He extended the church up the Hudson River Valley and into New Jersey so that by 1715 he reported serving seven congregations, traveling over 1,200 miles a year to do so. Only five years into Falckner's twenty-year tenure the Lutheran population of the Hudson Valley was dramatically increased by the arrival of immigrants from the Palatine, led by Joshua Kocherthal. Many of these newcomers moved on to Pennsylvania. Their experience is further examined in the next chapter, which treats that region. In New Jersey the first worship was held in response to an invitation from Are Van Guinea and his wife, Jora, former members of the Manhattan congregation and free blacks. The material resources of the Lutheran congregations continued to be minimal. Despite a contribution from the Lutherans of St. Thomas, Virgin Islands, toward a building fund, their property was in ill repair. They lacked adequate books for worship and instruction, and their pastor's salary was not always paid. By the time of Falckner's death in 1723, fourteen congregations in New York and New Jersey depended on his leadership. His work was continued after his death by Wilhelm Berkenmeyer, who came from Hamburg and had been trained at Altdorf, a university more inclined toward orthodoxy than Halle. The significance of the difference became evident in Berkenmeyer's cool response to Muhlenberg.

The polity set out in the Manhattan congregation's constitution reflected the influence of a Reformed environment and addressed the local situation of a free church with voluntary membership and no church taxes for financial support. These last conditions shaped the practice of all Christian groups in the United States, giving even the Roman Catholics a more democratic organization than in other nations. The Lutheran constitution adopted in 1686 provided for a solid core of lay leadership, including elected elders and deacons, and a lay reader and a bell-ringer. The elected officials served on the church council and had responsibility for church funds. In matters of "doctrine, faith, and morals" the elders and the pastor were to decide together.[7] Collection and distribution of alms for the poor were the deacons' distinctive charge. The lay reader led singing and read from prepared materials when the pastor was absent, likely serving in another congregation. The bell-ringers' tasks included the obvious one, as well as having the water ready for baptisms, sweeping the church, digging graves, and responsibility for the church-key. The importance of the last became violently apparent during a dispute between Berkenmeyer and a pastoral ''pretender.'' Although Berkenmeyer's rival lacked either adequate qualifications or proper authorization for the office he had assumed, he did have the support of the key-holder, so when Berkenmeyer arrived to lead worship the church door had to be broken down by force.[8]

Language disputes that arose in the Manhattan congregation in the 1740s provide an opportunity to observe the church's polity in action and are indicative of the struggles with language transition that continued among American Lutherans for over two centuries. The Lutheran population in the New Netherlands had always been a diverse group from several nations, with the Hollanders in the numerical minority. When the colony came under British rule, and as the number of Germans among them increased, due, in part, to Palatine immigration, it was perhaps inevitable that the members' satisfaction with using Dutch would erode. First requests for German preaching were addressed to the pastor, giving as their reason the need to prevent Lutherans from going to the Anglican Church. The pastor referred the matter to the council. Between 1742 and 1745 requests came before the council for regular use of German, and permission was granted, though not all services authorized were actually held. The German petitioners boycotted worship and then renewed their request. Four of them sponsored a German preacher who lacked proper credentials and then alienated half the council with their deceptions. A split in the congregation was averted only at the last minute by Berkenmeyer, who was no longer their resident pastor; he was firm in his support of providing German services. Only three decades later a second transition, this one from German to English, would be under way.

By the mid-1700s the Lutheran church of New York passed from Dutch to British government, from a meager toleration to a more open one. The legal situation that forced them to take part in Reformed activities produced some bitterness between the groups, but there were also indications of better personal relationships, such as intermarriages. The original multinational composition of the Lutheran community was sustained, even increased with the addition of African members, but the balance was tipped toward the Germans. Building upon the models brought from Amsterdam, a polity was in place, and a standard of worship practice was in use. For pastoral leadership the Lutherans of New York were still dependent on European sources and continued to be vulnerable to pretenders, unqualified for the office. With Lutherans in other places, particularly Pennsylvania, they were establishing relationships that would later support Muhlenberg's organizational efforts.

NEW SWEDEN

A Swedish colony was established in North America not long after the Dutch founded the New Netherlands. In New Sweden Lutherans were, however, in a quite different situation due to the Lutheran Church's established status in Sweden. That arrangement was the usual one for most European Lutheran churches, but in the Western Hemisphere this was one of the very few situations in which Lutherans were in charge of political life and government of the entire colony. The Swedish Lutheran Church's official responsibility for the spiritual well-being of those settlers was also unusual. Instructions to the governor and pastor made clear that this concern for spiritual matters was to be extended to the natives of the land as well. Like their coreligionists in the New Netherlands, the Swedes struggled with transitions in language, from Swedish to English, but unlike them the Swedes did not maintain their confessional identity in the process. These Swedish Lutheran congregations were absorbed into the English Episcopal Church.

The Swedish colony in the Delaware Valley was begun at the urging of a former governor of the New Netherlands in 1638. The unusual situation of Lutherans' having political control of an American colony lasted less than two decades before the Dutch took over in 1655, and the English followed nine years later. The Swedish settlers and their descendants maintained religious connection to their homeland several decades longer; indeed, it was renewed in the 1690s by the arrival of three Swedish clergymen charged to care for them as the royal instructions to Governor Printz had required a half century earlier. Johan Printz arrived in 1642 and was joined the next year by Pastor Johan Campanius. Queen Christina provided directions for how the colony was to be ruled, from mundane matters such as the care of livestock to the conduct of worship and tolerant treatment of the Dutch Reformed living in the colony.

Campanius was, of course, more directly involved with religious matters than was Printz, although the governor was the one who might have disturbed the Dutch in their exercise of their Reformed religion. Campanius had two primary audiences: the Swedish Lutherans and the native peoples of the area. For the former he was instructed to "take all good care that divine services be zealously performed according to the true Augsburg Confession, the Council of Uppsala, and the ceremonies of the Swedish church."[9] The last direction ensured that worship in New Sweden followed a more elaborate form than used by the Lutherans in New Amsterdam. Further, he was to see to the instruction of the youth and to maintain discipline. For the second audience his task was not unrelated. The governor having seen that they were treated with "humanity and respect," no doubt turned over to the pastor the charge to "gradually [instruct the natives] in the true Christian religion and worship and in other ways [bring them] to civility and good public manner."[10] The stated reasons for this evangelization effort were not entirely religious but included also the pragmatic need to gain the natives' loyalty. Campanius' efforts toward this end earned him the distinction of being the first Lutheran missionary, preceding even the famous Danish mission to India begun in 1705. Along with his face-to-face work, he translated Luther's Small Catechism into Lenni-Lenape, the Delaware language; predating John Elliot, this was the first effort to provide Christian materials to

Native Americans in their own language, though it was not published for half a century. That he translated a distinctly Lutheran document, rather than a portion of the Bible, is worth noting as an indication that he adhered to a more confessional sort of Lutheranism than those pastors trained at Halle would bring. After six years he and his family returned to Sweden, and his work among the Lenni-Lenape was left untended. Thus, this early effort to extend Lutheranism was a false start that bore no fruits.

After the Dutch assumed rule of the colony, the Lutherans continued to get their pastors from Sweden and to practice their religion freely, though their coreligionists in the New Netherlands were not allowed to do so. For nearly forty years they had the leadership of Lars Carlson Lock, who arrived during the last months of Campanius' ministry and died in 1688 in America. He traveled—sometimes by canoe—between three congregations in Christina (Wilmington), Tinicum Island, and Wicaco (Philadelphia). Two of these constructed wooden buildings, but the third met in a blockhouse, or fort, of which one of Lock's successors observed that it was "a place of defence for the body as well for the soul."[11] For a colleague Lock had Fabritius, who ministered to the Swedes after he left the New Netherlands. Before their deaths both men became infirm: Fabritius blind and Lock lame. Thus, as the seventeenth century came to an end, the Swedes in North America were without pastors. At Wicaco a layman read to the people from the Bible and a collection of sermons, and there was an old widow who taught children to read from the Bible. So, too, at Crane Hook a lay reader, Carl Christophersson Springer, was the mainstay of the congregation.[12]

Among the letters Springer wrote back to Sweden was one responding to a request for information about the settlers and pleading their need for a pastor. The colonists described themselves as "almost universally farmers, who plow and sow and practice agriculture, and live according to the laudable old Swedish customs in meat and drink. . . . Our wives and daughters also busy themselves much in spinning both wool and flax, many also with weaving." They went on to echo Article 7 of the Augsburg Confession: "God grant that we may also obtain faithful Pastors and watchmen for our souls, who may feed us with that spiritual food, which is the preaching of God's word and the administration of the Holy Sacraments in their proper form."[13] Through a connection with a nephew of Governor Printz, the colonists' need had come to the sympathetic attention of King Charles XI and aroused a renewed sense of responsibility for the Swedes in North America. In 1697 three pastors arrived, equipped with hymnals, Bibles, and copies of Campanius' catechism.

Anders Rudman, Eric Bjork, and Jonas Auren launched efforts to rebuild the beleaguered church both spiritually and materially. Among the new churches they built were Holy Trinity in Wilmington and Gloria Dei in Philadelphia, where Falckner was ordained. One hundred thirty men contributed 1,083 days' work to raise a building at Crane Hook. After the dedication members shared a festive banquet of lamb, calf, deer, and turkey; eggs, raisins, bread, and cake;

ale, red wine, rum, and coffee. The new church had seating for nearly 170, with a few more places designated for men than for women. A small pew rent was charged.[14] In the new Gloria Dei Rudman held services that lasted from eight in the morning into the early afternoon. These included a significant period of catechetical instruction as well as prayers, hymns, a sermon, and High Mass with communion.[15] Congregational records from the early 1700s indicate that expansion beyond the original membership had taken place; in addition to Swedes and Swedish-speaking Finns there were English, Irish, Germans, and "black servants," and among these members were former Quakers and Presbyterians. Before the Revolution two dozen pastors were sent from Sweden to the American mission with some financial support and assurance that they would receive calls when they returned to Sweden. Israel Acrelius wrote a history of the settlement. Carl Magnus Wrangel cooperated with Henry Melchior Muhlenberg in his efforts to organize the American church.

Renewal of the tie with Sweden did not bring all difficulties to an end. Money was in short supply. Members of single congregations lived on both sides of the Delaware River, creating logistical problems that gave rise to internal discord. Unauthorized and unqualified "pretenders" tried to set themselves up as pastors, stirring up congregations and causing trouble for duly called candidates such as Rudman's successor. Pastors who came from Sweden initially were unable to use English, and if they regarded the Delaware Valley only as a stepping-stone for return to Sweden, they had little motivation to learn. This was a real problem, as some services were being conducted in English by the early eighteenth century, and English was increasingly the language of social interaction. Perhaps if the Swedes had retained political control and sustained the religious link, things would have gone differently, but that is beyond knowing.

What is clear is that as English was used more and more and Swedish less and less, the Lutherans of New Sweden moved toward the British Episcopal Church, with which the Church of Sweden was in good relationship, rather than toward the German Lutherans. Cooperative interactions between the Swedish and Anglican clergy who exchanged pulpits and between the Swedish and English laypeople whose families became linked though marriage fostered the shift. In the Lutheran congregations the Episcopal Book of Common Prayer was used for English services, which were attended by neighboring English folk when they were without a priest. As early as 1742 the congregation at Penns Neck resolved to hold all their services in English, using the forms of the Church of England.[16] When consulted by Carl Wrangel on this general matter, Muhlenberg responded at length. Drawing upon his own experience among German Lutherans, he indicated that he preached "in English as well as German, and so we not only retain our members, but also win other men and women with their children. We should look at language as we look at a bridge over a river." He went on, "Whether it is made of oak or of 'kanuo' is not important, so long as it holds and enables us to get across and toward our goal."[17] After the Revolution the congregations petitioned to elect their own pastors rather than having them supplied by the Swedish Church. The Swedish king withdrew his support from the mission to the United States in 1789. By 1846 all seven of the Swedish Lutheran congregations joined the Episcopal Church.

The Swedish Lutheran mission to America came to an end. Although the Church of Sweden's mission responsibility for the Lutherans in the Delaware Valley might at first seem an advantage, in the changing circumstances of an English colony and then the new nation it appears to have been a burden. Few new immigrants arrived from Sweden, and the subsequent generations became ever more integrated into the English colonies. Insistence upon using the Swedish language and following Swedish forms no longer served the increasingly American membership. Similarities between Swedish Lutheranism and the Church of England encouraged the descendants of the settlers to cross over the bridge of language to another church. Neither of Johan Campanius' audiences—the Swedes or the Lenni-Lenape—continued as Lutherans. The legacy of this mission, therefore, is to be found hidden in the Episcopal "Old Swedes" congregations, in the lineage of Rudman's ordination of Falckner to serve in New York, and in the cooperation between Wrangel and Muhlenberg.

DANISH VIRGIN ISLANDS

The third scattered beginning of Lutheranism in the Western Hemisphere was not on the North American continent, but the subsequent relationship between Lutherans in the Virgin Islands and those in the United States warrants attention to this Danish colony. Like New Sweden, the Danish West Indies of St. Thomas, St. John, and St. Croix were colonized and governed by members of a Lutheran state church. The Danish West Indian and Guinea Company helped secure St. Thomas for Denmark in the mid-1660s, just after the British took over both the New Netherlands and New Sweden. Africans were brought as slaves within a decade, and St. Thomas became a busy slave market as well as a colony of Danish Lutherans. The population, however, included a wider range of nationalities and churches. Notable among them were German Moravians, whose mission work among the Africans challenged the Lutherans to alter their methods and give greater autonomy to the African members. Long before the 1917 transfer of the Virgin Islands to the United States, the majority of Lutherans there were African Americans.

The Danish Lutheran Church was established in the Virgin Islands by Pastor Kjeld Jensen Slagelse. He arrived with Governor Erik Nielsen Schmidt in 1666 and shortly thereafter founded a congregation, the second oldest in this hemisphere and the origin of the Frederik congregation in Charlotte Amalie, St. Thomas. After the governor died, Slagelse temporarily filled that office as well. The tribulations of meager supplies, disease, and death led Slagelse and many of the Danes to return to their homeland. The Danish West India Company recommenced the colony in earnest, in 1671, sending to the island a shipload of just over 100 Danes, nearly half of them convicts intended as laborers. Though Pastor Slagelse was among them when they set sail, he and more than eighty others died en route.

George Jørgen Iverson, the new governor, was busy with the tasks of organizing the colony, bringing together the Danish and Dutch residents, and attending to the people's physical needs. Quickly he saw that Fort Christian was made usable for conducting both Danish Lutheran and Dutch Reformed worship as well as for his own residence. In the absence of a pastor these services were led by a layman, likely Iverson himself on some occasions. Among his first set of orders were requirements that everyone who spoke Danish attend worship each Sunday or pay a fine; that "persons of all other nations" were to do the same; and that every householder "encourage his servants to be pious and have morning and evening prayers; and if he allows them to do work on Sundays which might have been done on Saturday, or if he occupied servants of other people in his employ, he is, for every offence, to pay fifty pounds of tobacco."[18] The fines were divided between the king, the complainant, and the church, thus providing the church with a source of income unavailable farther north where the Lutheran church was not established and therefore dependent on voluntary contributions from its members. Requests for a pastor yielded little; though men were sent, death, drunkenness, or disputes made many of them useless.

The Danes, like the Dutch Lutherans in the New Netherlands, were always in a numerical minority, composing perhaps one-sixth of the European population. The predominance of the Dutch made that language the most common one until the early 1800s, when English surpassed it. A treaty with the duchy of Brandenberg added more Dutch, German, and Flemish workers. A group of French Protestants increased the island's religious, linguistic, and national variety. Africans were first brought to the island as slaves in 1673. A free black population also developed, and before the turn of the century Africans were in the majority.

The first evidence of mission work among the Africans was the baptism of a slave in 1713. However, sustained Lutheran efforts did not begin until after the Moravians had been active for a decade. Moravians were prompted to undertake evangelization of Africans in the Danish Virgin Islands by the witness of Anton Ulrich, a baptized slave who traveled to Denmark in the party of the president of the Danish West India Company early in the 1730s for the king's coronation. There Count Nikolaus Ludwig von Zinzendorf met him, heard his plea on behalf of his fellow slaves, and was inspired to launch the Moravians' first foreign mission in the Virgin Islands. The work was largely conducted by men and women who earned their living in occupations such as potter or carpenter. Along with preaching, they provided instruction in blacksmithing, shoemaking, and other trades. That the Moravians from the outset did their evangelization in

Dutch Creole, the predominant language of the Africans, contributed to their enormous success. Lutherans also complained that their competitors for converts required less instruction and thus were more attractive.

The first serious Lutheran venture was the educational effort begun by Pastor Hans Jacob Otteson Stoud in the 1740s, but it, too, was short-lived. When the Danish crown bought out the Danish West India Company in the 1750s, a royal decree defined the church's task among the island's enslaved Africans. The Word of God was to be preached to them; they were to be instructed in Christianity; and children were to be baptized, thus becoming church members. Ten students were sent from Denmark to assist the pastors in this work, specifically, in its instructional phase. Before anyone could be baptized by the pastors, they were instructed by these men in religion and in the Danish language, which was largely unknown to the slaves, as Creole was unknown to the Danes. This linguistic requirement, imposed by the church in Denmark, hampered the Lutherans' efforts. Similarly, continued use of Danish in worship prevented many Africans from full participation in the services of the church.

A second phase of work began in the 1770s with recognition that the Moravians' less culture-bound methods of evangelization were producing greater results. Church authorities in Denmark gave permission for several significant changes, all of them more attentive to the specific circumstances of the African audience. Dutch Creole was substituted as the language both of instruction and of worship. Parallel congregations were established so that the Africans and the Danes might share a building, but worship at different times in different styles. For example, the pastor ceased wearing a ruff, and changes were made in some components of the liturgy. Within these specifically African congregations members held leadership positions similar to the lay reader of the New Netherlands, though more appropriately called the church clerk. Able holders of this office, such as Michael Samuelsen, allowed the African "mission" congregation to continue services during clerical vacancies, even when the Danes did not.[19] Finally, missionaries were directed to concentrate their efforts in the cities rather than attempting to travel between rural areas as they had done in the past. In the first five years these changes yielded about 200 new African Lutheran members per year.[20] By 1800 the mission congregation on St. Thomas had approximately 1,000 members divided equally between slave and free.

These changes in mission strategy and later educational projects required materials in the local Dutch Creole. Fortunately, the necessary translation project was begun even before 1770 by Johannes Christian Kingo. He arrived in 1757 and stayed a quarter of a century, receiving ordination specifically to work among the Africans. During his ministry Kingo earned a reputation for defending his parishioners even if he thereby antagonized the local government leaders and planters or the church authorities in Denmark. At his own initiative, he compiled a dictionary, translated Luther's *Small Catechism*, and then Matthew's gospel. In addition he prepared a grammar book. Additional linguistic work was done by J. M. Magens, a linguist and layman from a St. Thomas family, and by missionary Erik Røring Wold. Wold's work included a hymnal and Magen's the Bible.[21]

From the outset education was a critical part of both the Moravian and the Lutheran missions. Beginning in 1787, the Danes went further, introducing a plan for a system of free public schools for slaves. The schools were set up in towns, in conjunction with Lutheran congregations. Free blacks were appointed as the teachers, a position then linked to the church clerk's office. Creole was stipulated as the language of instruction. In 1839, expansion of these schools by extension into the rural areas and by making attendance compulsory prompted other modifications as well. The larger number of students created a need for more teachers, a need addressed by using Moravians as instructors. Early in the century two brief British occupations had encouraged a trend toward English. Rather than continue to offer instruction in Creole, the new ordinance directed that English be used. This gave Africans access to the language most commonly used by the Europeans, a minority but a minority with power.[22] The schools also helped prepare the way for the end of slavery and final emancipation of those Africans who were still slaves in the mid-1840s.

Slavery in the Danish Virgin Islands ended when Governor Peter von Scholten proclaimed emancipation on July 3, 1848. The immediate context was a slave rebellion on St. Croix, but preliminary steps toward emancipation had been taken the previous year. Indeed, since the Danes were the first nation to outlaw international trade in slaves in 1792, the movement had been in this direction. The educational measures discussed earlier were part of that movement. Von Scholten also instituted advances in the conditions of free Africans, such as giving them the right to secure licenses to engage in trade.[23] Like the Moravians, the Lutheran Church freed its slaves in advance of the general proclamation. The decision to free the seven adults and five children was made by the chancellery in Copenhagen in 1845.[24]

Although in subsequent years the proportion of Danes among Lutherans in the Virgin Islands dropped still further, when Denmark sold the Virgin Islands to the United States in 1917, contact between the Lutheran churches was established via a Danish American, Pastor A. G. Kildegaard. Unlike the case of New Sweden, where the missionary pastors' adherence to Swedish and the ready availability of an English alternative led Lutherans into the Episcopal Church, in the Danish Virgin Islands bold use of new languages was the means of expanding the church beyond its initial membership. Translation of Lutheranism there was not merely a matter of using Dutch Creole and then English. Changes in worship and development of leadership also contributed to the growth of Lutheranism among the Africans of the Danish Virgin Islands and thus to the continued life of this beginning. This is one of few examples in the United States of a fruitful transfer of Lutheranism from a European language and culture into another language and culture. The number of church members in the Danish Virgin Islands was relatively small (approximately 2,500 members from five congregations in 1917). Yet, the ministry there bore remarkable fruit. Deaconess

Emma Francis, for example, became a leader in social ministry and was among the founders of Transfiguration Lutheran in Harlem.

THE SALZBURGERS OF GEORGIA

This fourth beginning is removed temporally from the other three by several decades, bringing us close to Muhlenberg's arrival. It appears as a scattered beginning, nonetheless, because of the uniqueness of the case. The Salzburgers immigrated to North America as a group for religious reasons and initially lived communally. Thus, they provide an instructive contrast to most other Lutherans, who arrived from Europe individually or as members of small family groups and whose leaving was prompted more by economic concerns than religious ones. Although Lutherans often have settled near each other, rarely have they been so intentional in doing so. The Salzburgers, like the church members in the Virgin Islands, also provide a cautionary reminder that not all Lutherans are clustered in Pennsylvania and the upper Midwest, nor have they been so for two centuries.

Regionalism and the concentration of Lutherans in identifiable areas of settlement are, however, a good place to begin consideration of the Salzburgers, whose removal from that European area was prompted by a sudden, strict interpretation of the regional religious arrangements stipulated by the Peace of Augsburg and the Peace of Westphalia. These two treaties responded first to the upheavals of the Reformation and then to the violent conflicts of the Thirty Years' War by allowing for controlled religious variety among Christians on the basis of freedom of religion for rulers, in the first case for Lutherans and Roman Catholics and then in the second for Calvinists as well. The principle *cuius regio eius religio* granted the ruler of an area the right to determine the religion that would be practiced within its bounds. Thus, a Roman Catholic ruler would establish a Roman Catholic city or territory, while a Lutheran would establish a Lutheran one. The success of such a model of religious purity depended on the mobility of those who held to the "wrong" confession; their willingness to exercise that mobility; relative stability of governance; and some degree of practical tolerance within the official policy of homogeneity. This arrangement can hardly be regarded as religious toleration, as it maintained the Constantinian notion of a single church coinciding with a unified social unit, albeit on a smaller scale. Nonetheless, this regional approach did suggest the possibility that more than one expression of Christianity might be valid, thus anticipating more generally tolerant arrangements that would later develop.

The alpine territory of Salzburg, larger in those years than the present city, long had been ruled by the Roman Catholic archbishop acting as secular prince as well as a church official. Rich deposits of salt and silver made the post desirable to those interested in material wealth. In the sixteenth century the miners who harvested these natural resources were attracted to the Reformation teachings of Martin Luther, and by 1560 the population, especially in the outlying areas, was largely Lutheran. In contrast the archbishops who ruled Salzburg continued in the Catholic Church. Thus, when the Thirty Years' War came to an end, the Peace of Westphalia maintained, in this instance, a Roman Catholic ruler for a population that was more Lutheran than Catholic.

Although the Lutherans in Salzburg, like their coreligionists in the colonies of the Western Hemisphere, were without adequate pastoral leadership, they were firm in their commitment to what they knew of the teachings of the Augsburg Confession even in the face of opposition. As early as the 1680s, small numbers of Lutherans were expelled from Salzburg. Among them was Joseph Schaitberger, the author of the "Exiles' Song," a hymn beloved by later generations of his country folk. When Count Leopold Anton Eleutherius von Firmian became archbishop, opposition to the Lutherans became overt and aggressive. Though perhaps one-sixth of his subjects were Lutherans, they were fewer in the cities than in the countryside, so it is possible that he underestimated their strength in numbers as well as their devotion. In the summer of 1731, 150 deputies gathered to pledge their loyalty to the Evangelical faith, following local custom by sealing their oath with a lick of salt.[25] What they anticipated then happened: on October 31 an edict of expulsion was published, ordering all Lutherans without property to leave the territory within eight days and those with property to do so within three months. These harsh conditions were in violation of the treaty, and they were made worse by the fact that they were issued just at the outset of winter. Nonetheless, as many as 30,000 faithful Salzburgers set out in search of refuge in Protestant regions.[26]

Protection and aid came from several sources. Along the way the inhabitants of Protestant towns offered food, shelter, and spiritual comfort to these quaintly dressed sojourners. Twenty thousand industrious refugees were welcomed by Frederick William I of Brandenburg-Prussia. National and religious connections between Germany and England yielded an invitation to immigrate to the newly established English colony of Georgia. The king of England, George II, was also duke of Hanover-Brunswick and, though publicly head of the Church of England, privately a Lutheran. His chaplain, Friedrich Michael Ziegenhagen, was a member both of the Society for the Propagation of Christian Knowledge (SPCK) and of the Trustees for Georgia and thus well placed as an advocate for the Salzburgers. Pastor Samuel Urlsperger of Augsburg, a corresponding member of the SPCK, was charged with gathering 300 Salzburgers to go to Georgia. This invitation provided the exiles, who for religious reasons could not stay in Salzburg, with a promising alternative. The trustees would pay for their passage, land, seeds, and other material necessities, and the SPCK would pay the pastors' salaries. There would also be benefits for the English from the Salzburgers, who were to act as a buffer between the English settlements in South Carolina and the Spanish in Florida and as well as provide a source of raw materials.

The first group that made the journey to North America by way of Rotterdam and Dover was nearer to three dozen than the proposed 300. Subsequent transports would include other Germans in addition to Salzburgers and swelled their numbers toward 1,000. In Rotterdam the first transport of Salzburgers was joined by Pastors Johann Martin Boltizius and Israel Christian Gronau, both instructors at the Latin School in Halle; these two men accompanied them on their passage and gave both spiritual and secular leadership in Georgia. Thus, the Halle tradition of pietism, already represented by Justus Falckner of New York, was again introduced to American Lutheranism. After a two-month winter voyage, in March 1734 the Salzburgers arrived in Charleston and were met by the founder of the colony, James Ogelthorpe.

The Salzburger colony of Ebenezer was the site of numerous firsts in the history of Georgia. When the inadequacy of the initial location due to infertile soil and malarial conditions became evident, a second effort was made at Red Bluff about twenty-five miles upriver, or a six-hour horseback ride, from the major English settlement of Savannah's. The town was laid out on a plan similar to Savannah's. The exiles soon built a water-powered mill, the first in Georgia. By direction of their English patrons they also established a silk industry that endured as long as it was subsidized. In keeping with the practical piety of Halle, church, school, and orphanage were organized. Both the school and the orphanage were also the first of their kind in the colony. The example of the orphanage inspired George Whitfield to found a second such institution in Savannah.

The community was both civil and churchly. In other places and times, such as the upper Midwest in the late nineteenth century, the compact settlement patterns of Lutheran immigrant groups brought the religious and secular communities into close alignment; however, in Ebenezer the two were as nearly coincident as they would ever be. The membership of the congregation and the town overlapped to an extraordinary degree, with each member of the congregation being asked to subscribe to the Augsburg Confession and a set of regulations devised by their three religious patrons: Urlsperger of Augsburg, Zeigenhagen of London, and Francke of Halle.[27] The pastors provided a degree of leadership that bordered on theocracy. Boltzius extensive reports to Halle document the wide range of matters in which he was involved, from planting the mulberry trees for the silk industry, to supervision of the orphanage and the more expected affairs of worship.[28] He conducted daily worship in Ebenezer and regularly traveled to Savannah to minister to Germans there, both Lutheran and Reformed. When Muhlenberg arrived from Halle enroute to Pennsylvania, he was instructed to travel by way of Ebenezer and there consult with Boltzius. Later he would return to mediate in a dispute between two of Boltzius' successors.

At the outset the Salzburger colonists rejected slavery, and the trustees of Georgia prohibited both importation and use of slaves. However, after a only few years' experience with the agricultural conditions of Georgia, colonists pressed for reconsideration of slavery, which was the usual practice of the region. Eventually, in 1750, slaves were introduced, and even Boltzius succumbed to the system despite his early strong disapproval. In correspondence with his sponsors he came to the view that slavery could be turned to a good end if used as an opportunity for evangelism. The mixture of subversive and conservative impulses in the efforts made at Ebenezer doomed them to failure. The Salzburgers undertook to baptize African infants; between 1761 and 1767 the number of Africans baptized nearly matched the number of Salzburgers in the first transport a generation before. The German refugees instructed enslaved Africans, even teaching them to read German in direct violation of the law. However, parish records do not yield any evidence that the Lutherans circumvented the laws that prevented slaves from marrying and establishing durable family units. This strategy of evangelism put the converts in the untenable position of being German-speaking Lutherans in church and school and then returning to their work as slaves. Though some Salzburgers justified the introduction of slavery by the opportunity it provided to preach the gospel to those who were enslaved, the continuation of slavery itself undercut their evangelization.[29]

By the time of the American Revolution, less than half a century after the arrival of the first transport, the Salzburger colony of Ebenezer was on the decline. Boltzius' death in 1765 was followed by a period of intense internal conflict brought on by bad relationships among the three pastors and then by an interim without pastoral leadership. The communal property arrangement had proved ineffective and been abandoned, allowing individual families to move away from the town onto their own land. Many of the residents favored the Revolutionary party and so fled when British forces occupied the town, used Jerusalem Church for a hospital, and shot a bullet hole through Luther's swan atop the steeple.[30]

That swan still flies above Jerusalem Church, now surrounded by a retreat center rather than by a lively communal settlement. The colony's significance is in its experiments rather than in its long-term consequences. The contemporary presence of Lutherans in the southeastern United States resulted from later migrations from Pennsylvania more than from expansion of Salzburger beginnings. As a mission outpost for Lutherans in Halle and for the British SPCK as well as a political entity, the Salzburgers were involved in political matters to a greater degree than Lutherans in other North American settings. Their efforts to run the colony with an established church that granted wide authority to the clergy were finally not worthy of emulation. While their concerns about slavery and attempts to evangelize African Americans are notable, there are few enduring results. Slavery was adopted in the colony, and the church membership remained largely German. The Salzburgers shared Muhlenberg's connection with Halle and were the first to welcome him to this continent. That hospitality does not give them responsibility for what he accomplished; nonetheless, it does point to their characteristic that was most widely shared among Lutherans in subsequent generations, namely, having been influenced by the pietism of that place.

SUMMARY

The yield from these four beginnings was uneven but always relatively meager. The dependence of Lutherans in this hemisphere upon leadership and resources from Europe hampered their ability to respond to the American context and to develop mature churches. In the Virgin Islands continued use of languages other than the dominant one in their area raised barriers to evangelism for decades; the transition to English in New Sweden was the bridge out of the Lutheran Church. Nonetheless, there was life in these churches. Extreme circumstances encouraged pragmatic ecumenical efforts, particularly with the Reformed and Anglicans in North America. Relations with Moravians were less cooperative. Despite linguistic differences Lutherans did attract some newcomers as well as continuing to nurture their own faith.

NOTES

1. Lars Pederson Qualben, *The Lutheran Church in Colonial America* (New York: Thomas Nelson, 1940), p. 126.

2. E. Theodore Bachmann and Mercia Brenne Bachmann, *Lutheran Churches of the World* (Minneapolis: Augsburg Publishing House, 1989), p. 577.

3. Qualben, *Lutheran Church*, p. 126.

4. F. H. Knubel and M.G.G. Scherer, eds., *Our Church: An Official Study Book* (Philadelphia: United Lutheran Publication House, 1924), p. 43.

5. Knubel and Scherer, *Our Church*, p. 47.

6. Arnold J. H. VanLaer, trans., *The Lutheran Church in New York, 1649–1772: Records in the Lutheran Church Archives at Amsterdam, Holland* (New York: New York Public Library, 1946), p. 909.

7. Qualben, *Lutheran Church*, p. 277.

8. New York Evangelical Church of St. Matthew, *Protocol of the Lutheran Church in New York City, 1702–1750* (New York: Synod [i.e., United Lutheran Synod of New York and New England], 1958), pp. 116–117. The incident took place in New Jersey. The key was held by Hendrykje, suggesting either that a woman was the bell-ringer or that she was the wife of the bell-ringer. In any case, she also threatened Berkenmeyer, saying that she would "smash his brains in." Procession of the communion cup was also at issue.

9. Trygve Skarsten, "Johan Campanius, Pastor in New Sweden," Appendix I: "Instructions for the Governor of New Sweden, Johan Printz," *Lutheran Quarterly* 2 (Spring 1988): 80.

10. Ibid., p. 76.

11. Israel Acrelius, *A History of New Sweden*, 2d ed., trans. William M. Reyonolds, Memoirs of the Historical Society of Pennsylvania, vol. II (Philadelphia: Historical Society of Pennsylvania, 1966), pp. 176–177.

12. Richard Hulan, "New Sweden and Its Churches," *Lutheran Quarterly* 2 (Spring 1988): 11.

13. Acrelius, *History*, pp. 187–188.

14. Eric Peter Mouritz Larson, *The Virgin Islands Story* (Philadelphia: Fortress Press, 1950), pp. 89–90.

15. Conrad Bergendoff, *The Church of Sweden on the Delaware, 1638–1831* (Rock Island: Augustana Historical Society, 1988), p. 9.

16. Suzanne Geissler, *Lutheranism and Anglicanism in Colonial New Jersey: An Early Ecumenical Experiment in New Sweden*, Studies in American Religion, vol. 29 (Lewiston, New York: Edwin Mellon Press, 1988), p. 1.

17. Henry Melchior Muhlenberg, Letter to Carl Magnus Wrangel, 12 August 1761, trans. Milan von Lany in *The Lutheran Church Quarterly* 13 (January 1940): 82.

18. Larson, *Virgin Islands*, p. 18.

19. Jeff G. Johnson, *Black Christians: The Untold Lutheran Story* (St. Louis: Concordia Publishing House, 1991), p. 43.

20. Ibid., p. 41.

21. Larson, *Virgin Islands*, pp. 113–114.

22. Neville A. T. Hall, *Slave Society in the Danish West Indies: St. Thomas, St. John, and St. Croix*, ed. B. W. Higman (Baltimore: Johns Hopkins University Press, 1992), p. 199.

23. Larson, *Virgin Islands*, Chapter 14.

24. Ibid., p. 185.

25. George Fenwick Jones, *The Salzburger Saga: Religious Exiles and Other Germans along the Savannah* (Athens: University of Georgia Press, 1984), p. 6.

26. E. Clifford Nelson, ed., *The Lutherans in North America* (Philadelphia: Fortress Press, 1975), p. 33.

27. These regulations are reproduced in P. A. Strobel, *The Salzburgers and Their Descendants*, Foreword, Appendix, and Index by Edward D. Wells, Jr. (Athens: University of Georgia Press, 1953 (first published Baltimore: T. Newton Kurtz, 1855), pp. 94–99.

28. Samuel Urlsperger, *Detailed Reports on the Salzburger Emigrants Who Settled in America*, 9 vols. (Athens: University of Georgia Press, 1968–1988).

29. Johnson, *Black Christians*, pp. 55–66 provides an instructive account of the Salzburgers' shifting response to slavery and their evangelization efforts.

30. A legend asserts that at his execution John Huss called out from the flames, "You kill a goose but a swan will arise." The words for goose and swan pun on the names Huss and Luther.

3
PLANTING A CHURCH

A century after the beginnings in New York, New Sweden, and the Virgin Islands and just as the Salzburgers were getting settled in Georgia, the number of Lutherans in North America began to grow rapidly, and the churches took on more definite shape. Membership in those churches was increasingly German as immigration by groups and individuals from southwestern Germany accelerated. The religious life of Lutherans was given clearer form in local settings, connections between congregations and pastors were made more formal, and as Lutherans moved beyond their initial concentration in eastern areas, the church also expanded into the South and the West.

The impetus to describe these changes as the church being planted comes most specifically from a phrase used by one of the chief gardeners, Henry Melchior Muhlenberg, who arrived in Philadelphia in 1742. *Ecclesia non planta, sed plantanda*[1]: whether one reads this as "the church must be planted" or "is being planted" is not nearly as important as the fact that in the second half of the eighteenth century it was planted, its roots reached more deeply into the American soil, and it bore fruit. By the early 1800s the Lutheran Church in the United States was far less precarious and fragile than it had been a century earlier, and it was well on its way to being firmly established.

Looking back from the late twentieth century, Muhlenberg's role in this process both as pastor and as organizer of the Ministerium of Pennsylvania was crucial, but he was not alone in the work. He had forerunners and contemporaries in Pennsylvania and the other colonies, some of them allies and others competitors. As the church and its organization expanded in numbers and geography, other men provided leadership parallel to Muhlenberg's: in New York, his son-in-law John Christopher Kunze; in the Carolinas, John Bachman; and on the western frontier, John Stough.

BEFORE MUHLENBERG

In the century prior to Muhlenberg's arrival the Lutherans in the Western Hemisphere were found in several scattered locations. They were largely dependent on more established European churches for clergy, and their contact with each other was episodic. In 1703 one of those episodes of cooperation took place—the ordination of Justus Falckner at Gloria Dei in Philadelphia by Swedish pastors to serve the New York congregations. Because it not only provides a glimpse of the situation at the turn of the century but also anticipates developments of the eighteenth century, it is worth returning to this event.

Though it was not evident at the time, Philadelphia would in the next decades come to be an important center of American Lutheranism as well as of the infant nation. The Church of Sweden had recently revived its mission responsibility for Swedes living in the now English colonies and sent clergy to see to their spiritual needs, but the situation among Lutherans in New York was less satisfactory. No European church bore responsibility for Lutherans from several nations who lived there; nor had connections with the Constitutory of Amsterdam assured a reliable source of clergy. Consequently, the lay members were left to conduct their own worship—likely by reading a printed sermon and definitely without the sacraments—or to attend the services offered by another church. The Swedish clergy stepped into the gap; first Anders Rudman served the New Yorkers himself, and then three of the Swedes ordained a pastor for them. Justus Falckner, known to Rudman as a member of the latter's former parish, had studied at the newly founded University of Halle before immigrating and was influenced by its pietism. That same influence would be spread still further, though not without challenge, in the second half of the century by several pastors associated with the university and other Halle foundations. These men were sent from Halle to serve the Lutheran population, which was ever more German, due to a surge of immigration and the movement of the Swedish-founded congregations into the Church of England.

Falckner's parish extended from New York City up the Hudson River, including more than half a dozen local congregations by 1715. The arrival of thousands of Palatines, many of them Lutheran, early in the 1710s swelled the number of potential members for those congregations. Like the Salzburgers, who would come to Georgia three decades later, though not as intensely, some of the Palatines left southwestern Germany in response to religious conditions. The bitter winter of 1708–1709 contributed to their desire to leave, as did the detrimental effects of war and taxes that followed. The attraction of the American colonies as a more prosperous location was fostered both by the willingness of the English to sponsor German immigration and by land agents' efforts to promote the advantages of the colonies, especially Pennsylvania. Two organized waves of Palatines made the journey in 1708 and 1709.

The first, smaller group of just over fifty traveled via London with Pastor Joshua Kocherthal as their leader. In the spring they were settled up the Hudson

River with the dual purpose of providing naval stores such as tar and hemp to the English and acting as buffer between the British and the natives. To plead for better conditions, Kocherthal returned to London, where he discovered that the large influx of Palatines was wearing out their welcome. Queen Anne was sympathetic to the Germans, but her subjects found giving hospitality to more than 10,000 refugees burdensome and increasingly irksome. Nearly 800 families were relocated in Limerick, Ireland, to support the Protestant cause; another party of several hundred individuals was sent to the Carolinas, where they founded New Berne. Ten shiploads, almost 3,000 passengers, set sail for New York, where they were to produce naval stores in exchange for their passage.[2] The rough crossing cost dozens of lives before the group reassembled on Governor's Island, and more people succumbed to disease. In the spring they were taken about 100 miles up the Hudson, where they established West and East Camp on either side of the river. Despite their failure to produce naval supplies in the anticipated quantities, the English continued a subsidy until the fall of 1712.

The Palatines were nearly equally divided between the Reformed and the Lutheran, both of a moderate sort and each with their own religious leader. At the outset the Reformed were served by John Frederick Hager. The Lutherans were served by Kocherthal until his death in 1719 and subsequently by Justus Falckner, his brother Daniel, and others who traveled up and down the valley between Albany and Manhattan. In 1730 they were able to raise a log structure, twenty feet square, and hang the bell given them by Queen Anne. Thus, worship was moved out of private homes and into a public church building. However, after the end of government subsidy the settlers began to move away from the area, and by 1751 so few Lutherans were left that the building was given over to the Church of England.

Settlers relocated to Pennsylvania, New Jersey, New York City, and other areas of New York. One hundred and fifty families moved to Schoharie, west of Albany. The English aggressively disputed their claim to this land, proceeding as though it did not exist and finally offering the occupants the options of buying, leasing, or vacating. In an effort to press their case, a delegation of three was sent to London in 1718, but the mission was in vain. Those who stayed in Schoharie were forced to purchase or lease the land they already occupied. Others relocated again, this time to the Mohawk Valley, to Palatine Bridge, and to Tulpehocken, Pennsylvania. Conrad Weiser, the influential Indian agent and future father-in-law of Muhlenberg, was among the group that moved to Pennsylvania.

After the first quarter of the century Pennsylvania was the principal destination for German immigrants. By the American Revolution as many as 750,000 million had come to the colonies; by 1790 a third of Pennsylvania's residents were German.[3] Germantown, now part of Philadelphia, predated the Palatine migrations by a generation. It was founded in 1683 by sectarians of several sorts led by lawyer Franz David Pastorius. Another seventeenth-century settlement was established by Johan Kelpius, a mystic and millennialist. In 1717 three ships landed with 363 German passengers, signaling the beginning of the major influx of Germans. In contrast to the 1708 and 1709 groups, subsequent immigrants tended to travel in families and small groups rather than the large, organized parties of the Palatines and the Salzburgers.

The religious identity of these immigrants varied from Roman Catholic, to Lutheran, to Reformed, to Moravian, to members of smaller sectarian groups. Ephrata Cloisters, a celibate, mystical community in the same tradition as Kelpius', was founded by Johann Conrad Beissel, who immigrated in 1720. Located near the Palatine settlement in Tulpehocken, it attracted Germans of various religious backgrounds, including temporarily Conrad Weiser and Daniel Falckner, who later returned to the Lutheranism of his family and was ordained as a pastor. Less far removed from Lutherans but ultimately more troublesome were the Moravians and their leader, Count Nicolaus Ludwig von Zinzendorf. With the German Reformed, relationships were usually friendly between both individuals and groups. In many instances two congregations—one Lutheran and one Reformed—joined their resources to construct a building that they used in turn.

Among the Lutherans who came directly to Pennsylvania were the Henkel (Henckel) family party, which arrived in 1717; they provide an instructive glimpse at conditions early in the 1700s. The group included Pastor Anthony Jacob, his wife, Maria Elizabeth, their seven children, aged 6 to 29, and some in-laws. Though he came without an official call from a congregation or authorization from any European church, Henkel did provide pastoral care to his fellow German Lutherans in New Hanover and in Germantown, congregations that would later become the charge of Muhlenberg.[4] At midcentury Muhlenberg described what his predecessor had found:

At first the people were isolated and poor, but withal true to their word, helpful, sober, humble, and diligent in their callings. According as they had been more or less well instructed in the fundamentals of the Christian religion in their fatherland, they had tried to put it into practice here, seeking to foster the little light and life by using the prayers they had learned in youth and the few books, such as Bibles, catechisms, and hymnals, they had brought with them. When they were occasionally visited in their loneliness by a Swedish or German preacher [HN: Pastor Henkel] and brought the Word of God and Holy Sacraments, they considered it a great privilege.[5]

Many, if not most, of Henkel's parishioners and neighbors had come as redemptioners who paid for their boat fare by indenturing themselves for years of labor. They were neither well educated nor prepared to assume what would usually be the pastor's responsibility for religious life. In his efforts to respond to these needs, Henkel drew criticism and disdain from his more orthodox colleague in New York, Wilhelm Christopher Berkenmeyer, who arrived in 1725.

Berkenmeyer's area of activity returns us to New York, where he was the successor of both Falckners and Kocherthal, whose daughter (Benigna Sibylla) he married. His career in New York was marked by conflicts that highlight the difficulties facing colonial Lutherans as well as the tensions that surfaced between orthodox and pietist impulses within Lutheranism as those difficulties were addressed. Berkenmeyer came to North America in response to the New York congregations' request to the Consistory of Amsterdam asking that body once again to send a qualified pastor to serve them. Despite the facts that the oldest congregation was now several decades old and that Justus Falckner had been ordained in North America, the colonial church was still not able to supply itself with pastors. Falckner had been trained prior to his immigration, and the clergy who ordained him did so as an emergency measure. The scattered Lutherans lacked either the educational resources needed to prepare a candidate or a regular body to authorize and then carry out an ordination. A layman from New York carried the request to Holland, where he was advised to look for a pastor in Hamburg as no pastors were available in Amsterdam.

Berkenmeyer was then serving at the City Prison as a teacher, not as a prisoner. He was at first unwilling to accept the call, but following an illness he agreed and was ordained by the Amsterdam body in May 1725. Unlike many others who came to America when quite young, Berkenmeyer was thirty-eight when he arrived in New York. His preparation for the task that faced him included his practical work in Hamburg and study at the University of Altdorf, an institution associated with the orthodox school of Lutheranism. Thus, he brought to the colonies a dual commitment to right teaching and right practice in the church without the attentiveness to personal religious life that characterized the Pietists trained at Halle.

These concerns for doctrine and order propelled him into disputes with his colleagues and prompted his efforts to bring the church into a more definite organization. Beyond depreciating Henkel for his lack of an official call and accusing him of ordaining without authorization, Berkenmeyer also opposed John Bernard van Dieren, his rival in Hackensack, New Jersey, who claimed that Henkel had ordained him.[6] Further, Berkenmeyer regarded his potential colleagues, Muhlenberg and John Christopher Hartwick, as tainted by pietism and thus unworthy of cooperation.[7] His theological judgment was confirmed by his encounters with the eccentric Hartwick and by Muhlenberg's intervention in a dispute between the Raritan congregation and its pastor. Berkenmeyer's organizational efforts were of two sorts, securing additional pastors whom he regarded as sufficiently orthodox and proposing specific plans. Once worthy colleagues arrived, Berkenmeyer divided the New York congregations, taking responsibility for the northern cluster. He suggested that all the congregations be linked with supervision from the Church of Sweden, which he judged adequately orthodox as well as better able than any German body to provide oversight. When this proposal was not taken up, he wrote a constitution to unite the congregations of the Hudson River Valley and New Jersey. This group met once in 1735 with three pastors and nine laymen representing orthodox Lutheranism in North America. These valiant efforts, however, had little lasting effect and were overshadowed by the Halle school and its representatives.

In summary, by the mid-eighteenth century, Lutherans were to be found in several North American locations, most notably, in the Hudson River Valley and Pennsylvania, with other concentrations in the Virgin Islands, Georgia, and the Carolinas. Although Lutherans had come from several European nations, and some converts had been made among both Africans and European colonists, increasingly, the majority of Lutherans had German origins, though they lived in English colonies. In that setting the oddity that the English monarchs, who were the head of the Church of England, had Lutheran associations worked to the German Lutherans' benefit, opening the way for material support in the cases of both the Salzburgers and the Palatines. Further, the connections between the court chaplain in London, the English Society for the Propagation of Christian Knowledge, and various German church leaders formed a conduit for spiritual support in the persons of Boltzius, Kocherthal, and others. To a degree all Lutherans in the Western Hemisphere were in a mission situation, an ecclesial parallel to a colony. No church had direct responsibility for them, as would have been the case for regular parishes; rather, they received financial support and pastoral leadership through the generosity of various bodies far removed from their specific circumstances.

This produced a haphazard situation in which groups of Lutheran laypeople gathered themselves into local congregations that were usually unconnected to other congregations and frequently without pastoral leadership. The scarcity of men with adequate training, proper authorization, and worthy lives made congregations vulnerable to the ploys of unqualified men passing themselves off as pastors. Some pastors simply stayed too short a time for their colonial career to be effective. Congregations lodged complaints about pastors who charged for conducting funerals and who could not preach without a manuscript. Other men served long and well. The pastors who did serve in the 1700s were of several types: those, like Dutch Bernhard Arensius and Swedish Anders Rudman, who were ordained in Europe and sent by a recognized authority, usually in response to a specific call; those, like German Anthony Jacob Henkel, who were ordained in Europe but came without a regular call; those, like the Falckner brothers, who had some training in Europe and received authorization for their work in America; those, like van Dieren and John Caspar Stoever (both father and son), who had neither license nor ordination, some of whom might be called pretenders to the office; and those, like John Nicolas Kurtz, who received some of their training in America and whose work was sanctioned by an American authority.[8] Pastors suffered from too much travel, willful and uninformed congregations, and lack of pay. In 1733 Pastor John Spaler made a house-to-house visitation in rural New York, inquiring about the family life, conduct, and religious activities of his parishioners. He reported to the Amsterdam Constitutory that he "found people who either knew nothing at all, or who could hardly recite the Lord's Prayer and the Apostle's Creed, and just as ignorant as they were, were also their children. . . . Some had never, others only many years ago, attended the Lord's Supper.'' To temper his dismal account he also noted meeting ''a few, whose parents brought a good education with them from Germany, who had some information.''[9]

The shortage of clerical leadership and the minimal organization, characteristics akin to a mission field, encouraged a sort of pragmatic ecumenism in which groups of Reformed and Lutheran believers united their material resources, and individuals took part in any religious activities available. Conrad Weiser's extremely fluid religious affiliation, which ranged from Ephrata Cloister, to the Moravians, to his son-in-law's Lutheranism, is but a notable case in point. Though language hampered many German-speaking Lutherans from full participation, the Great Awakening that spread through the colonies in the second quarter of the century also fostered a spirit of cooperation that downplayed distinctions between religious groups.

MUHLENBERG AND THE MINISTERIUM

By the 1730s Lutherans in the Philadelphia area were gathered in three congregations: one in the city, one in New Hanover, and one in Providence (Trappe), together known as the United Congregations. Though they had been served intermittently both by German pastors such as Henkel and by visiting Swedes, in 1734 they were without a pastor and appealed through Frederich Michael Ziegenhagen, the German court chaplain in London, to Halle for one to be sent to them. Despite the eight-year delay before a positive response to their request arrived, the congregations had found a reliable source of good leadership. Gotthilf August Francke and others associated with the Halle institutions were interested in mission work, and men trained there were committed to the teachings of the Lutheran Church and concerned for the religious life of Lutherans. This combination produced the firm grounding tempered by flexibility that was needed for effective ministry in the colonial situation.

No doubt the delay between the request and its fulfillment would have been shorter had communications been easier. Nonetheless, several exchanges between the congregations and Europe still would have been required even had communication been swifter as each party pressed its view of how the agreement between pastor and congregation should be settled. The Europeans insisted that a salary be guaranteed along with a return passage to Germany, if that were needed. The congregations were unwilling to commit themselves to this financial responsibility without having a chance to assess the pastor firsthand. No doubt, their reluctance reflected their limited resources and was a response to experiences with less than satisfactory pretenders to the pulpit. It also is indicative of a pragmatic difference between the European Lutheran situation and that developing in North America. The old way, in established churches, was that taxes or a patron paid the expenses; the new way, in a voluntary church, was that everyone needed to contribute something willingly. For good or for ill, the American church depended upon the lay members to pay the pastor's salary and other expenses. This financial responsibility, though frequently paid in kind, had the potential to give each member a sense of ownership with the attendant right to evaluate the services received for the outlay. Like all the European churches and societies, Halle had many enterprises closer to home than Pennsylvania. Response to the request from the United Congregations was delayed also by other concerns pressing for Francke's attention. In the interim, he was informed by ongoing correspondence with other parties in the colonies about conditions there. Finally in 1742, perhaps spurred by information about the advance of Moravians in Pennsylvania and Zinzendorf's plan to visit there, Francke turned to Henry Melchior Muhlenberg, a man just turning thirty, and gave him the call.

Muhlenberg had previously expressed an interest in going to India as a missionary; at the time he received the call to North America, he was a pastor in Grosshennersdort and inspector of a financially troubled orphanage. Though of humble background himself, Muhlenberg had patrons among the aristocracy, including Zinzendorf's aunt. He was trained at the University of Göttingen and attached to the Halle Foundations through additional study and his work as an instructor. His early career was ordinary, but his later record suggests that his gifts and preparation were well suited to meet the challenges of ministering to a young and still unformed church. Muhlenberg followed the path of the Palatines and the Salzburgers and fellow Hallesian Boltzius through London, where he, too, consulted with Ziegenhagen. As instructed, he traveled via Georgia to visit Ebenezer and meet Boltzius, who was to accompany him to Philadelphia. The treacherous fall conditions convinced Boltzius to stay put, but Muhlenberg declared that his call was to Pennsylvania, not Georgia, and prevailed upon a ship's captain to take him aboard for the coastal journey.

With the dangers of sea travel behind him, the young shepherd arrived in Philadelphia and found wolves among his sheep. In all three of the United Congregations Muhlenberg faced rivals. Thus, from the outset it was obvious that the task he had been called to do would entail more than ministering to the needs of his members; he would also have to build the fold and determine with whom the care of the flock could be shared. As in these first instances, the challenges would come from within and without. Assisted by the sympathetic Swedish clergy, he faced the New Hanover and Trappe congregations as well as pastor Valentine Kraft and pretender George Schmidt with his credentials and after some discussion won his post. Zinzendorf in Philadelphia proved to be a more difficult case.

The Moravians traced their lineage to reformer John Huss, who was executed at the Council of Constance in 1415. Following the Thirty Years' War, in the 1720s a group of these Bohemians took refuge at Zinzendorf's family estate, Herrnhut. Their noble patron, a Lutheran influenced by pietism more radical than that of Philipp Jacob Spener, his godfather, was attracted to their joyful religious ways. In addition to his Lutheran ordination he eventually was made a Moravian bishop and saw no conflict between the two offices. In the colonial setting with its dearth of organized religion, Moravians' concern for the spiritual well-being of their German country folk was appealing to many previously attached to Lutheran or Reformed churches. The Moravians' attention to the subjective aspects of religion had clear affinities with the Great Awakening sweeping through the early eighteenth-century American colonies with the leadership of native-born preachers such as Jonathan Edwards and Gilbert Tennent and Englishmen John Wesley and George Whitfield.

In 1741 Zinzendorf joined the Moravians in Pennsylvania and reached out among the larger German population in an ecumenism born of greater concern for spiritual life than for uniformity of confession. He attempted to organize all the Germans into one body, to be called the Congregation of God in the Spirit, and established himself in the Lutheran pulpit in Philadelphia. The more moderate Muhlenberg rejected the national, or ethnic, basis of the Congregation of God in the Spirit as too slight, giving insufficient weight to the need for right teaching and common practices as well as a worthy life. Having faced Zinzendorf in an unpleasant encounter, he also recovered the Philadelphia congregation's record book and chalice. Zinzendorf returned to Germany. Over the years relations between Lutherans and Moravians in Pennsylvania improved, particularly once the Moravians were better defined as a church and stayed within their own flock. In other regions, such as the Virgin Islands and the southern states, the two groups had a friendlier, even cooperative relationship.

Once Muhlenberg's call was cleared, and his place in the United Congregations was secured, he was able to take up his work as a pastor. He promptly abolished irregular customs practiced by "vagabond preachers" who accepted special payment for baptisms and received an offering for their own pocket when they administered communion. In two of the congregations he encouraged the people to construct adequate church buildings; the third had just done so, and there a school was built. In addition to his pastoral duties, he served as teacher for the children. Initially called to three congregations, his field soon expanded to include Germantown and then enlarged further as other groups asked him to come to them. A visit to the Lutherans at Tulpenhocken also brought him to the Weiser household, where he displayed his musical skills and met Anna Maria, the eldest daughter of the family. They were married in 1745.

Muhlenberg's detailed journals and reports to Halle reveal the wide range of his work and give us access more generally to the life of the church in the years preceding the Revolution. Because his congregations were located at substantial distances from each other, and he traveled also to others that invited him, even those congregations with a "resident" pastor did not have public worship weekly, and others were likely to have their worship on a weekday. Muhlenberg himself noted that the pastor often "combine[d] in his own person the duties of several offices . . . serv[ing] simultaneously as preacher, schoolmaster, cantor, sexton, bell-ringer, catechist, rector, and his own *substitute* or *deaconus*."[10] His preaching was intended to awaken his hearers to their spiritual condition as well

as instruct them. Particularly at funerals, when the congregation might include
non-German speakers, Muhlenberg used English for preaching or at least to add
a comment about the sermon. He and his clerical colleagues were called on to
officiate at life cycle rituals—baptisms, weddings, and funerals—for persons
who were not members of their congregations, or even Lutheran. Like his predecessors in the colonies, Muhlenberg noted that he baptized Africans, though
unlike Wilhelm Berkenmeyer he did not own any slaves. When he visited in
people's homes, he inquired after the state of their souls and catechized them.
His ministry was not limited to matters of the soul; he also provided medical
attention and medicines from the Halle dispensary. Payment for all these services
came in kind as well as occasional cash.

Lutheran congregations in Pennsylvania, like those in other colonies, were
most often organized at the initiative of a group of laypeople or by a traveling
pastor who gathered them together. In addition to their desire for access to the
ministrations of a pastor for baptisms and for public worship with a sermon
proclaiming the gospel and communion, perhaps three or four times a year, they
also hoped for a school where their children could learn and for a place to bury
their dead. Indeed, the existence of an established graveyard sometimes determined the location of a church building, which came later. Unlike the Swedes,
who were initially all Lutherans, or like the congregation in Manhattan, which
always included Lutherans from several nations, the Lutherans in Pennsylvania
were mostly German, though not all Germans were Lutheran. A great many of
the Germans were Reformed. Relations between these two sorts of Christians
were likely more cooperative in North America than they had been in Germany.
By 1776 almost half of the congregations were union arrangements in which
two groups shared responsibility for, and use of, a single building.[11] The distinctive confessional identity of each was maintained by separate governance,
leadership, and worship, though it was not uncommon for the members of one
family to be divided by their membership in different congregations. Or, put the
other way, membership in different congregations was not regarded as a bar to
marriage.

The organization of the Lutheran congregations was influenced by the same
Amsterdam model used in New York. It had also been adopted by the Lutheran
Savoy congregation in London and from there carried to Ebenezer, Georgia, and
Pennsylvania. In the latter colony it was the basis of the 1762 constitution for
St. Michael's, in Philadelphia, and thus became the model used by many other
congregations. Though there is variety in details, the major characteristics are
similar. Lutheran congregations in North America were not only not controlled
by the state, but governed by their lay membership. The laity, men and women,
paid the bills, and the men either made decisions as a group or elected some of
their number as trustees, elders, and deacons to act on their behalf. The office
of lay reader, cantor, or clerk seems to have been less important in these congregations than among the Africans in the Virgin Islands; nonetheless, a layman,

often a schoolteacher, could substitute for a pastor in certain circumstances such as emergency baptisms.

Individual laymen were notable for their efforts to secure pastors or represent the interests of their community. The activities of women, however, seem largely to have been overlooked by the records. No doubt they—like their brothers, cousins, fathers, husbands, and sons, most of whom were ordinary church folk— listened to sermons, learned their catechism, sang hymns, and said their prayers. A few women came into view as the daughters and wives of pastors. Women such as Anna Maria Weiser Muhlenberg, born in North America and the daughter of a prominent provincial Indian agent, provided their clerical husbands with an intimate connection to the people the men served. The women who were both daughter and wife to pastors, such as Benigna Sibylla Kocherthal Berkenmeyer and Margaret Henrietta Muhlenberg Kunze, linked the clergy together by personal as well as professional bonds.

Muhlenberg's credentials as a trained clergyman, legitimately ordained, and in good standing with the European church were enhanced by his growing reputation as one who could respond constructively to difficult situations. As a result, he was asked to intervene in several controversies that might have been referred to an authority such as a bishop had one been available. This happened in Raritan, New Jersey, where he was able to negotiate an agreement in a long-standing dispute between the people and their pastor. Unfortunately, his success irritated Berkenmeyer, who regarded Muhlenberg as having interfered in his field. Muhlenberg also made a return visit to Ebenezer, at the request of their common sponsor in Halle, to mediate between the clergy there. Clearly, even the day-to-day work of attending to the United Congregations was more than one pastor could do. Muhlenberg appealed to Halle for helpers. The first group of three—one pastor and two catechists—arrived in 1745, just as the volume of German immigration was increasing.

In addition to these fellow laborers from Halle, Muhlenberg had other colleagues in his work both Lutheran and non-Lutheran. His churchly piety inclined him toward those Christians whose awakening animated their beliefs rather than overshadowing them. This was the basis of his affinity with both Presbyterian Gilbert Tennet and Anglican George Whitefield. Though he had doctrinal disagreements with Whitefield, Muhlenberg described the Englishman as a "sharp saw to cut through knotted, gnarled, streaky hearts" and invited him to preach at the confirmation service held in conjunction with the 1760 meeting of the ministerium.[12] Just prior to Muhlenberg's arrival in North America, Tennet had published a famous sermon entitled, "The Danger of an Unconverted Ministry"; in it he expressed sentiments not unlike those articulated by Spener, the founder of the Halle institutions. On more than one occasion Tennet and Muhlenberg corresponded in a cordial tone. Together they lent their support to German Reformed pastor Michael Schlatter in a dispute with his congregation. Perhaps Muhlenberg's most sympathetic colleague was the Swedish Lutheran Carl Wrangel, whose tenure as provost among his country folk began in 1759. Not only had he been instructed to maintain a good relationship with the German Lutherans, but his personal religious character was akin to Muhlenberg's. Unfortunately for him, it was not pleasing to his Swedish colleagues, who agitated for his recall. With other Germans Muhlenberg's relationships were various. His conflicts with Berkenmeyer have been mentioned. Following the advice of his diplomat father-in-law that it was better to include than to exclude them, he came to work more closely with men such as John Caspar Stoever Jr., whose training and authorization for ministry were less regular but who nonetheless played an active and important role in the late colonial period.

Beyond his informal leadership, Muhlenberg moved the American church toward organization by convening a nucleus of Halle men to form the Ministerium of Pennsylvania. This body, founded in 1748, is generally taken as the first synod linking American Lutherans to one another beyond local settings. The group Berkenmeyer convened in the previous decade did not endure, and the suggestions of Philadelphia merchants Henry Schleydorn and Peter Kock in 1744 that a synod be organized were never pursued. In contrast, this ministerium had a long and fruitful existence. In the early years it was primarily an organization of ministers, to which lay representatives were invited in order to report upon conditions in their congregations. Initially, the pastors included were those sent out from Halle who had been meeting informally to consult about the work in their common field. Later the group was expanded to include other Germans as well. Few Swedes were sympathetic to the pietist approach characteristic of the ministerium's members. Wrangel was an exception, and he encouraged the revival of the ministerium in 1760 after a period of dormancy.

The first meeting of the ministerium, called by Muhlenberg, already pointed toward the functions that the body would assume. The September gathering coincided with the dedication of a new church building in Philadelphia and was the occasion for the ordination of John Nicolaus Kurtz, one of the two catechists who had arrived three years earlier. Prior to his ordination, Kurtz was closely examined as to his suitability and preparation for the office he was to be given. Many years would pass before the American church provided a school to train pastors, but examining and setting apart pastors would continue to be a central task of the ministerium throughout its entire existence. From the outset attention was given to conditions within the congregations and their schools. Among the topics of concern was the manner in which worship was conducted. Lay representatives made the practical suggestion that on cold days services be shortened. The uniform order proposed by Muhlenberg and his associates for use in all congregations associated with the ministerium was adopted. In devising this service, the pastors had access to a copy of the Dutch Antwerp order as translated and adapted for use by London's Savoy Lutheran congregation. The order they prepared—circulated in less than four dozen handwritten copies—showed these influences and followed the basic liturgical pattern common in Saxony, northern German, and Scandinavian churches. A combined service book and hymnal was published in 1786. Thus, the American Lutheran Church began to assume greater responsibility for its own life by organizing its governance, providing itself with clergy, overseeing its own worship life, and defining its identity. In the year that the ministerium was organized, there are estimated to have been 7,000 Lutherans in seventy congregations served by twelve pastors.[13]

The Lutherans whose call Muhlenberg answered were German-speakers living in an English colony. By the time of the Revolution, as many as one-third of the population of Pennsylvania were German in origin. When the war broke out, Lutherans, like their neighbors, had to decide where they stood—with the rebels or with the monarch. Individual Lutherans throughout the colonies made their own choices, which ranged from one extreme to the other. As two German Lutheran pastors in New York gave their support to the British, it seems likely that some lay folks did, too. Within the Muhlenberg family, the father would have preferred to stand apart from such matters, but the sons gave dramatic support to the Revolution. Whether Peter Gabriel Muhlenberg did or did not ascend his pulpit, declare that there is a time to preach and a time to fight, and then throw open his preaching robe to reveal his military uniform, the legend makes clear that there were Lutherans whose loyalty to the rebel cause was firm and whose American identity was well established. In a sort of civic parallel to Lutheran teaching about vocation—that one serves God in whatever station one finds oneself—Christopher Ludwig, a Philadelphia layman, became baker-general for the colonial forces. Further evidence of that shift toward primary identification with the United States, rather than Europe, came after the war, when Frederick Augustus Muhlenberg exchanged his pulpit for a political career and was elected first Speaker of the U.S. House of Representatives. Because Lutherans' connections with England were based on affinities and more informal than official, the Revolution and American independence did not create the same organizational difficulties for them as for the Episcopalians. Rather, Lutherans continued their gradual development of a structure independent from the European churches and societies and of their own distinctive customs.

Known as its patriarch, Muhlenberg's importance for the American Lutheran Church now rests not only on what he actually did but also on what is thought about him. Almost without exception he has been regarded as worthy of his title and the respect given him. A few critics have regarded his friendly relations with contemporaries such as Whitfield and Tennent as examples of doctrinal indifference, and others have judged the Pietist strand of Lutheranism he brought with him lacking in theological rigor. More positively, Abdel Ross Wentz identified four characteristics that the American Lutheran Church has inherited from him in varying degrees: the warmth of heart and breadth of spirit typical of Halle pietism; a genius for practical affairs both benevolent and administrative; confessional orthodoxy; and a churchly taste in liturgy and hymnody.[14]

EXPANSION—NEW YORK, SOUTH CAROLINA, OHIO

In the decades after the Revolution the Lutheran churches in the young United States grew in numbers, in area, and in self-sufficiency. Developments that had taken place in the earliest congregations were repeated as new groups gathered and organized themselves. Movement beyond the original areas of concentration prompted formation of both special conferences of the ministerium and new synods. Extended residence in North America and slowed immigration encouraged Lutherans to think of themselves as citizens of the new nation and to look among themselves, rather than to Europe, for leadership. These widespread developments can be seen through attention to a few specific cases beginning with a return to New York, the location of one of the first congregations.

Lutherans had been among the first European residents of the New Netherlands, though the Dutch government was officially unfriendly toward their confession. Once restrictions on public exercise of non-Reformed religious practices were eased, the Lutherans secured a pastor, put up a building, and commenced worship. When the English took control in the late 1600s, the Lutherans secured official permission for their activities. Most often their pastors came to them through the Consistory of Amsterdam, but the pastors who came were seldom Dutch, and the people themselves had various national origins. They were also served temporarily by a Swede, and the first Lutheran ordination in North America provided them with Justus Falckner. When Wilhelm Berkenmeyer arrived in 1725, the Lutheran population in New York and the Hudson River Valley had grown in numbers and become predominantly German. His efforts to impose good order and establish orthodox teaching were vigorous but without long-term effect. Even before Berkenmeyer's death in 1751 Muhlenberg had been invited to mediate disputes in congregations both in Manhattan and in New Jersey. In subsequent years, the influence of the Pennsylvania patriarch and his ways increased through the leadership of his son-in-law, John Christopher Kunze.

Kunze's training was similar to Muhlenberg's, though he was a more accomplished scholar than the older man. He, too, had associations with the Halle institutions and some experience as a teacher before responding to a call to serve in Pennsylvania. On his Atlantic journey he was accompanied by two Muhlenberg sons who were returning from a period of study in Halle. Upon his arrival in 1770 he shared the care of the Philadelphia congregations with Muhlenberg, who became his father-in-law the next year when Kunze married Margarthe Henrietta. Recognizing the need to train pastors in North America, rather than relying upon those sent from Europe, he began a pretheological school, which functioned until the Revolution. In 1784 Kunze accepted a call to Christ Church and entered into a new arena of leadership among the heirs of the Dutch congregations.

As in Pennsylvania, so, too, in New York, Kunze extended himself beyond his congregation to teaching and to other tasks that required attention if the Lutheran Church was to secure its existence in the new nation. Though somewhat more successful than his attempt to found a German Institute at the University of Pennsylvania, his appointment as professor of Oriental languages at Columbia College turned out to be more a recognition of Kunze's linguistic talent than an avenue for widespread pedagogical influence. A bequest from pastor John Christopher Hartwick provided funds for theological education as well as to found a school for Native Americans. Rather than establishing a single institution, the money was used at the outset to support tutors in various locations. Kunze's private instruction of students such as Philip Frederick Mayer was supported with the moneys. Though he could supervise only a small number of students, Kunze's effort set the pattern of informal tutoring that trained many pastors in the decades before Gettysburg Seminary was founded. Unlike Kunze and most of the men in his generation, many of the pastors he prepared were native-born and more able to move toward an American church. Mayer, as a notable example, was called to serve St. John's in Philadelphia when it was founded in 1806 as an English-speaking alternative to the older congregations that persisted in using German. Because his colleagues in Philadelphia were not enthusiastic about the work of this new congregation, Mayer continued in closer contact with the New York pastors than might otherwise be expected.

As Mayer's experience suggests, one of the challenges for Kunze and his students was guiding the churches' transition from using German to using English. In New York the congregation had made a similar change from Dutch to German not many years before. By the late eighteenth century, after more than a century of British rule and the American Revolution, the time had come for the Lutherans of various national origins to face the reality that fewer and fewer of their number used German easily. Kunze recognized the necessity of the change, though his own difficulties with English pronunciation persuaded him to cease using it for preaching. He facilitated the transition with publication of an English hymnal and prayer book, which also contained the first translation of Luther's Small Catechism into English.[15]

In addition to his educational and linguistic contributions, Kunze supplied organizational leadership in the Ministerium of New York. The need for a forum for cooperation among the pastors and congregations of the New York area had been recognized by Berkenmeyer earlier in the century. Just prior to the Revolution, Kunze's brother-in-law, Frederick Augustus Muhlenberg, had also contemplated the need for a synod; however, his obvious patriotic leanings made it imprudent for him to remain in the city, and he returned to Philadelphia before taking any action. In 1785, on the occasion of the dedication of a church building, Kunze convened a small group of pastors and laymen in Albany to found the Ministerium of New York. No rupture from the older Pennsylvania synod was intended. Indeed, the purposes of the New York Ministerium and its establishing documents were almost indistinguishable from those of the older body, and Kunze maintained his membership in both while serving as president of the new synod. The new organization made cooperation more convenient for the pastors and lay delegates as well as formalizing the movement of the congregations they represented into the orbit of the Philadelphia tradition. In two matters the new body did differ from its parent. From the outset lay delegates were given both voice and vote in all matters except those related to the certification of clergy; and, as might be expected with Kunze as the senior member, the New York Ministerium moved more quickly to use English. The constitution was printed in English in 1796, as were the proceedings after 1807.

Following Kunze's death the New York church moved into a new stage characterized by changes in membership and leadership. Another wave of immigration shifted the composition of the congregations back toward recent arrivals from Germany and reintroduced linguistic challenges. In response the ministerium returned its official language to German. Frederick Henry Quitman, Kunze's successor as theological tutor and senior of the ministerium, brought a different theological emphasis than the confessional center of Kunze's pietism and Berkenmeyer's orthodoxy. Like Kunze and Muhlenberg, he had close associations with the University of Halle, but Halle of a later generation that was influenced by the rationalism current in European intellectual life. Often reviled as the epitome of rationalism, Quitman might also be described as a supernaturalist who was influenced by the Enlightenment and its concerns while not rejecting those aspects of Christianity that remain outside the realm of human reason.[16] His *Evangelical Catechism* departed from the model of Luther's Small Catechism in the materials included, their arrangement, and their content. Overall, Quitman's volume projected a more positive anthropology than classic Lutheranism and was more concerned for human happiness than for holiness.

A similar shift was evident in worship, where alterations in the service removed many of the responsive elements from the liturgy and highlighted the sermon at the expense of active congregational participation. The collection of hymns Quitman published in 1814 lacked the doctrinal grounding of older Lutheran texts. The hymns included drew heavily on Anglo-American sources and were reflective of popular evangelical themes rather than rationalistic ones.[17] Of course, these trends cannot be attributed to Quitman alone; the New York Ministerium authorized his catechism, and, like the Ministerium of Pennsylvania, it removed explicit references to the Lutheran Confessions from its organizing documents in the final years of the eighteenth century.

Even as Lutherans in the central areas of Pennsylvania and New York were developing their organization, worship life, and leadership, so, too, were Lutherans in the South and West. John Bachman, one of Quitman's students, provided Carolina Lutherans with leadership parallel to Kunze's in New York, while Lutherans in Ohio appealed to John Stough, a devout layman in their midst, for pastoral care. The careers of these two men illustrate the growth of the church in two distinct geographic areas, each with its own challenges as well as demonstrating two ways that the church supplied itself with leaders, though both were American-born and -trained.

Several generations of Bachman's father's family were resident in North America before his father fought in the Revolution. His mother's family were more recent immigrants. He grew up on a farm in New York state, where he was often found roaming the countryside. His training for the ministry followed the pattern of tutoring practiced by Kunze and was supported by the Hartwick legacy as he studied successively with Anthony Theodore Braun in Rensselaer County, then with Quitman in New York, and then with Philip Mayer, Kunze's student and Quitman's stepson, in Philadelphia. Bachman's move to Philadelphia in 1810 was prompted, at least in part, by his need to earn an income by teaching.

After three years he received a call to succeed Braun as pastor of the congregations of Gilead Parish and was licensed by the Ministerium of New York. Thus, he returned to the congregation of his childhood, living with his parents. Bringing a local boy home, did not, however, mean that things in the parish continued completely as before. Bachman's first language was English, so in contrast to his former teacher, he was well equipped to introduce regular English preaching. Throughout his career he would also preach frequently in German. The congregations and their pastor were well suited, but illness required that Bachman remove himself to a warmer climate. First he traveled to the Caribbean, then took a leave of absence to serve Saint John's in Charleston, South Carolina. Though formally only on leave from Gilead, Bachman was ordained before departing for the South, where he spent the rest of his ministry.

From his arrival in 1814 into the 1860s Bachman was a prominent figure in southern Lutheranism. His local ministry extended to the African population and the German-speakers as well as the white, English-speaking majority. He played a key role in the organization and ongoing life of the Synod of South Carolina and in the founding of both a college and a seminary. In addition, his work as a naturalist earned him a respectable reputation. This last interest was foreshadowed by his childhood activities and was not without precedent. Muhlenberg's son Henry Ernest, for example, was a reputable botanist as well as a pastor. Bachman's studies of local plants and animals led to collaboration with John James Audubon as well as publications in his own name.

The congregation Bachman came to serve had its beginning in the mid-1700s. Though known as St. John's, its legal name—the Lutheran Church of German Protestants—was indicative of its origins. However, by 1814 the members were accustomed to English services, which Bachman was qualified to provide for them. Nonetheless, many Sundays at least one of the three times he preached was in German. In 1816 he consulted with the lay vestry about a request he had received from a group of people who were not yet members of the congregation; several African Americans had approached him asking for instruction and access to communion. The vestry authorized their pastor to respond positively to those persons who had favorable recommendations from ''respectable white persons,'' and thus began the most successful urban Lutheran ministry among African Americans in the nineteenth century.[18]

Though St. John's was an effective and important effort, it was unusual and is perhaps best considered in comparison to other work by early nineteenth-century southern Lutherans. By the turn of the century little, if anything, remained of the Salzburgers' evangelism among slaves. Only scattered baptisms were recorded in the various states in subsequent years. However, by the second decade of the century, the North Carolina synod was beginning to wrestle with how best to respond to the presence of African Americans. A series of resolutions passed between 1809 and 1817 moved from a limited willingness to respond to requests for baptism to a carefully articulated Five-Point Plan. Initially, pastors were given permission to baptize enslaved persons whose owners asked for it to be done. The 1814 resolution expressed the church's "duty to preach the gospel to Negroes, and after proper instruction to admit them to all the means of grace of the church, and for this purpose to make room for them in the churches."[19] The five points addressed issues such as the status of marriage between slaves and their participation in the sacraments. Although willing to perform weddings for slaves, this policy condoned the owner's prerogative to separate married persons by sale. While allowing African Americans to serve as baptismal sponsors and requiring even slaves to have their children baptized, the policy imposed additional requirements on these members before they were admitted to communion. No specific instruction was given about how to make room in the churches. This plan was implemented more vigorously in the upper South than in the lower South.

Two decades after its adoption and with the spur of abolitionist antagonism to the system of slavery growing more pointed, the South Carolina Synod adopted two strategies, one in keeping with the Five-Point Plan, the other not. The first continued to rely upon the Lutheran owners as the point of access to enslaved persons and thus established some connection between new African American Lutherans and existing congregations. The second emulated the method used by many other Protestants, sending evangelists to preach on plantations without regard to the proximity of any Lutherans. In the fifty years prior to Civil War these various approaches yielded perhaps more than 10,000 new members; by 1859 African Americans—enslaved and free—constituted 20 percent of the communicant members in the South Carolina Synod and 10 percent in the Georgia Synod.[20] This growth took place in churches that gave tacit and sometimes explicit support to the system of slavery.

At St. John's in Charleston, where Bachman was the pastor, by 1860 a third of the membership was African American. These members had their own separate organizations, educational program, leadership and twice-weekly worship. Two parallel congregations operated in a manner similar to the arrangement among Lutherans in the Virgin Islands in the same years. As in the Caribbean, so, too, in South Carolina, the division seems to have encouraged development of capable leaders. From St. John's, three men are notable for their work in other places. Jehu Jones, Daniel Payne, and Braxton Drayton all were considered as possible missionaries to the African American settlement in Liberia. Following his ordination by the Ministerium of New York in 1832, Jones went instead to Philadelphia, where he founded an independent African American Lutheran congregation. With encouragement from Bachman, Payne attended Gettysburg Seminary and was ordained by the Franckean Synod; however, most of his contributions were made as a pastor and bishop in the African Methodist Episcopal Church. In 1845 Drayton did go to Liberia, sponsored by the African American mission society at St. John's; he was the first Lutheran missionary in Africa.

How much credit can be given to John Bachman for the success of St. John's ministry with African Americans is difficult to assess. His contribution to the organization of southern Lutheranism and its institutions, in contrast, is evident and significant. The first southern synod, North Carolina, was founded in 1809 and thus functioning when Bachman arrived. Nonetheless, he maintained his membership in the Ministerium of New York but was unable to attend any of its meetings between 1815 and 1825. Nor was he present at the first meeting of the South Carolina Synod in 1824, but that fall at its second he was elected president and held the office for ten years. During that decade Bachman visited congregations, served on most synodical committees, and preached at, and chaired synodical meetings. Unlike the Tennessee Synod, whose founders withdrew from the North Carolina body in the heat of controversy, the South Carolina group parted peacefully, and the two maintained friendly relations. Bachman's interest in education and his concern for the quality of pastoral leadership available to the church were expressed in his active support for the founding Southern Seminary in 1830 with Ernest Hazelius as professor. Before long the need to provide preparatory work was clear. That project proceeded, and in 1856 Newberry College was chartered with Bachman as the first chair of its Board of Trustees.

While Bachman was busy among southern Lutherans, others were responding to the needs of those Lutherans who joined the accelerating movement into the frontier. Migration to the South continued through the Shenandoah Valley, and others went west into Ohio. Among those who moved west were both the descendants of colonial immigrants and people who were themselves newly arrived in the United States. In areas far distant from the eastern seaboard and the old established congregations in places such as Pennsylvania and New York, these pioneers found themselves in conditions quite similar to those that faced German immigrants in the early 1700s. They, too, lacked material resources and organization; pastors were available only intermittently; and responsibility for church life fell upon those laypeople who showed the ability to take it.

The clergy in Ohio came to their calling by paths other than those followed by Kunze, who was trained in Europe and sent to serve in North America, or by Bachman and Mayer, who were first trained by American tutors and then authorized to serve existing congregations. Most of them were born in North America. Many were identified by their neighbors as likely candidates for ministry and began their work unofficially as laymen—leading prayers, perhaps conducting baptisms, weddings, and funerals—and then sought authorization from the synods. The synods authorized ministerial leadership in a series of grades from catechists, to licentiates, to ordained pastors. With each grade the standards increased as the degree of supervision and the restrictions on the leader's work were reduced.[21] The system allowed for the uneven preparation of potential leaders to be addressed while also responding to pressing needs. Rather than staying put in one place, these men often traveled long distances seeking out Lutherans and gathering them into congregations. John Stough was a prime example of this sort of American Lutheran pastor on the western frontier.

Stough came from a pious, poor family. He learned to be religious at home and trained to be a wagon-maker as well as a farmer, but he received little formal education. His call to ministry came from his (West) Virginia neighbors, who asked him to read to them from a sermon book and lead prayers and later prevailed upon him to perform weddings. Thus, without a local constitution defining the office, he took on some of the quasi-pastoral tasks assigned to the lay reader of colonial New Amsterdam or the church clerk in the Virgin Islands. After his wife died in 1793, he delivered to the Ministerium of Pennsylvania a petition from several congregations in Virginia asking that he be given the office of catechist and allowed to serve them. His only training was what he had received on the job. The request was granted. The next year he presented two sermons as evidence of his qualifications for the task. He was preaching at ten places in rotation, traveling about 160 miles every four weeks. At the 1804 ministerium meeting he was ordained and two years later moved to Ohio, where he had already traveled. His work in Ohio had three emphases: organizing and caring for congregations, encouraging potential pastors, and developing a larger structure for cooperation.

In the first case he sought out Lutherans and German speakers. To them he provided the sacraments as well as preaching. He helped them form themselves into congregations, some of these in union arrangements with Reformed congregations reminiscent of those in Pennsylvania. The conditions of the frontier created a need for pastors that was not being filled by the informal tutoring arrangements operative in the eastern states. Perhaps the example of Methodists and Baptists, who made frequent use of unschooled, but devout, preachers, and certainly his own experience prompted Stough to observe the men in the congregations, looking for those who might have the gifts to follow his path. These he urged on and helped them to secure places to preach and to obtain authorization for their work from the ministerium. These men, along with Stough, formed the core of what would become the Ohio Synod.

As congregations were organized, and the numbers of pastors grew, Lutherans in Ohio began to look to one another rather than back east. The trip to attend a ministerium meeting in eastern Pennsylvania was a long one that required pastors and lay representatives to be absent from their usual work for many days. The convenience of meeting together closer to home appealed to them, as it had to Kunze and others in New York. First in 1812 they petitioned for, and were granted, permission to organize a special conference as provided for in the 1792 constitution of the ministerium. Stough was elected president. This body could send a single representative to ministerium meetings. Because the older body retained authority to ordain pastors, the Ohio Lutherans were still dependent upon it, as neither the Ministerium of New York nor the North Carolina synod was, until the Ohio Synod was organized in 1818. Over the next century Ohio Lutherans supported two colleges and two seminaries, which represented distinctive approaches to the proper cultivation of Lutheranism in North America. Several times they reorganized into new synodical bodies and realigned themselves within the larger Lutheran spectrum; often Lutherans in Ohio articulated central concerns in a controversy so that their positions highlight what was at stake while standing between two extremes.

By the early nineteenth century, Lutherans in the young United States had spread from their initial locations into the frontiers. Not only had the seeds of their faith and church been scattered, but those seeds were cultivated by gardeners such as Muhlenberg and his successors, and the plants were increasingly productive. In addition to the expanded geographic range from New England to the South and into the Northwest, Lutherans were growing in the number of members, in organization, and in self-sufficiency. The next decades would bring a harvest of continued growth but also of controversy as divergent responses to the American environment came into conflict.

NOTES

1. Theodore G. Tappert, "Was Ecclesia Plantanda Muhlenberg's Motto?," *Lutheran Quarterly* 5 (1953): 308–311.

2. Two thousand eight hundred is given by Kathleen Neils Conzen, "Germans," in Stephen Thernston ed., *Harvard Encyclopedia of American Ethic Groups* (Cambridge: Harvard University Press, 1980), p. 407.

3. Conzen, "Germans," p. 407.

4. On Henkel see Charles H. Glatfelter, *Pastors and People: German Lutheran and Reformed Churches in the Pennsylvania Field, 1717–1793*, vol. 1 (Breinigsville: Pennsylvania German Society, 1981, pp. 19–22; Henry Eyster Jacobs, *A History of the Evangelical Lutheran Church in the United States* (New York: Charles Scribner's Sons, 1893), p. 187; Raymond M. Bost and Jeff L. Norris, *All One Body: The Story of the North Carolina Lutheran Synod, 1803–1993* (Salisbury: North Carolina Synod, 1994), p. 86.

5. Henry Melchior Muhlenberg, *The Journals of Henry Melchior Muhlenberg*, vol. 1, trans. Theodore G. Tappert and John W. Doberstein (Philadelphia: Muhlenberg Press, 1942), pp. 271–272.

6. See Glatfelter, *Pastors and People* entry for "Dieren," vol. 1, p. 30.

7. David Jay Webber, "Berkenmeyer and Lutheran Orthodoxy in Colonial New York," *Concordia Historical Institute Quarterly* 60 (Spring 1987): 19–31, especially 27–30.

8. Glatfelter, *Pastors and People*, vol. 2, p. 189.

9. Amsterdam Records, pp. 198–199 *Lutheran Church in New York, 1649: Records in the Lutheran Archives at Amsterdam, Holland*, trans. Arnold J. H. Van Laer (New York, New York Public Library 1946) cited by Webber, "Berkenmeyer," p. 24.

10. Tappert, "Was Ecclesia Plantanda Muhlenberg's Motto?," p. 310.

11. There were seventy-eight union churches, 45 percent of the total. Glatfelter, *Pastors and People*, vol. 2, p. 163.

12. Muhlenberg, *The Journals*, vol. 2, p. 442.

13. *The Lutheran World Almanac and Encyclopedia, 1934–37* (New York: National Lutheran Council, 1937), p. 371. The figures on this chart for the early decades appear to be estimates or at least to have been rounded.

14. Abdel Ross Wentz, "Muhlenberg and the United Lutheran Church," *Lutheran Theological Seminary Bulletin* 72 (Fall 1992): 41–48. Reprinted from *Lutheran Church Quarterly* (1942).

15. *A Hymn and Prayer Book, for the Use of Such Lutheran Churches as Use the English Language* (New York: Printed and sold by Hurtin and Commardiger, 1795).

16. Raymond Bost, "The Reverend John Bachman and the Development of Southern Lutheranism" (Ph.D., Yale University, 1963), pp. 56–60; Arthur C. Repp, *Luther's Catechism Comes to America: Theological Effects on the Issues of the Small Catechism Prepared in or for America Prior to 1850* (Metuchen, NJ: Scarecrow Press, 1982), 121–126.

17. Paul Westermeyer, "What Shall We Sing in a Foreign Land? Theology and Cultic Song in the German Reformed and Lutheran Churches of Pennsylvania, 1830–1900" (Ph. D., University of Chicago, 1978), p. 18.

18. Jeff G. Johnson, *Black Christians: The Untold Lutheran Story* (St. Louis: Concordia Publishing House, 1991) p. 116.

19. Ibid., p. 106.

20. Ibid., pp. 128–129.

21. Jacobs, *A History of the Evangelical Lutheran Church in the United States*, p. 312.

4
AN AMERICAN CHURCH?

In the nineteenth century the Lutheran churches struggled to adapt to, and thrive in, the environment of North America. That adaptation is the subject of this chapter. The church, planted by patriarch Muhlenberg and his contemporaries and spread into the frontier, struggled with being an American church in the 1800s. Thus, we are concerned here with the character of American life in those years as it impinged upon the internal life of Lutheranism, particularly, remnants of Puritanism, revivalism, slavery, and war as well as some aspects of increased immigration. We are concerned with both the formal debate about how Lutheranism could be made American and the ways that the Lutheran Church extended and supported itself. The next chapter covers approximately the same time period but introduces into the plot the new set of characters that appeared with increasing immigration from Europe and then changed the membership of Lutheran churches.

A major manifestation of this struggle was the so-called American Lutheranism controversy, in which the proponents of significant adaptation of Lutheran doctrine and practice were opposed by a growing Confessionalist group that favored less extreme changes. The controversy was played out in church publications and synodical meetings and, no doubt, on trains and in private homes. Perhaps the central episode in the controversy was the publication in 1855 of the Definite Synodical Platform, laying out revisions in the Augsburg Confession. Though, as we will see, the controversy had been building to this point and would continue after, this document provided a focus for the debate. In subsequent years the Confessionalist position solidified and took organizational form in a new seminary and a new cooperative synod. While much energy and ink were consumed by the American Lutheranism controversy, not all of Lutheran church life was about debating. Lutherans were also busy with organizing, publishing, educating, and giving care. These activities could be said to have sunk the church's roots deep into the American soil insofar as they were quite similar to the activities of other American religious groups at the time. In some cases the more "Americanist" of the Lutherans went so far as to join in cooperative ventures with other Protestants such as the American Bible Society and the Sunday School Union. But the same activities might also be regarded as the fruits borne by a tree well tended.

THE PEOPLE

As the century began, Lutherans in the United States numbered in the tens of thousands.[1] Nearly all of the members in these congregations were descendants of earlier immigrations, largely from Germany, though some remnants remained from the Dutch and Swedish congregations, and some "converts" had been made among both other European Americans and African Americans. During the middle of the century economic and religious conditions in Europe contributed to a dramatic increase in immigration. The Lutherans who arrived from Germany and Scandinavia as part of that resurgence are primary characters in the next chapter; here they appear at the periphery of the action. The central characters here are from what might be called the Muhlenberg stock, who had moved beyond their initial settlements in Pennsylvania and New York, spreading west and south with their countryfolk, especially into Ohio, the Carolinas, and Virginia.

Among these Lutherans were many removed from their immigrant origins by several decades, perhaps by two or three generations, as the Henkels, a family prominent in the controversies of the time, can illustrate. In 1717 the family came to colonial Pennsylvania from the Palatinate. When they arrived, their party included Pastor Anthony Jacob, his wife, and seven children. Pastor Henckel (as the name was then spelled) served congregations in New Hanover and Philadelphia. Son Johann Justus was eleven when they landed. In 1751, at age forty-five and with nine children (ages one to eighteen), he and his wife, Maria Magdelena (Eschman), moved south to North Carolina. Before a decade had passed, fear of danger from the Catawba tribe prompted their son Jacob to take his wife, Barbara (Dieter), and their four children (ages one [?] to six) and move again. Before settling near Riverton, (West) Virginia, they spent short periods in other locations in Virginia and Maryland, including some time in a fort. Others from the family had settled nearby in Staunton, Virginia, where they built a fort that saw service in the American Revolution. By 1801 Jacob's family included eight adult children; his eldest son, Paul, was an ordained pastor with ten children and at least one grandchild, the sixth generation of Henkels in the United States.

As might be expected in families even less distant from their European heritage and their original settlements, Lutherans in the nineteenth century were adapting themselves to the American environment. One of the most obvious changes, use of English, had begun in the previous century, and the transition continued, not complete or without controversy. Paul Henkel, for example, who was born in Pennsylvania, as was his father, spoke and wrote both English and German, though his written German was not good. He deplored the loss of German among the people he preached to. Nonetheless, he also preached in English. The press he founded with his sons published religious materials in English as well as German and German-language instructional items such as an ABC book with grammatical information.[2] By the early 1800s congregations, such as St. John's in Philadelphia, were founded explicitly as English-speaking. The New York Ministerium changed its official language to English in 1806.

There were, however, opponents of this trend. Notable among them was Justus Henry Christian Helmuth in Philadelphia. When members of Zion congregation proposed introduction of English in worship, he and a majority of members refused their request. With Helmuth's leadership, the Ministerium of Pennsylvania backed the prohibition, though allowing the possibility of new congregations' using English. Together with Germans—Moravians and Reformed—as well as Lutheran, he advocated establishment of German schools as a means of preserving their shared language and culture. To the same end he published the short-lived *Evangelisches Magazin* with cooperation from John George Schmucker, though Schmucker later shifted his views on the possibility of preserving a German-speaking church.

The efforts of Helmuth and the Henkel Press to preserve and advance German language use show an awareness that language is not separate from a larger cultural matrix, manifested, for example, in literature. Those who advocated transition to English by Lutherans knew that such a shift required worship, education, and theological materials in that language. Most realized that becoming an American church was not accomplished merely by speaking, singing, and praying in English. Indeed, other aspects of American life were also working their way into Lutheran consciousness in the early decades of the century, and the proper response was the topic of vigorous debate.

THE AMERICAN SCENE

Beginning at the turn of the century outbreaks of religious enthusiasm animated American religious life, beginning on the frontier and spreading throughout the nation. Characteristic of this Second Great Awakening were protracted meetings, several days in duration. The crowd heard continual preaching from numerous pulpits as well as spirited singing and fervent prayer. Conviction and conversion were often dramatic, sometimes accompanied by wild physical manifestations. Paul Henkel described what he observed in 1802: "At first several preached in due rotation but as the crowd could not be moved in this way, three or four preachers harangued at the same time with the most fearful expressions that they could invent until finally two young women rushed on the platform among the preachers, began to sink on the floor and to cry out with much agony and agitation."[3] Conversion was to be followed by a reformed life marked by moral behavior and attention to the salvation of others and reform of the social order. Individual salvation fueled formation of societies for missionary work and social reforms such as abolition and woman's rights. Among the controversial innovations of the era were New Measures: the anxious bench for those nearly ready for conversion; allowing women to pray aloud in public meetings; and the protracted meetings themselves. These methods and their outcomes were in keeping with a theology that gave more importance to human participation in salvation than allowed by the classic Calvinist theology previously espoused by Presbyterians and other denominations involved. But the fine points of doctrinal disputes were devalued in the midst of such an outpouring of the Spirit. No doubt enthusiasts regarded this as a return to the unity of the primitive church; opponents judged it to be indifferentism.

Among Lutherans the revival received responses ranging from pietist sympathy to explicit endorsement by some American Lutherans, from reserved clerical participation to outright opposition. On the frontier, far from established congregations with regular religious services, English-speaking Lutherans were attracted to camp meetings and the preaching of revivalists along with their neighbors. Some congregations incorporated new measures into their regular life combining catechetical instruction with the expectation of a revival-style conversion. The frequently pietist character of colonial Lutheranism provided points of affinity between the Lutheranism that migrants brought with them from Pennsylvania and the revivalism developing on the frontier. Both emphasized the need for a clear conviction of sin, for an experience of receiving God's forgiveness, and for a moral life. There were also differences in doctrine, in particular, Lutheran insistence on the primacy of God's grace conferred at baptism and reluctance to even suggest that any human action has an effect in salvation. Differences in worship style would also have been noticeable, as Lutheran worship tended to be far more subdued, though less fully liturgical than it would become by the end of the century.

Pastors John Stough and Paul Henkel ministered to people in areas where revivals were common. Their response was mixed. Henkel did participate by preaching on some occasions. His comments in journals and letters make clear that his action was far from a wholehearted endorsement. To the contrary, he took part in an attempt to moderate what went on. Stough's opinion of the revivals was more positive, and he made use of some of their methods, even under pressure.[4] Back east in Maryland, editor Benjamin Kurtz supported revivals in *The Lutheran Observer*. Other Lutheran leaders, unmoved by the success of revivalism, opposed both its methods and its theology. In keeping with the emerging Confessionalist view, they endeavored to preserve distinctly Lutheran teachings and to restore historic practices. Some opponents, such as William Julius Mann, depicted the advocates of the American Lutheran position as overly influenced by Puritanism as well. In this charge they pointed to heightened concern for a virtuous life marked, in particular, by strict Sabbath observance and attention to issues such as temperance and abolition.

By the nineteenth century slavery had a nearly 200-year history in the United

States, though not without opponents from Quaker John Woolman forward. In the first decades of the 1800s antislavery and abolitionist forces were growing, becoming ever more powerful; pro-slavery proponents responded with their own arguments. The developing debate and the war it contributed to preoccupied Americans for most of the century. Having produced neither prominent political nor military leaders, Lutherans are not among the major figures in this controversy. Nonetheless, Lutherans were affected by these events whether as slaves or slave owners or merely as residents in a nation engaged in a furious and violent controversy.

The popular view that Lutherans were not involved in slavery is quite simply wrong. As has been noted along the way, European Lutherans came into contact with slavery and individual slaves on St. Thomas and in Georgia. The Salzburgers overcame their initial objections to slavery and acquired their own slaves. Other lay and clerical Lutherans are known to have been slave owners, as were some parishes.[5] Some Lutherans were slaves, as indicated in synodical actions by the North Carolina and South Carolina synods authorizing baptism of slaves and providing for reception of slaves into the church.[6] Parochial reports such as those submitted by David Henkel and John Bachman confirm that such actions were taken.[7]

There was no uniform or official Lutheran stance toward slavery. Reactions by Lutherans took several forms: individual advocacy, synodical action, and theological debate.[8] Among individuals two—Samuel Simon Schmucker and John Bachman—are remarkable for the positions they took. Bachman was a South Carolina pastor with scientific interests. In his volume *The Doctrine of the Unity of the Human Race*[9] he argued the unpopular opinion that all humans are one species sharing a single origin; or put the other way, that the so-called races are not distinct species of separate origins. This thesis he supported by numerous inferences from other species. Though ahead of many of his contemporaries on this biological matter and active as a pastor among African Americans, Bachman was not free from racial stereotypes; indeed, although his scientific thesis could be, and was, used by abolitionists to support their views, Bachman himself was not an opponent of slavery.

Schmucker shared Bachman's views about the origins of the human race, but, unlike the South Carolinian, he was steadfast in his condemnation of slavery on biblical and political grounds. In particular he relied upon Acts 17:26, which asserts that all nations are made by God of the same blood. To encourage others to this position Schmucker employed the means readily available to him: sermons, the classroom, and various publications as well as his remarks at church meetings. In addition he was long a member of the American Colonization Society while simultaneously advocating immediate emancipation. His service in Virginia congregations and his marriage into a slave-owning family prevented Schmucker from treating slavery in the abstract. He was compelled to respond to both slave owners and enslaved persons in his own home. He had occasion to consider the best way to treat slaves as well as how to free them. When the family moved to Pennsylvania, he worked out a compromise with his wife that allowed for the eventual manumission of her "servants."

Few synods took official synodical actions on the issue of slavery. Such unsurprising quiet is consistent with a general corporate silence by nineteenth-century Lutheran churches on social issues with the exception of temperance.[10] While Schmucker was a member, the Maryland and Virginia synod passed a resolution recommending that its members support the American Colonization Society. Stronger action was taken by the Franckean synod, whose name honored Hermann Augustus Francke, the German pietist leader. This small synod in upstate New York organized in 1837 with a firm abolitionist commitment. The constitution forbade slaveholders from serving as lay delegates and made opposition to slavery a condition of clerical membership in the synod. In subsequent years more rigorous resolutions were passed, including one suggesting that slave owners and slave traders be barred from receiving the Lord's Supper. These regulations set the Frankeans apart from their fellow Lutherans but were in keeping with the come-outer strategies common in revival-saturated New York state.

Most Scandinavian Lutherans lived in areas removed from concentrations of slavery; nonetheless, their pietist convictions predisposed them to oppose it even from a distance. Brief organizational alliances between some Scandinavians and the Frankean synod appear to have reinforced that view.[11] On the other hand, contact between the leaders of the Norwegian Synod and the Synod of Missouri, both more Confessional than pietist, contributed to a long debate among the Norwegians about how the badness of slavery is to be understood. Either it was a sin and thus an evil as well, or it was merely an evil but not a sin. Some pastors, more sophisticated in their biblical interpretation and anxious to maintain biblical authority, were inclined to support the latter view—an evil but not a sin. They articulated their view in a resolution at the 1861 synodical meeting: "Although according to the Word of God, it is not in and by itself a sin to keep slaves, nevertheless it is in itself an evil and a punishment from God. We condemn all abuses and sins connected therewith, and furthermore, when official duties require it and when Christian love and wisdom demand it, we will work for its abolition."[12] Led by farmer Erik Ellefsen, laypeople were interested in the reality of slavery as it existed in the United States and boldly declared it a sin "in direct conflict with Christian love." The debate continued for years, fueled by opinions solicited from theologians in Norway and precipitating congregational withdrawals from the synod. Though the issue of slavery was legally settled by the state, the underlying issues about the relationship between the Word of God and the Bible continued within the church.

Once war broke out, Lutherans, like all citizens, were drawn into the conflict in new and unescapable ways, both individually and corporately. Though they had previously avoided an organizational division such as separated the northern and southern Baptists, the secession of southern states and the formation of the Confederacy lead to a break within the General Synod. In 1863 several regional synods withdrew to found the General Synod of the Confederate States. This weakened the General Synod's tenuous claim to link all Lutherans in the United States and introduced a division that would endure until 1917.

As citizens many Lutheran men fought in the armed forces. Students from the college and seminary in Gettysburg formed Company A of the Twenty-sixth Pennsylvania Emergency Regiment.[13] As is usually the case, the war provided newcomers with an opportunity to demonstrate their loyalty to the nation. From the Norwegians came the Fifteenth Wisconsin Regiment, led by Hans Christian Heg. Among the few official responses to the war, the General Synod in its 1864 meeting passed a resolution to set aside on the second day of their meeting an hour to pray "for the forgiveness of our national sins, for [God's] blessings upon our Armies and Navy in the Opening campaign, for victory in the coming struggle, and for the speedy suppression of the Rebellion and the restoration of peace to our distracted land."[14]

One of the most famous battles of the war took place near, and on the campus of, Gettysburg College and Seminary in the summer of 1863. Historian Henry Eyster Jacobs, then a young man in his twenties, was living in Gettysburg, where his father was a professor at the college. He observed the battle through the college's telescope as well as by its occurrence all around him. His vivid accounts indicate the extent to which the battle intruded into everyone's life. At the end of the first day, "The town was one vast hospital. The churches were full of wounded. The seminary was a Confederate and the college a Federal hospital. Many private dwellings held men of both armies. . . . Night fell, and on its damp air were wafted the cries of the uncared-for on the field. The dead lay on the pavements and in the streets for days."[15] A Federal soldier was shot on the Jacobs' doorstep, and others were taken prisoner from their cellar. Late in the battle, his sister Julia stood amid flying bullets warning the Union forces of pickets below them.[16] After the battle three months passed before all the dead were well buried. Though the organizational repercussions of the war were small among Lutherans, as were the personal consequences for Jacobs, he points to the profound effects for those Lutherans who fought on both sides and were injured or killed and for their families and friends.

Throughout the nation and in most churches the legal end of slavery moved questions about racial relationships out of the political realm and into the social realm, leaving church members to act on their own convictions. Lutheran response was predictably in keeping with general trends. At its 1866 convention the Tennessee Synod moved toward segregation. The language of the resolution assumed that the whites constituted the synod even as it asserted that "some of them [colored people] were formerly members of our congregations and still claim membership in them." This situation called for some action, "so that every one could worship God with the least possible embarrassment." Therefore, the synod established a procedure to license black lay preachers and voted to support organizations of separate congregations.[17]

For several years the North Carolina Synod retained responsibility for this work within its territory while authorizing separate black congregations with their own leadership. A few men were licensed to preach and carry out other pastoral acts prior to David James Koontz's ordination in 1880.[18] As the work grew, the North Carolina Synod requested aid from the general bodies but was turned down. In 1889 a handful of black leaders petitioned the synod to organize a "colored Evangelical Lutheran Synod." The Alpha Evangelical Synod of Freedmen in America was formed almost immediately, with five congregations totaling 180 members and with David J. Koontz as president.[19] Initially, this independent body was an effort to keep the congregations alive. However, within a few years a request for aid from the Synodical Conference opened the way for it to assume responsibility. Nils Jules Bakke took charge, and the leaders of the Alpha Synod were removed, with the result that a mission to blacks continued, but largely under white leadership. Between them the resolutions of the Tennessee Synod and the actions of the Synodical Conference were indicative of the official attitudes and actions of Lutheran churches for several decades.

THE AMERICAN LUTHERANISM CONTROVERSY

Within Lutheranism the nineteenth century was marked by the American Lutheranism controversy, a war of words about the role that distinctly Lutheran teachings should play in American Lutheran church life. Although "American" has come to designate this debate among Lutherans, it is worth noting that among American churches only the Lutherans would have it on just these terms, in particular, with such attention to the Augsburg Confession. The controversy was waged on two fronts: doctrine and practice. Although language continued to be an issue for American Lutherans, it is not a useful indicator of positions in these debates. The American Lutherans, as would be expected, used English by preference, but even most of the strongest Confessionalists wrote and spoke in English, often as their native tongue; indeed, they prepared liturgical and educational materials in English. Anticipating the use of both German and English at the Lutheran Theological Seminary in Philadelphia, Charles Porterfield Krauth, a Confessionalist leader, remarked: "It is the one want of our Church that the two tongues should work together—sisterly harmony. . . . Let the German and English elements of Church throb heart to heart in faith and life, and the tongues will no longer make the old practical difficulty."[20] In this way he expressed his view that language is the servant of the gospel, not the reverse.

The parties in the controversy are generally indicated by the labels American Lutherans (or Platformists) and Confessionalists. The former included most prominently Samuel Simon Schmucker along with his students Benjamin Kurtz and Samuel Sprecher and also Schmucker's brother-in-law. Schmucker's position as professor of the recently founded seminary in Gettysburg and his leadership in the General Synod provided the base of his extraordinary influence throughout the church. Indeed, Schmucker's importance in the first half of the century was comparable to Muhlenberg's in the 1700s, though he has not been as consistently revered in the ensuing years. His friend Kurtz, a pastor in Maryland, published the *Lutheran Observer*, giving a printed voice to their position. Samuel Sprecher, president of Wittenberg College in Springfield, Ohio, carried it to the western areas of the church. All three men were native-born Americans, eager for their church to adapt itself to its current environment.

The Confessionalists were a more diverse group, including Schmucker's son, Beale Melanchthon, and Charles Porterfield Krauth, both American-born, among its leadership. Krauth's father, Charles Philip Krauth, a colleague of Samuel Schmucker at the Gettysburg Seminary, was claimed by both sides; however, his moderately conservative position was more in continuity with a more definite Confessionalism than with the American Lutherans. Also among this party were recent arrivals in the United States such as William Julius Mann, a friend of historian Philip Schaff. Mann's initial work in the United States was in German-language publication and in a German Reformed setting. However, he soon returned to the Lutherans and provided important leadership for the moderates through his writings, translations, and teaching at the Philadelphia Seminary. This group Philip Schaff termed the moderates in contrast to the neo-Lutherans such as Schmucker.[21] They took organizational form in the General Council (1866).

The Henkels, Confessionalists all, did not join the General Council and so provide a bridge to a third subgroup to the theological right of the Confessionalists, what Schaff called the old Lutherans. This party is not always brought into discussions of the American Lutheranism Controversy because it did not play a major part at the time. Nevertheless, these Lutherans must be mentioned to provide the full spectrum of views then current. This position is well represented by the Saxons, who immigrated to Missouri to avoid doctrinal indifferentism and unionism between Lutherans and Calvinists. Lead by C.F.W. Walther, these Lutherans formed the synod of Missouri, a group that has consistently defined the conservative confessional boundary of Lutheranism by requiring conformity on all aspects of doctrine and practice as conditions of fellowship. They also supported parochial schools using German as the language of instruction. Their influence extended into the Scandinavian immigrant communities and was formalized in the formation of the Synodical Council (1872). A similar position was taken by Johannes Grabau and the Buffalo synod.

That observer Philip Schaff was able to identify and name these three parties within American Lutheranism in the 1850s indicates that by midcentury the positions were coalescing, though they had not yet assumed institutional form. The emerging divergent views can be discerned earlier in the careers of the principal participants in the episodes that erupted in the 1850s and 1860s. The early development of Samuel Simon Schmucker is particularly important due to his central role in the events that would follow. He was the son and nephew of clergymen who had been tutored by Paul Henkel. John George Schmucker, his father, was a prominent churchman and well read in German theology. The younger Schmucker received his training both in the informal way usual until then and at recently established schools. He was taught by his father and J.C.H.

Helmuth, who provided one of the few remaining links to Muhlenberg's generation. He also attended the University of Pennsylvania and Presbyterian Princeton Seminary. Thus, his education put him in contact with both the legacy of colonial Lutheranism and contemporary developments of American Protestantism. Unlike most of his classmates at Princeton, Schmucker was able to read current German theology without waiting for translations.

When Schmucker was ordained by the Ministerium of Pennsylvania at age twenty-two, he was recognized as a learned man and given responsibilities usually reserved for older leaders. He preached at synodical meetings and was given charge of training half a dozen aspiring clergymen. Of his own initiative he conceived of a three-part plan for the American Lutheran Church: to translate into English a major work of Lutheran theology; to establish a theological seminary; and to found a preparatory college.[22] In part because of his commitment to scholarly activity he took a small parish whose demands would leave time for other work. While translating Gottlob Christian Storr and Karl Christian Flatt's *An Elementary Course in Biblical Theology*, he exerted himself to assure the formation and survival of the General Synod. In 1819 the Ministerium of Pennsylvania proposed bringing all American Lutherans together in one cooperating organization, a purpose akin to the one that had motivated the founding of the ministerium nearly eighty years before. As will become evident, this organizational effort helped to precipitate the debates about the Confessions. Once the General Synod was in place, Schmucker urged the establishment of a theological seminary to prepare pastors. This was done in 1826 with Schmucker himself as the sole professor at the school in Gettysburg.

Because he was the author of the oath he took when inducted into his teaching post and of the seminary's constitution, the man and the institutions he led mirrored each other to an uncommon degree. These documents demonstrate that at this stage, Schmucker was a proponent of distinctive Lutheranism. He was not eager to meld Lutherans into one of the churches he had come to know through his fellow students and teachers at Princeton. However, he was interested in a Lutheranism defined by a lean set of criteria. Lutherans have long agreed that uniformity on all matters is not required for unity; some things are *adiaphora*, or matters of indifference. Schmucker placed much in this category, though his terminology was of fundamentals and nonfundamentals. Though by midcentury he was regarded as an opponent of the Confessions, in the 1820s Schmucker's work called for renewed attention to these documents, which had been removed from the constitution of the Ministerium of Pennsylvania in 1792. Thus, he gave impetus to the very movement that eventually passed him by.[23]

Farther south, disagreement about how Lutheranism was to be defined and practiced was already brewing in the North Carolina Synod, whose membership included several of the Henkels as well as pastors with other denominational origins, for example, Gottlieb Schober, from the Moravians. In the first years of his career Paul Henkel worked peacefully with men from other traditions, displaying an openness in keeping with awakened concern for the state of souls more than for the details of doctrine. However, over the years his views shifted, and those of his son, David, were even stricter. Publications from the Henkel Press in New Market, Virginia, trace the shift. These moved from works that could be read as confessionally indifferent in the 1810s to the first English edition of the Book of Concord in 1851. The change is also marked by Henkel's suggestion in 1797 that the conference of pastors in Virginia print and distribute copies of the Augsburg Confession, a project carried out eight years later by his son Solomon, and by the document he wrote for the Ohio Synod in 1818 to differentiate its Lutheran teachings from those of other Christian bodies.

David Henkel's views and his desire to be ordained were the occasion for the fault line in the North Carolina Synod to quake apart. Though still young and largely self-taught, David Henkel sounded the charge for a return to the confessional basis of Lutheranism; his writings defended baptismal regeneration, the real presence of Christ in the Lord's Supper, and conventional Christology. While still a candidate for ordination, he had already challenged Schober's position. Then at the 1819 meeting of the North Carolina Synod, the men's disagreement led to Henkel's being put on trial. Neither his brothers nor his father was present because the meeting date had been moved forward in order to authorize a delegate to represent the synod at the meeting to consider the plan for the General Synod, a plan Henkel opposed. On the original date, Trinity Sunday, David was ordained by his brother, Philip. In July of the following year the Henkels, together with a few others, constituted the Tennessee Synod, popularly known as the Henkelites. The first such body founded on theological grounds rather than geographical ones, it subscribed to the whole of the unaltered Augsburg Confession. Perhaps of longer significance, the synod's members—namely, the Henkel family and their press—made that Reformation document and the entire Book of Concord more widely available in English.

The General Synod was formed in 1820 despite Henkelite opposition. Its purposes had been modified from those set out in the *Plan Entwurf* so that the body had less control over its members than initially proposed. In his *Carolina Herald of Liberty*,[24] David Henkel asserted that Lutheran unity proceeds from a common confession of faith, not from uniformity in matters such as forms of worship. In so doing he emphasized an internal, rather than an organizational, understanding of unity, even as he denied that the internal sort could be present among those who did not subscribe explicitly to the Confession and those who did. Henkel's apparent preference for internal unity and the General Synod's effort to secure organizational unity represent two positions that would reappear in subsequent discussion of Lutheran cooperation. When it was constituted, the General Synod membership included the New York, the North Carolina, the Maryland, and the Virginia Synods in addition to the Ministerium of Pennsylvania. Only three years passed before the Ministerium of Pennsylvania withdrew its membership; reasons suggested for the move include unwillingness to support a seminary for training clergy and general reluctance in rural areas to participate in a body that might reduce cooperation with the Reformed such as had taken place since colonial years.

Though the General Synod did not encompass all the regional synods, a quarter of a century after its founding its membership spanned a wide variety of theological positions that became more evident as greater attention was paid to theological matters. Thus, a not unreasonable request was made at its 1845 Convention in Philadelphia for "a clear and concise view of the doctrines and practices of the American Lutheran Church."[25] As is so often the case, the committee appointed to write the statement determined what sort of statement it would be; the committee consisted of Schmucker, Benjamin Kurtz, and others who argued that the historic Lutheran Confessions needed to be altered in ways consistent with then-current American religious life and that Lutheran practice should be similarly adapted. When the committee's work was presented to the 1850 convention, it was tabled, and the committee dismissed from further attention to this task.

At the same meeting in 1850, Schmucker's colleague on the Gettysburg Seminary faculty, Charles Philip Krauth, called "for us to go back to our father's house." He continued alerting his hearers that "[i]t is our duty to exert a conservative influence."[26] This appeal was in keeping with the concerns expressed by his son the previous year in "The Relation of Our Confessions to the Reformation," published in the *Evangelical Review*. The younger Krauth wrote,

Is there a conflict between the two [Lutheranism and America] when carried to their farthest limits? Must Lutheranism be shorn of its glory to adapt it to the times of our land? No! Our land is great and wide and glorious and destined, we trust, under the sunlight of her free institutions long to endure, but our faith is wider and greater and is eternal. . . . In my heart these excite no conflict but blend harmoniously together. . . . No church can retain her self-respect or inspire respect in others, who is afraid or ashamed of her own history, or who rears a dubious fabric on the ignorance of her ministers and her members.[27]

Three years later, the Ministerium of Pennsylvania returned to the General Synod after a thirty-year absence, with the contingency that if the synod took actions that the ministerium's representatives judged out of order, they would withdraw. The ministerium also founded a professorial chair at Gettysburg Seminary in an effort to provide for a sufficient supply of German-speaking pastors for its congregations.

In the midst of these developments two English editions of the entire Book of Concord were issued by the Henkel Press. The first was largely the work of southeastern pastors, though the initiative was from lay members of the Henkel clan. Its appearance was greatly anticipated, especially by the Confessionalists associated with Capital Seminary in Columbus, Ohio. This initial edition was intended as a sort of first draft and was immediately revised with cooperation from more learned authorities, including those at Columbus and both Krauths.

Then, in 1855, the American Recension of the Augsburg Confession appeared in a small booklet titled, *Definite Synodical Platform, Doctrinal and Disciplinarian.* In its first printing the *Platform* was anonymous, though its American Lutheran content pointed to Schmucker, who later claimed major authorship. Here were laid out the errors of the Augsburg Confession. Prominent among them were these five, which suggest the influence of Protestantism shaped by Puritanism and revivalism: lack of Sabbath observance; failure to condemn the abuses of the mass; failure to reject private confession; adherence to the real presence of Christ in the Lord's Supper; and assertion of baptismal regeneration. The pamphlet focused the debate, which was conducted in both church periodicals and other publications, such as William Julius Mann's *Lutheranism in America.*[28] This revised version of the 1530 Augsburg Confession was proposed for adoption, as a whole, by regional synods. Less than a handful of small synods did so, but the debate continued.

In the 1860s a series of events solidified the positions that became associated not only with individuals but also with rival seminaries and synods. Withdrawal of southern synods to found the General Synod of the Confederate States in 1863 weakened the General Synod's claim to unite Lutherans in the nation. Yet the claim was still strong enough to attract an application for membership from the abolitionist Franckean Synod, a body that had never subscribed to the Augsburg Confession in any form. When its request came before the General Synod's convention at York, Pennsylvania, in May 1864, the debate led first to a vote refusing the application and then to one granting admittance with some conditions. This vacillation demonstrated that a large middle ground existed. But the final vote prompted the representatives of the Ministerium of Pennsylvania to withdraw in order to report to their home synod. This was in accord with the reservations made when the ministerium rejoined in 1853.

A third event finally prompted the moderate Confessionalists to organize their own institutions. When Samuel Schmucker retired from his position on the Gettysburg faculty, the Confessionalists had hoped that Charles Porterfield Krauth would be appointed in his place and thus shift the weight of that institution away from the Platformists. The man named to the post, James Allen Brown, was not a Schmucker disciple, but neither was he the younger Krauth. The combination of this disappointment and the General Synod's admission of the Franckean Synod convinced Confessionalists within the Ministerium of Pennsylvania of the necessity of establishing their own seminary at Philadelphia in the fall of 1864 and two years later to organize the General Council, bringing like-minded regional synods together into a larger body.

The renewal of confessionalism in the nineteenth century was accompanied by a like renewal of interest in more traditional forms of worship. As would be expected, of the two northeastern bodies, the General Council moved toward a liturgy and hymnbook that reflected sixteenth-century German Lutheran practice.

These included a more active role for the congregational members in liturgical response and the selection and arrangement of hymns. Both hymns and the service with music were printed together in one book. Beale Melanchton Schmucker and Charles Porterfield Krauth both contributed to this movement, the former perhaps more than the latter. Krauth's sister, Harriet Krauth Spaeth, also made a mark in the area as music editor of the *Churchbook with Music* (1893). A move toward more distinctly Lutheran forms of worship was being made by many in the General Synod and the United Synod of the South. The impetus for working together on a common order of worship came from the southerners in 1884. Beale M. Schmucker was joined by George Unangst Wrenner and Edward Traill Horn in this venture. The Common Service of 1888 helped to draw these three bodies toward one another. This service was printed by each synod in its own book with slight variations. But the versions were close enough to one another that a member of a General Council congregation in Pittsburgh would have had an easy time finding the way through worship in a North Carolina, United Synod, South congregation. The service was prepared with careful attention to the liturgies of the sixteenth century as their model while also drawing upon the English text of the Anglican Book of Common Prayer. In subsequent decades immigrant synods adopted the Common Service as their English order of worship.

Despite the truism that similarity of worship practice has given Lutheran people a shared experience and cultivated in them common expressions, Lutherans have also assumed that "confessional unity can persist in the face of liturgical diversity."[29] Indeed, the suggestion that the General Synod intended to regulate a common order of worship was one of the points that had stimulated Henkelite opposition earlier in the century; Article 7 of the Augsburg Confession was cited as requiring a more limited basis for unity. James William Richard of Gettysburg Seminary was critical of the Common Service for other reasons. He particularly objected to the suggestion that centuries-old forms could be lifted out of their particular settings and put to use in very different situations without attention to the "wants and needs" of the contemporary worshipers.[30] This double debate, about the role of worship forms in defining Lutheran identity and about which forms are to be regarded as both authentic and essential, persisted in several episodes well into the twentieth century. Indeed, there are no signs that either aspect of the debate has been settled.

The underlying issues of the American Lutheranism controversy were no more solved by the Common Service than by the formation of competing synods and institutions. Those organizations contained, for a time, the parties in the disputes. Various channels, such as committees to prepare worship resources and exchanges of official visitors, fostered greater familiarity among those least different from each other. Nonetheless, disagreements about specific issues arose again and again. Here the more concrete debate about worship points to the basic issues that remained. Lutherans in the United States continue their ongoing and likely never-ending negotiation of their confessional and national corporate identity. While nearly all agree that historic Lutheran teaching and practice must be considered, the weight given in relation to contemporary cultural concerns is shifting balance.

THE WORK OF THE CHURCH

The doctrinal debate that embroiled theologians and pastors also drew the attention of some laypeople and their congregations; however, to give the impression that the whole of church life in the nineteenth century was consumed by this controversy would be a distortion. While the Schmuckers and the Krauths and the Henkels discussed the doctrinal foundations of the Lutheran Church in the United States, they and others were also busy with establishing mechanisms for the church to do and expand its work. In addition to new congregations being formed in areas of migration, synodical bodies were organized, periodicals were published, schools and charitable institutions were founded, missionaries were sent out in the United States and overseas, and women's groups were begun. By this means Lutherans in the United States strengthened the self-sufficiency needed if they were to be a church, not a mission field.

Lutheranism was extended into areas newly occupied by Lutherans migrating from the east by their presence and by the organization of congregations. The movement south and west placed more established congregations and the Ministeriums of Pennsylvania and New York in a position similar to the one occupied by the European churches in the colonial era. Appeals came from groups of laypeople asking for qualified pastors to minister to them. We have seen the need in the career of John Stough, who was pressed into pastoral service before he had either training or authorization. The Ministerium of Pennsylvania determined to appoint traveling missionaries to seek out and attend to the needs of Lutherans isolated from a congregation. When Paul Henkel was thus appointed to travel in Ohio, he found many Lutherans eager for more sustained access to preaching and the sacraments. Before he took a parish in Virginia, Samuel Simon Schmucker also considered joining in the migration; his brother George did go west, eventually as far as Iowa, where he died in the 1880s. If the church was to survive and flourish, however, an arrangement other than itinerary was needed. John Stough reported in his journal for 1806 that on November 29 he preached "to fifteen people who told me with tears that many of them had lived there for six years without hearing a single German sermon."[31] Lutherans needed stable congregations with well-trained resident pastors.

Organization of synods was an important step in developing self-sufficiency. Cooperation between congregations and pastors provided the necessary authority and resources for ordaining pastors, sponsoring schools, and preparing worship materials. As was discussed in the previous chapter, the first effort in this direction was the Ministerium of Pennsylvania, though initially it took a far more ambitious name, the Ministerium of North America. As the geographic spread of Lutherans increased, the distances involved made participation in the annual meetings of the ministerium burdensome. Even in the late 1700s distance prompted formation of additional synods in South Carolina, North Carolina, New York, and Virginia. By the late 1800s the number had multiplied to several dozen, not always in a peaceful fashion.

The synod of Ohio emerged from a special conference of the Ministerium of Pennsylvania, organized, in part, to allow the pastors of the area to send a single representative to the ministerium's annual meeting. Responsibility for examining ministerial candidates and conferring ordination remained with the parent body, despite requests to grant it to the conference. A compromise allowing the local body to examine the first two grades of ministry—catechists and candidates— while retaining ordination as the prerogative of the ministerium did not settle the issue. The older men, such as Henkel and Stough, who had personal connections to the ministerium were inclined to accept the arrangement, but the younger men prevailed, and the new synod of Ohio was organized in 1818. Before long this synod divided itself into two geographic districts—east and west. Then in 1836 the English District was added, indicating an increasing divergence between the English-speaking and the more theologically conservative, German-speaking groups.

The contentious beginnings of the Tennessee Synod have been described. It emerged from the doctrinal debates within the North Carolina Synod and in opposition to the proposed General Synod. The Tennessee synod was the first formed for theological reasons rather than as a matter of logistical convenience. Within a few years this motive would become more common. The hasty organization of the West Pennsylvania Conference into a body independent of the Ministerium of Pennsylvania in order to save the General Synod might be taken as a second example. Certainly, the Franckean Synod's insistence on purity of practice, though not of confession, provides a variation on the theme of synods defined by teaching rather than location.

When Muhlenberg led in the formation of the first synod, there was hope that it would unite all Lutherans. By the late 1810s this hope was obviously in vain, and the desire to bring the regional synods into a more cooperative relationship was expressed. Before the century was out, three/four general bodies existed, each one linking regional synods and representing the three theological positions characterized by Schaff as the neo-Lutheran, the moderate, and the old Lutheran.

The first, the General Synod, has already appeared several times in this chapter. Initially, it was not proposed to represent a specific theological position but rather to bring together in a visible way all Lutherans whose regional synods increasingly fragmented. Indeed, its rather indefinite doctrinal statement was an attempt to allow for the wide variety present among Lutherans. The need for some sort of cooperative body was recognized by many, but the specific plan and invitation to consider it came from the Ministerium of Pennsylvania. The *Plan Entwurf* was issued in 1819, over the signature of its president, John George Schmucker. As we have seen, the Proposed Plan met with extreme reactions from the opposition of the Henkelites, to the support of Schmucker's son Samuel. The original proposal gave the General Synod authority to introduce liturgical forms and to regulate grades of ministry. In response to criticisms, these powers were reduced in the constitution. The constituting convention, held in October 1822, was attended by representatives of four of the six existing regional bodies. Membership of at least three was required and was tenuously maintained. When the parent Ministerium of Pennsylvania withdrew, Schmucker convinced his father and others to disassociate themselves and form the Western Pennsylvania Synod, thus preserving the General Synod. In the midst of the American Lutheranism controversy, the General Synod included two-thirds of the Lutherans in the United States. However, losses to the General Synod of the Confederate States and the second departure of the Ministerium of Pennsylvania reduced this number significantly. Once the General Council formed, the General Synod marked the boundary of "liberal" (neo-Lutheran) Lutheranism characterized by its similarities in belief and practice to other American Protestant groups—less structured liturgy, more emphasis upon morality, and willingness to adapt the historic confessions.

The General Council took the middle ground, gathering in those bodies whose leaders and members were committed to a more conservative reading of their doctrinal heritage. Two meetings of the older General Synod led up to its formation. The first was the General Synod's 1864 meeting in York, when the Frankean Synod was admitted to membership, and the protesting Ministerium of Pennsylvania delegation withdrew to consult with the ministerium, as the terms of its membership allowed. The second was the next General Synod meeting two years later in Fort Wayne, Indiana, when Samuel Sprecher, a Platformist, was president. Interpreting the Pennsylvania delegation's withdrawal at York as from membership in the synod, not merely from a single meeting, he refused to seat the delegates. Despite disapproval from some delegates, the chair's decision held, and the way was opened for another general body. In 1866 the ministerium again took the lead, issuing an invitation to all Lutherans loyal to the Unaltered Augsburg Confession to consider a new general body with, on one hand, a more strict doctrinal standard and, on the other, a less centralized organization. The faculty of the new Philadelphia seminary gave leadership. At the December meeting in Reading, Pennsylvania, Charles Porterfield Krauth's Theses of Faith and Polity provided the basis of conversation. Eleven months later (November 1867), back in Fort Wayne, the General Council was formed with participation by eleven regional synods. Initially, these included the slightly more conservative Ohio and Augustana; these two regularly stood at fluid border between general groups embodying the dynamic, ongoing negotiation of doctrinal positions with a matrix of other relationships.[32] The Norwegian Synod and Missouri stood outside, regarding the General Council as too lax in its Confessional position and too willing to allow variations of practice. These groups gathered into a third general body, the Synodical Conference, that marked the opposite extreme from the General Synod.

Mention of the Norwegian Synod and the Swedish Augustana anticipates another basis for synodical organization that appeared in the second half of the century, shared national origins. Each of the immigrant groups formed at least one general body that used a common, non-English language. In the environment of American religious voluntarism, the Lutheran Swedes confined their organizational efforts largely to what became the Augustana Synod, while other ethnic groups multiplied synods on the basis of varieties of piety and doctrine. This development contributed to a rapid increase in synodical organizations: nearly sixty new ones were formed between 1840 and 1875.[33]

Each of these synods would eventually spawn a full complement of supporting mechanisms including periodicals, schools, and charitable institutions. Periodicals were of particular importance, as the printed voice of specific theological positions as well as for spreading information about the churches' work and cultivating support for it. Among the earliest to appear were publications sponsored by individuals. The *Lutheran Observer* was started by John Gottlieb Morris and long published by Benjamin Kurtz in Baltimore. Its editor was a strong supporter of the American Lutheran party, and thus it, too, was associated with that position and with the General Synod. A more moderate position was espoused by the *Evangelical Review* from Gettysburg and the *Lutheran and Missionary*, begun by William Passavant and later edited by Charles Porterfield Krauth from Philadelphia. The Lutherans farther west also had their own publications, including the English *Lutheran Standard* and the German *Kirchenzeitung*, both connected with the Confessionalists at Capital Seminary in Columbus, Ohio. As an important forum of doctrinal debate, these periodicals and others such as *The Young Lutheran*, a monthly for Sunday schools, contributed to the theological stratification of Lutherans in the United States both by defining the points of divergence and by consolidating the parties. But this should not overshadow the value of their less polemic contributions, spreading information about the work of the churches' various workers and enterprises and fostering Christian life.

Educational endeavors in these years ranged from local German schools, to seminaries and colleges, to schools for women. Among the Muhlenberg descendants German schools were primarily a project of the early decades, though such parochial projects would long receive support from the Lutheran Church Missouri Synod and will come to our attention again. Greater effort was given to establishment of seminaries to prepare men for pastoral service. From the days of Muhlenberg American Lutherans recognized the need to provide themselves with pastors, not to rely upon the European churches to provide for them. The patriarch himself purchased land in Philadelphia with this purpose in mind, but nothing long-lasting came of his forethought. John Christopher Hartwick left his estate earmarked for theological education, especially for training of Native Americans. In the 1810s his legacy was used to support Hartwick Academy in upstate New York and John Kunze's teaching in New York City. Nonetheless, most pastors received their training by informal tutoring from established men. Consequently, the Lutheran expectation of an educated ministry imported from Europe and found in the generation of pastors who immigrated after completing their training was difficult to maintain without sending young American students abroad, as the Muhlenberg sons were sent. Such prominent leaders as John George Schmucker were without formal theological education. This situation was not unlike what was found in other American churches, though they moved more quickly in establishing theological seminaries.[34]

By attending Presbyterian Princeton, Samuel Simon Schmucker distinguished himself from others of his age group and gained an appreciation for the value of such an education. Both Schmuckers were strong supporters of Gettysburg Seminary, founded by the General Synod in 1826 largely through the son's efforts. In his four decades as a professor, at first the only one, he had a significant role in shaping more than a generation of pastoral leadership. Though several of his students took a different theological position than he, his solid teaching equipped them to move beyond indifference and to carry on an informed debate.

Before those students and their allies founded the rival seminary in Philadelphia in 1864, nearly half a dozen others had been established: Capital in Columbus, Ohio; Southern in Newberry, South Carolina; what would come to be called Hamma at Wittenberg College in Springfield, Ohio; Concordia in St. Louis, Missouri; and Wartburg, now in Dubuque, Iowa. Each school served a particular constituency defined by a combination of geographical, ethnic, and theological factors. There were, nonetheless, similarities among them with regard to the challenges they faced and the methods they employed. Books were less available in those years than now, so professors often used in-class time to dictate for students who copied out in their own hand what became a textbook. If time remained, the professor might expound upon the material thus transmitted. Topics covered included exegetical, systematic, historical, and practical theology. Standards for preparation of candidates were not strictly defined, so there was a temptation for students, who faced financial pressures and the immediate prospect of God's work waiting for them, to leave before completing the whole course. As Schmucker soon discovered, students came to the seminary with uneven preparation.

Throughout the United States, the nineteenth century was a boom time for college founding by religious individuals, churches, and government.[35] Students' need for a better general education prior to undertaking theological study prompted Lutherans to start colleges as well as seminaries. Prior attempts were made in this direction, some in cooperation with the German Reformed, but none of those endured long. The first to survive (and to continue to the 1990s with Lutheran affiliation) was the college founded in Gettysburg, then named Pennsylvania College. Its importance for Lutheran education was not limited to the model it provided but extended to supplying founders, presidents, and teachers to other colleges, thus forging connections between institutions. The schools founded in the next decades included Capital University in Columbus and Wittenberg in Springfield, Ohio; Susquehanna in Selingrove and Muhlenberg in

Allentown, Pennsylvania; Roanoke in Salem, Virginia; Lenoir-Rhyne in Hickory, North Carolina; and Newberry in Newberry, South Carolina. In addition, the newly arriving Scandinavian and German Lutherans were establishing schools.

The two Ohio colleges were associated with opposite parties in the American Lutheranism controversy and on language issues as well as representing two quite different approaches to education. Wittenberg's founder, Ezra Keller, a Schmucker student, pointed to the Lutheran heritage of education but deliberately followed the American model, combining theological and college departments as one school. The Lutheran notion that education is valuable for carrying out one's vocation in various occupations, not only the pastoral office, was a motivating factor. The founders of Capital were associated with the more conservative party and favored greater effort to provide German-language education. In contrast to Keller, they hoped to replicate the European model university with faculties of medicine and law in addition to theology and letters.

Thiel College, now in Greenville, Pennsylvania, was different in being coeducational from the outset, an innovation untried by schools devoted largely to preministerial preparation. Three girls and two boys constituted its first student body. The college was founded by Pastor William Passavant with $4,000 donated by A. Louis Thiel, a layman who had made good investments in oil. At the laying of a cornerstone in 1872, Passavant's remarks highlighted the importance of education to equip laypeople to carry out their vocations.

We can conceive of nothing more praiseworthy in the service which men can perform for their fellow men, than to send back to his home, at the end of his college course, the young man in the dew of youth, healthful in body, ingenuous in heart, pure in life, cultivated in intellect and established in the faith of Christ. The world needs such men and the Church needs them. They are wanted at the bar, in the ministry, in the healing art, in the editorial chair, in the school room, in every department of business, commerce, trade, in agriculture and the mechanical arts, everywhere, men of piety, of a positive faith, of a true manhood, who know in whom and in what they believe, and stand up in their place as God's witnesses among their fellows![36]

Unfortunately, Passavant's language obscures the importance of such education to the women who were part of the student body. Though none survive into the late twentieth century, several schools were founded for female students. Among these was a female college attached to what became Susquehanna and Lutherville (Maryland) Female College with J. G. Morris as a patron. The last operating women's school was Marion College, the successor of a girls' school started in 1855; its final graduating class was in the 1960s.[37]

William Passavant was involved in nearly every aspect of nineteenth-century church life from congregational ministry, to editorial work, to synodical organization, to several sorts of philanthropy. His founding of congregations, his responsibility for the *Missionary* and the *Workman*, and his leadership in the organization of the Pittsburgh Synod and in the General Council were important but do not set him apart from his fellows as distinctly as his diligent advocacy of an active, practical expression of religion. Passavant was born in 1821, the year after the General Synod was founded; he grew up among German Lutherans in western Pennsylvania, where he was influenced by the revivalism then sweeping the frontier. He was educated at Jefferson College, a Presbyterian school, and went off to Gettysburg Seminary ready to continue his development along American Lutheran lines. Though he would devote himself to causes in keeping with the evangelical concerns of Professor Schmucker, Passavant moved toward the theological position of Professor Krauth and Krauth's son, with whom Passavant collaborated. Passavant's charitable and missionary work put him in contact with the newly arriving immigrants, for whom he served as a link to the older Muhlenberg Lutherans and who were made welcome at the seminary he founded in Chicago.

Philanthropic activities, along with educational endeavors, were a sign that the American church was becoming more self-sufficient and securely enough rooted to attend to the material needs of its members, even to extend its efforts beyond its members. Based on his wide-ranging activity and his prominence among his contemporaries, Passavant can stand as a remarkable, but not unrepresentative, example of this work sometimes called inner missions.[38] His concern for the well-being of others appeared early in his life, as did a particular attentiveness to African Americans. After his ordination the energetic young pastor launched into work that took him into the far western areas of the United States. He was instrumental in founding three orphanages and four hospitals. The latter were located in Pittsburgh, Chicago, Jacksonville, Illinois, and Milwaukee, Wisconsin. Having traveled to Europe and seen the work of the deaconess community established by Theodore Fliedner, Passavant introduced the modern deaconate to American Lutherans in 1849, when he brought four German women to serve at the hospital in Pittsburgh. Some of their number gave nursing aid to Dorothea Dix during the Civil War.

As we have already noted, Lutherans' movement away from the older settlement areas in the East required older congregations and synods to assume responsibility for sending out missionaries to gather the scattered members into congregations and larger bodies. John Stough and Paul Henkel were early workers of this sort. Later in the century, Passavant and Johann Christian Friedrich Heyer (affectionately known as Father Heyer) took up the task. Heyer began his travels in Indiana and Kentucky and went as far west as Minnesota. He also was sent out by the Ministerium of Pennsylvania as a missionary to Guntur, India, in 1842. This was the beginning of American Lutherans moving beyond self-sufficiency to take responsibility for spreading the gospel into new lands. There will be more to say about inner, domestic, and foreign missions in the next chapter.

Though little has appeared here about women's participation in the life of the church, that is not to suggest that they were not active. A most obvious sort of contribution came through the faithful partnership of pastors' wives in their husbands' ministry. Not all wives took this role, but those who did, like Elizabeth Henkel, who traveled with her husband, Paul, served not only to support their husbands but also to encourage other women. More unusual was the liturgical and hymnological work of Harriet Krauth Spaeth. The day-to-day ministry, some days ordinary and some days extraordinary, of female members of congregations in their homes and their communities cannot be overlooked. Susan Henkel sewed together the books published by her in-laws' press; uncounted women sewed clothing for seminarians or quilts to be auctioned in support of mission work. By midcentury some of those local women were joining together to give tangible form to their support for the church and its mission. There is a record of a women's organization in Meadville, Pennsylvania, as early as 1817. These women supported the church through their prayers, their funds, and their educational efforts. In 1883 Anna Sarah Kugler went to Guntur, India, the site of Heyer's early work, as the first woman sent into foreign missions by American Lutherans.

NOTES

1. Edwin Scott Gaustad, *Historical Atlas of Religion in America* (New York: Harper and Row, 1962), p. 18, Figure 15 indicates that in 1780 Lutherans had just under 250 congregations. In reference to the nineteenth century Gaustad writes, "From a membership of about 35,000 the Lutheran communion rose to approximately 1½ million baptized members in 1900" (p. 70). For 1798 *The Lutheran World Almanac and Encyclopedia, 1934–37* (New York: National Lutheran Council, 1937), p. 371 gives a membership of 20,000 in 300 congregations. These appear to be estimated, or at least rounded, figures.

2. *Das Kleine ABC-Buch* (New Market: Solomon Henkel's Druderep, 1819).

3. Cited by Raymond M. Bost, "Catechism or Revival?," *Lutheran Quarterly* 3 (Winter 1989), p. 415.

4. Willard D. Allbeck, "John Stough, Founder of Ohio Lutheranism" *Lutheran Quarterly* 12 (Fall 1960), p. 42 cites remarks to this effect from Stough's autobiography published in C. V. Sheatsley, *History of the Joint Evangelical Synod of Ohio and Other States from the Earliest Beginnings to 1919* (Columbus: Lutheran Book Concern, 1919).

5. William Edward Eisenberg, *The Lutheran Church in Virginia, 1717–1962* (Reannex, VA: Trustees of the Virginia Synod, 1962), p. 45.

6. Paul P. Kuenning, *The Rise and Fall of American Lutheran Pietism: The Rejection of an Activist Heritage* (Macon, GA: Mercer University Press, 1988), p. 134 notes that in 1809 the North Carolina synod authorized baptism of slaves provided that their owners did not object; and in 1815 the South Carolina synod provided the procedure for receiving slaves into the church.

7. In 1821 Henkel recorded that he confirmed sixty-nine slaves. Socrates Henkel, *History of the Evangelical Lutheran Tennessee Synod* (New Market: Henkel, 1890), p. 47. In 1830 Bachman baptized forty African Americans. Kuenning, *The Rise and Fall*, p. 137.

8. Kuenning, *The Rise and Fall*, treats abolitionism in Chapters 4–7; and I have relied heavily upon this work.

9. John Bachman, *The Doctrine of the Unity of the Human Race Examined on Principles of Science* (Charleston, SC: C. Canning, 1850).

10. Christa R. Klein and Christian D. von Dehsen, *Politics and Polity: The Genesis and Theology of Social Statements in the Lutheran Church in America* (Minneapolis: Fortress Press, 1989), pp. 13–15.

11. The Eielsen synod, a small group of Norwegians with some connections to the Franckeans, included an antislavery statement in its 1846 constitution. E. Clifford Nelson and Eugene L. Fevold, *The Lutheran Church among Norwegian-Americans: A History of the Evangelical Lutheran Church*, vol. 1 (Minneapolis: Augsburg Publishing House, 1960), p. 171.

12. Ibid., p. 175.

13. Henry Eyster Jacobs, *Lincoln's Gettysburg World-Message* (Philadelphia: United Lutheran Publication House, 1919), pp. 27–28.

14. Proceedings of the twenty-first Convention of the General Synod, York, PA, May 1864.

15. Jacobs, *Lincoln's*, p. 42.

16. Henry E. Horn, ed. and annotator, "How an Eye Witness Watched the Great Battle: Henry Eyster Jacobs Relates His Impressions of the Battle of Gettysburg," in *Memoirs of Henry Eyster Jacobs* (Huntington, PA: Church Management Service, 1988), p. 48.

17. Synod minutes quoted in Henkel, *The History of the Evangelical Lutheran Tennessee Synod*, p. 69.

18. Raymond M. Bost and Jeff L. Norris, *All One Body: The Story of the North Carolina Lutheran Synod, 1803–1993* (Salisbury: North Carolina Synod, 1994), p. 191.

19. Jeff Johnson, *Black Christians: The Untold Lutheran Story* (St. Louis: Concordia Publishing House, 1991), pp. 144–145.

20. *Lutheran and Missionary* (August 11, 1864) cited in Adolph Spaeth, *Charles Porterfield Krauth*, vol. 2 (New York: Christian Literature, 1898–1909), p. 150.

21. Cited in E. Clifford Nelson, ed., *The Lutherans in North America* (Philadelphia: Fortress Press, 1975), pp. 211–213.

22. Abdel Ross Wentz, *A Basic History of Lutheranism in America* (Philadelphia: Muhlenberg Press, 1955).

23. See the oath he composed for his inauguration to Gettysburg Seminary, cited by Richard H. Baur, *Paul Henkel: Pioneer Lutheran Missionary* (Ann Arbor: University Microfilms, 1989, 1968), p. 141, as well as the constitution he also wrote for that institution. Note, however, that even at the early stage his subscription was qualified by his view that the Augsburg Confession was "substantially" correct and that latitude was allowed with regard to nonfundamental doctrines.

24. *Carolinian Herald of Liberty, Religious and Political* (Salisbury, NC: Krinder and Bingham, 1821).

25. Proceedings of the Thirteenth Convention, p. 54, cited by David A. Gustafson, *Lutherans in Crisis: The Question of Identity in the American Republic* (Minneapolis: Fortress Press, 1992), p. 121.

26. *Evangelical Review* (July 1950) cited by Gustafson, *Lutherans in Crisis*, p. 122.

27. *Evangelical Review* 1 (October 1849) cited in Adolph Spaeth, *Charles Porterfield Krauth*, vol. 1, p. 168.

28. W. J. Mann, *Lutheranism in America: An Essay on the Present Condition of the Lutheran Church in the United States* (Philadelphia: Lindsay and Blakiston, 1857). See Nelson, *Lutherans in North America*, pp. 211–214 for Schaff's typology.

29. Eugene L. Brand, "The Lutheran 'Common Service': Heritage and Challenge," *Studia Liturgica* 19 (1989): 79.

30. See Michael B. Aune, "Making Sense: An Exploration of Worship in Word and Sacrament," Typescript, 1995. In Chapter 4, " 'The Liturgical Question': What Is and What Is Not Evangelical Worship," Aune quotes Richard, "The Liturgical Question," *Lutheran Quarterly* 20 (1890): 124.

31. Theodore G. Tappert, "The Diaries of John Stough, 1806–1807," *Lutheran Quarterly* 12 (Fall 1960): 48.

32. Ohio is more conservative than its social association with Muhlenbergers suggested but less so than its ethnic association with Synodical Conference indicated; Augustana was more liberal than its ethnic association with other immigrant synods might have indicated.

33. Nelson, *Lutherans in North America*, p. 175, Table 2.

34. Christa Ressmeyer Klein, "Immigrant Lutheran Theological Education in Nineteenth Century America," *Lutheran Historical Conference* 9 (1982): 38–59.

35. Richard W. Solberg, *Lutheran Higher Education in North America* (Minneapolis: Augsburg Publishing House, 1985).

36. Cited by Ibid., p. 92.

37. Mary Markley, *Some Chapters on the History of Higher Education for Lutheran Women* (New York: Board of Higher Education, United Lutheran Church in America, 1923).

38. Klein and von Dehsen, *Politics and Policy*, pp. 8–16.

5
NEW BEGINNINGS

By the second third of the nineteenth century the Lutheran descendants of Muhlenberg were relatively secure in the United States. They traced their North American presence further back than the patriarch into the mid-seventeenth century, though many families and individuals were newer to the United States or to Lutheranism. Some congregations were more than a century old, as was the first synod. Colleges and seminaries were training local men to take leadership. Educational and worship resources were being produced. A debate about being Lutheran in the United States was carried on with surprisingly little reference to ethnic identity. This was a debate about accommodation of theological positions, moral values, and social practices, not about retaining a German ethnic identity. Into the church, boiling with this discussion and the possibilities of the age, were poured several ladles of cold water.

Between the 1830s and the mid-1920s a revival of European immigration brought an influx of German and Scandinavian Lutherans whose presence required adjustments in American Lutheranism as well as their own adjustments to the United States. These Lutherans departed Europe primarily for economic and social reasons and relocated largely, though not exclusively, in midwestern areas only recently open to settlement. To a certain degree their experiences echoed those of the earlier arrivals, though with variations due to changes in both the American and the Lutheran context and to the differences they brought with them. Each group faced challenges of leadership and organization; each one wrestled with its identity as Lutheran and American as well as ethnic; and many new synods were formed. Efforts were made to cooperate across synodical lines on the basis of similar ethnic heritage or theological commitments. In the late nineteenth century a major controversy about the way God effects salvation broke out and broke up previous alliances.

Meanwhile, all the challenges and opportunities of the nineteenth and early twentieth centuries in the United States and the world beckoned, prompting both the older Lutheran groups and the younger ones to expand their activities, to take on new projects, and to develop new ways of doing their work of proclaiming the gospel and being little Christs in the world. Concern for education continued and yielded a bumper crop of schools, colleges, and seminaries. Passavant's efforts in inner mission were multiplied by hospitals and homes of various sorts, by city missions, and by evangelism directed toward specific groups from Apaches, to Jews, to formerly Lutheran, to Danish Mormons. Foreign missions also grew, with each Lutheran group associated with specific fields. Support for mission close to home and far away was the principal purpose of the women's societies, which were developed in local congregations and then federated within church bodies. Deaconess communities provided staff to domestic institutions and mission endeavors in other countries.

THE NEWCOMERS

Renewed immigration in the nineteenth century changed the composition of the U.S. citizenry as well as of the Lutheran Church. It slowed or perhaps even halted what had been gradual, but steady, movement toward a cohesive nationality defined by the country's English foundations and the concentration of political, social, and economic power in the hands of male citizens of British descent. Lutherans, largely of German origin, were not at the center of power, but their numbers were significant, and they, too, had been on their way to finding a place in the society and nation. The arrival of thousands of newcomers who spoke languages other than English and lacked a common memory of the Revolution required reconsideration of the relationship of political identity—that is, citizenship or nationality—and ethnic identity. This took place over several decades, usually informed by an Enlightenment anthropology that assumed that in the proper circumstances anyone could learn to be an American citizen. Cultural similarities between the Northern European newcomers and their American hosts encouraged this view, as did relative economic prosperity.

While each group and each individual had specific and personal reasons for the dramatic decision to leave behind an old home, travel across the Atlantic, and establish a new life, certain sorts of motivations were especially common. Industrialization, agricultural reform, and natural disasters—in various combinations—prompted many rural people to consider the possibility that a better living could be made elsewhere. Inheritance customs and accelerating population growth also contributed to the difficult conditions. In some cases political or religious factors entered into the equation. For example, in the 1880s a military draft provoked many German men to emigrate. Most of the emigration was undertaken by individuals or small family groups, though there are notable examples of larger groups, and chain migration often resulted in many persons from a single European village or region clustering together in their new country.

The decision to leave was followed by a second decision about where to go. When the Salzburgers were exiled in the 1700s, only a small portion of them came to Georgia; others went to Prussia, whose ruler made an earlier offer than Ogelthorpe's. The reasons nineteenth-century immigrants chose the United States included advertising, transportation, availability of land, and personal contacts. Descriptions of conditions in North America had circulated in Europe for many years.[1] Some were written by authors who had actually seen what they described; others were not. Some were personal efforts to inform the folks back home about the opportunities available in the United States; others were prepared by commercial interests, such as the railroads, urging immigration to a specific location. By the middle of the century technological developments made steam-powered ships the usual mode of transportation, reducing the length of the journey and the cost of the fare. The Homestead Act of 1862 made vast expanses of good farmland available at a low cost. "America letters" written by friends and family members already in the United States highlighted the advantages of relocation and promised aid to those who joined them. Like the New Testament epistles, these letters were circulated far more widely than their intended audience; they were passed hand to hand and published in newspapers.

Thousands and thousands of people were convinced that the benefits in the United States were worth the risks of the new and the cost of leaving behind the old, even in a time when leaving was so final a separation that some parents held funerals for children who emigrated. Of course, some did return either for triumphant visits or, having reconsidered their earlier decision, as prodigals. German immigration picked up in the 1830s with a major peak in the 1880s and continued with surges in the new century caused by wartime displacement. The Scandinavians, a bit behind the German curve, were led by Swedes and Norwegians, who come earliest and in largest number. A few individuals arrived early in the century; the numbers increased in midcentury, slowed during the Civil War, and continued into the early decades of the twentieth century. The largest volume of Danish, Finnish, and Icelandic immigration began slightly later. Among these immigrants, the number who boarded the ships as Lutherans and the number who maintained that religion in the United States can only be estimated. Because the Scandinavian countries had established Lutheran churches, most of their emigrants were likely to have been at least nominally Lutheran, but estimates of how many remained Lutheran suggest that perhaps as many as 75 percent of Norwegians and more than 90 percent of Danes abandoned that church in the United States.

These Lutherans came to a situation both similar to, and unlike, what had greeted the colonists of New Sweden and the Palatines of Pennsylvania. A most obvious difference was the presence not only of other Lutherans but also of a maturing, increasingly self-reliant Lutheran Church organized into several regional synods supporting various institutions. Whether or not this would be an advantage was not immediately clear; the relationships between these newcomers and the older churches was complicated not only by differences of language and culture but also by developments within Lutheranism. The debate about the role of the Lutheran Confessions within the Muhlenberg tradition had its analogue in Europe, and each new group had either a position or an internal debate about topics such as pietism, confessional subscription, the clerical office, liturgy, and ecumenical cooperation. No doubt some Lutherans arriving in the nineteenth century simply joined an existing Lutheran congregation, but no group allied itself completely with either the General Synod or the General Council or with one of the regional synods, nor did it rely upon these bodies to provide all its needs.

Despite the differences, the newcomers did face conditions that would have been familiar to Muhlenberg and his contemporaries. Because these Lutherans had left behind their churches and come to a nation that stipulated institutional separation of church and state, they needed to devise ways to organize, govern, and support their own churches without the aid of either their former or new government. They often relocated in frontier areas where distances were great and travel difficult. There groups of lay folks gathered as they could to worship and were glad on the infrequent occasions when a pastor came their way to baptize, confirm, marry, preach, and give communion. As they were able, they built log churches rather than meeting out-of-doors, in homes, or in barns. Like their eighteenth-century coreligionists, they quickly found that they could not rely upon the old church to supply them with pastors; few were sent, and not all who came were appropriate for the peculiar situation. Thus, they, too, moved from local congregational organization, to synods, to founding schools in order to provide themselves with pastors. Like Lutherans in New Sweden and the Virgin Islands and Philadelphia and New York, these Lutherans who spoke Swedish, German, Norwegian, Danish, or Finnish had to figure out what to do about English and the American culture it stood for.

The particular way ethnic identity, based on country of origin, played out relative to religious identity and citizenship in specific cases depended on ideological and demographic variables. For the Germans who formed the Lutheran Church Missouri Synod, for example, using German was judged to be crucial to preserving the pure doctrine they came to Missouri to protect. Norwegians came from a country just developing its own national identity after centuries of being the "little brother" to Denmark or Sweden. In both these instances a propensity to conserve ethnic culture was reinforced by settlement patterns that kept members of the group in close proximity to each other and reduced opportunities for external contacts. Compact, isolated, rural communities in which congregation was coincident with civil community were most likely to transform the official European connection between nationality and religion into a strong affinity between ethnicity and religion in the United States. Diffuse, permeable, or urban settlements provided greater opportunities for exposure to other Lutherans and non-Lutherans, so ethnicity tended to be less persistent in them. Additionally, continued contact with the country of origin, especially by means of ongoing immigration, encouraged continued use of the native language and retention of additional aspects of that culture. The consequences of these dynamics and the persistence of ethnicity in conjunction with Lutheranism are still not entirely concluded.

Like these new immigrants, the colonial-era Lutherans of the New Netherlands had been a nationally various group without a supportive political government. Initially, they rather quickly adopted the language of the colony, namely, Dutch, and even when the majority of worshipers were German-speakers, they continued to use it. The threat of schism contributed to a move to German and then to English. Through each transition, the multiethnic group shared a common doctrinal confession and used one language. In the nineteenth and early twentieth centuries people were spread over a larger geographic area, and their development was more diverse, with the variations among the Lutheran immigrants providing the basis for many new synods and institutions. They brought with them a common Lutheran heritage shaped by factors that included different degrees of commitment to confessional standards, different concerns for spiritual awakening and moral life, different languages, and different liturgical standards. These factors, combined with the voluntary character of religion in the United States and with the location of most of these groups in the Midwest, far removed from the eastern centers of Lutheranism, produced at least one synod and usually more synods for each language group. For all the groups the general plot of organization and institution building was similar and followed a pattern like that of synods already discussed. The details that distinguish one from another are available elsewhere. Here our concern is more with distinctive features of a few, rather than with the whole story of every group.

THE LUTHERAN CHURCH MISSOURI SYNOD

The Germans who founded the Lutheran Church Missouri Synod in 1847 stood at the extreme boundary of allegiance to Lutheran confessional identity; they also developed a system of supportive institutions that fostered strong connections between German ethnic and Lutheran religious identity. The result was a cohesive, relatively homogeneous church that resisted realignments by either merger or division well into the twentieth century. According to the scheme outlined in the previous chapter, the Lutheran Church Missouri Synod stood as the definitive example of the old Lutherans, with the General Council as the moderates and the General Synod as the neo-Lutherans at the opposite end. Their commitment to orthodoxy was both an affirmation of the historic confessions in the Book of Concord and a rejection of pietism and rationalism, which they regarded as dual threats to true Lutheranism. More specifically, they rejected doctrinal indifferentism such as undergirded the uniting of Lutheran and Reformed churches in the Prussian Union of 1817.

In contrast to the generalizations made thus far, the Saxons, who were the core of the Lutheran Church Missouri Synod, migrated as a group for explicitly religious reasons. Under the direction of Martin Stephan, pastor of St. John's in

Dresden, they formed an emigration society in 1836. Three years later five boatloads set out, and four (about 700 people) arrived in Perry County, Missouri. A few of the Saxons remained in St. Louis; most of them located in rural areas; and they set about the work of building a community that encompassed not only the religious, but also the secular, aspects of life. Stephan was made bishop but soon proved himself ill suited to the office by his extravagant life, fiscal mismanagement, and alleged sexual misconduct. After exiling him across the Mississippi River, the group experienced a crisis of leadership and identity that reinforced the propensity for clear definition that they brought with them. Particularly at issue was their status as a church. Young Carl Ferdinand Wilhelm Walther emerged as the influential leader who would provide formative direction.

Walther, the son of a Lutheran pastor, had passed through several phases of development before rising to this position of leadership. His time as a gymnasium student exposed him to rationalism; during his university studies he read the pietist classics with a small group of friends influenced by Stephan; a period of illness in his father's house gave him opportunity to read Luther and his interpreters more closely. When Stephan was removed, Walther spent another convalescence reading Luther and contemplating the questions facing the Saxons. With this preparation, he formulated eight theses concerning the scriptural view of church and ministry, which he presented at a debate in Altenberg in April 1841. There he persuaded his hearers that they were indeed a true manifestation of Christ's church and that neither ministers nor bishops were required for that to be the case. Rather, in keeping with the Augsburg Confession, the church is found where believers hear the Word preached and receive the sacraments. Walther's influence was through his sermons, his official posts, and his publication after 1844 of *Der Lutheraner*.

A second important component in the Lutheran Church Missouri Synod was the influence of the Loehe men, missionaries sent to Germans in the United States by Wilhelm Loehe of Neuendettlsau in the 1840s. Loehe's interest had been sparked by reports from Frierich Conrad Dietrich Wyneken, a German serving as missionary for the Ministerium of Pennsylvania. His experiences on the frontier, in conditions like those Stough and Henkel confronted, had persuaded him of the orthodox position as well as of the need for more workers. Loehe responded by sending missionaries to work among the Germans and Chippewa in Michigan. These men shared Wyneken's views about the importance of the historic Confessions. Loehe, observing the situation from across the Atlantic, suggested that the time had come for those who shared this "old Lutheran" position to join together and form a synod.

After several preliminary discussions the two groups—the Missouri Saxons and the Loehe men and their parishioners—joined to form the German Evangelical Lutheran Synod of Missouri, Ohio, and Other States. The name the synod selected emphasized its dual ethnic and religious identity as well as indicating its North American regions of strength. Its structure responded to the Saxons' earlier crisis, making the congregation the primary unit of the church and the synod an advisory body. The commitments shared by both groups were articulated in the constitutional expectation that "every member of the Synod, accepts without reservation" the Bible as God's written Word and the entire Book of Concord as a "true and unadulterated statement and exposition of the Word of God."[2] This synod had much in common with the Buffalo Synod founded only two years earlier by Prussian Lutherans led by Johannes Grabau. They, too, opposed the Prussian Union, but their understanding of ministry was higher, emphasizing the pastor's divinely given authority rather than the congregation's. Nonetheless, when the Buffalo Synod split in 1866, the largest party united with Missouri.

The doctrinal center so clearly stated in the constitution was preserved within the Missouri Synod and guided relations with those outside it. Members were instructed through a system of parish schools, teachers' colleges, and seminaries, the largest such system maintained by Protestants. Many of these were named Concordia, drawing attention to the synod's commitment to the whole of the Book of Concord. Continued use of German as the language of instruction in local schools and publications in German kept that language functional inside the church community and reduced contact outside with other churches, Lutheran or not. Those contacts that were cultivated were subject to tests of doctrinal purity and right practice reminiscent of Berkenmeyer's desires in New York a century before.

Not surprisingly, the Missouri Synod regarded the neo-Lutherans in the General Synod as too lenient in their adherence to the Confessions and too willing to compromise Lutheran distinctiveness and thus were not interested in any sort of relationship with that body or its members. Missouri Synod leaders did take part in preliminary discussions leading to the formation of the General Council, but they judged its organization as premature and based on inadequate agreement about matters of doctrine and practice. Then, in 1872, the Lutheran Church Missouri Synod participated in the formation of the Synodical Conference, which brought the other conservative synods into closer cooperation. Added to the already existing General Synod and General Council, the Synodical Conference completed a triad of cooperative bodies giving institutional form to the three major sorts of Lutheranism. The southern synods—joined together in the United Synod, South—stood between the General Synod and the General Council, leaning a bit more toward the latter, without significantly changing the three-part pattern.

Among the synods with which Missouri joined in 1872 were the Joint Synod of Ohio and the Norwegian Synod. In the pre-General Council meetings, the Ohio Lutherans had pushed the issues of altar and pulpit fellowship with non-Lutherans, membership in secret societies, and chiliasm: the Four Points. They had been disappointed by the General Council's Akron Rule (1872), which they viewed as too accommodating in its allowance of exceptions to the rule of Lutheran pulpits for Lutheran preachers and Lutheran altars for Lutheran communicants. Thus, Missouri regarded these Ohioans, who supported Capital Seminary in Columbus, as orthodox. In addition they had their German ethnic heritage in common. The Norwegian Synod, the more confessional of the several Norwegian groups, also had theological affinities with the Missouri Synod. They relied upon the Missouri Synod's seminary in St. Louis to train pastors for their congregations until the debate about slavery sparked opposition. Despite initial agreement, relationships within the Synodical Conference were disrupted by the theological controversy about election, which erupted in the 1880s.

THE NORWEGIANS

Nineteenth-century Norway was emerging from centuries of political and social subordination to Denmark and Sweden as well as beginning modernization. Its nineteenth-century rate of emigration was second only to that of Ireland, and many of those who left came to the United States, where they located in the upper Midwest. Others gathered with country folk in Texas, Brooklyn, or Seattle. The religious freedom of their new country gave Norwegians the opportunity to express and perhaps to exaggerate differences that in Norway were held together within the one state-supported church. In the United States government restraints were removed, and every sort of religious impulse or program had the opportunity to organize itself. Initial alliances with Swedes, Danes, or Germans were left behind when there were sufficient numbers of Norwegians to sustain Norwegian congregations and synods. Thus, at the expense of their other characteristics, Norwegian Lutherans rightfully gained a reputation for their tendency to multiply congregations and synods. Not all synods were, however, formed by division. If the Norwegian Lutherans multiplied, they also began in the 1890s to move back together by reclaiming their common religious and ethnic identity. This common identity was based in a shared national origin that was cultivated by a lively press and societies devoted to activities ranging from singing, to athletics, to promotion of temperance.

To understand the variety of positions Norwegians brought with them requires some understanding of religious developments in Norway. At the turn into the nineteenth century, more than fifty years after the height of Spener and Francke's influence in Halle, Norwegians were enlivened by a revival of pietism. It was sparked by a young Norwegian who experienced an awakening while plowing his father's field. As his dutiful activity might suggest, Hans Nielson Hauge was not a wild youth; nonetheless, he came to an intense awareness of his sinfulness, followed by an equally profound sense of God's grace, and then by a call to live a moral life and share this knowledge. He commenced his career as a lay preacher, traveling up and down the length of Norway, holding religious meetings, disseminating technical information, and contributing to the ordinary people's growing political self-awareness. Because he ignored laws prohibiting religious gatherings other than those held by the state-supported pastors, Hauge was jailed. Those who heard his message were known for their pious rejection of sinful behavior and immoral activities such as drinking, dancing, and card-playing. A second pietist revival occurred in the 1850s. Led by Gisle Johnson, this wave extended into the ranks of the clergy and the faculty at the newly established University of Christiana (Oslo) and was more theologically articulate than the earlier movement. The Lutheranism these revivals fostered was characterized by a churchly piety that affirmed orthodox teaching and emphasized Christian service. It was informed by Danish Bishop Erik Pontoppidan's pietist, double explanation of Luther's Small Catechism, which was in wide use throughout Norway even after it went out of favor in Denmark.

Norwegian immigrants spoke dialects of a common language, sang the same hymns, had received the same sort of catechetical instruction, and read the same devotional books, including Arndt's *True Christianity*. They represented the entire spectrum of religious experiences and views from the most Pietist, low church, to the most orthodox, high church. Social class was also a factor, particularly among those clergy families who were associated with the Church of Norway. The ordinary church life among Norwegians had much in common with Lutherans in Ohio during the decades between the Revolution and the Civil War and with other Lutherans who came to the United States in the nineteenth century. In the early years pastors and lay preachers such as Claus Clausen, Herman Amberg Preus, and Elling Eielsen traveled long distances to gather scattered Lutherans and provide them with the most basic of spiritual care. When no pastor was available, the Norwegians drew on their confirmation training and pietist practices to hold worship conducted by a *klokker*, a layperson who read a sermon and led the singing. In extreme cases the *klokker* was prevailed upon to perform marriages and burials and, in ordinary ones, reverted to the role of assistant to the pastor.

The synods Norwegian Americans founded beginning in 1846 can be plotted along a continuum according to their position on matters such as the necessity of a personal awakening, required abstinence from immoral activities, the possibility of lay preaching, and use of vestments and liturgy. Low church pietism characterized the earliest group, the Eielsen Synod, and its larger offspring, Hauge's Synod (1876). Defining the other end was the Norwegian Synod (1853) led by university-trained men, ordained by the Church of Norway. After the two extremes were organized, the moderates came together. After 1890 the middle was occupied by the United Norwegian Lutheran Church in America, which combined three moderate groups. This early instance of American Lutherans moving toward greater institutional unification was based on a common ethnic identity and religious similarity but did not remove all differences of piety and theological emphasis.

Along with the Missouri and Ohio Synods the Norwegian Synod was part of the Synodical Conference. Like them, in the 1890s its leaders and, to a lesser extent, its congregations were consumed by a debate about how God saves, the election or predestinarian controversy. The controversy began at a Missouri district convention where Walther presented his understanding of God's action to elect those who are saved. Walther did not deny the classic Lutheran view that salvation comes by God's grace through faith; he did emphasize God's gracious action over the believer's faith. His opponents, also staunch Lutherans, placed more weight on the importance of the faith God foreknew that believers would have. The debate between Walther's position and his opponents' raged on and on. It broke up the Synodical Conference when both the Ohio and Norwegian Synods withdrew; it divided the Norwegian Synod when some members formed the Anti-Missourian Brotherhood; and it split congregations. Because both positions could be defended on the basis of Lutheran teaching generally and more specifically on the basis of Pontoppidan's catechism, neither one triumphed immediately. Indeed, both had advocates into the next century, when the Madison Agreement (1912) recognized the validity of each view, ensuring recurring debate. This settlement helped to clear the way for a second uniting of synods while preserving the ongoing discussion. When the Norwegian Lutheran Church of America formed in 1917, a small group rejected the settlement and continued as the "Little" Norwegian Synod; the low church, pietist wing was continued by the Lutheran Free Church, which had withdrawn from the United Church.

THE DANES

There were fewer Danish immigrants than Norwegians. Their arrival was a bit later. Consequently, they tended to settle a little farther west, with centers in Iowa and Nebraska as well as Wisconsin. Initial organizational cooperation with other Scandinavians gave way to distinctly Danish congregations, synods, and schools when the numbers were large enough to warrant it. Like the Norwegian situation, the Danish one was characterized by division; this one, however, was into two parts, which also can be described only with reference to developments in Europe as well as in the United States.

The towering figures of nineteenth-century Danish Lutheranism were Søren Kierkegaard and Nikolai Frederik Severin Grundtvig. While Kierkegaard continues to be well known and to inform contemporary theological and philosophical discussions, Grundtvig is less remembered. His awakening was of a different sort than Hauge's, leading to a vigorous, life-embracing piety rather than an austere one. Theologically, he emphasized the Apostle's Creed, which he regarded as the most ancient source of Christianity. He also urged an alliance of Danish culture and Christianity and wrote many fine hymns. The folk schools he founded cultivated religious and cultural identity in their students by attention to intellectual, cultural, and spiritual growth in a residential setting. In about the same years another impulse stirred other Danish Lutherans in a revival more like Hauge's. Those influenced by it organized in 1861 a Church Society for Inner Mission, whose purpose was to encourage repentance and moral rigor among the Lutherans of Denmark.

Among the Danish immigrants were folks influenced by Grundtvig as well as those aligned with the Society for Inner Mission. The Church Mission Society was organized in 1872 and two years later became the Danish Evangelical Lutheran Church. Like the Church of Denmark, it contained both impulses, though Grundtvigians, such as Frederik Lange Grundtvig, provided much of its leadership. Those more sympathetic to Inner Mission first allied themselves with similarly inclined Norwegians but later, in 1884, formed the Danish Evangelical Lutheran Church Association. In the 1890s, the older group divided in a dispute over the relationship between the Bible and the Word of God, the possibility of conversion after death, and the centrality of ethnic cultural identity. The "North Church" withdrew and joined with the other church, then renamed the United Church. These two churches were also known by references to the characteristic tone of their piety: the Danish Church, Grundtvigians were called Happy; the United Church, Inner Mission group were called Holy or Sad.

The Grundtvigian understanding that Christianity is expressed in the culture of a particular time and place was the basis of the Danish Church's commitment to preservation of the Danish language and culture in the United States. Half a dozen folk schools were founded for this purpose, and in the 1880s efforts were begun to gather Danes together into colonies. These were located not only in the predictable midwestern states but also in Montana, Oregon, and California. While the Danish Church supported preservation of Danish culture, the United Church, perhaps in reaction against that emphasis, put more stress on its Lutheran identity and moved more quickly to use English and to define its mission as unbound by ethnic boundaries. Nonetheless, it, too, was slow to add non-Danish members.

The developments that led to the formation of these two Danish churches and the dynamics that supported their continued existence into the 1960s are indicative of the several bases upon which Lutheran identity is built. Initial cooperation with Norwegians was based on both common religious characteristics and shared national history and culture. However, when growth in numbers made possible churches in which these characteristics were defined more narrowly, they were formed. Then concerns about piety, moral life, and doctrine combined with attitudes about the relationship between cultural life and religious life for another realignment. Simply to know that a person was Danish and Lutheran was not nearly enough to predict to which church that person might belong. In fact, it was precisely the question of what each term—Danish and Lutheran—meant and how they related to one another that was at stake. So, too, for most American Lutherans, it is precisely the question of what each term—American and Lutheran—means and how they are related to one another that is at stake in the struggle to be both at once.

THE SWEDES

The third major Scandinavian group, the Swedes, arrived beginning in the 1840s, with a swelling after the Civil War and into the 1920s. They located in the Mississippi River Valley of the upper Midwest and out into Kansas. Many of them chose rural areas, but more Swedes than Norwegians went to cities. Unlike either the Danes or the Norwegians, the Swedes who remained Lutheran formed a single, relatively steady synod. However, there were also a significant number of Swedish immigrants who retained church affiliation by joining a non-Lutheran church with or without a Swedish ethnic identity. These groups included the Swedish Mission Covenant and the Evangelical Free Church with Lutheran roots and the Swedish Methodists and Baptists. Because the descendants of New Sweden's colonists were no longer Lutheran, these newcomers could not appeal to them for aid, but they were willing to consider cooperation with Lutherans from the Muhlenberg stream, more so than were either the Missouri Germans or the Norwegian Synod.

Differences between the revivalism and piety of nineteenth-century Sweden and that in Norway and Denmark help to account for the Swedes' adaptation to religious freedom in the United States. The *läsare*, or readers, who gathered in homes to read the Bible and other pious literature were not unlike others throughout Scandinavia. However, the "preaching sickness" that animated Smaland in the early 1840s had more in common with the Second Great Awakening in the United States than did other pietist movements. An obvious connection to Anglo-American revivalism was George Scott, an English Methodist who served a congregation in Stockholm. His influence extended into the Swedish church, in particular to Carl Olaf Rosenius, who became the leader of Swedish pietism after Scott was expelled in the early 1840s. Rosenius refused ordination. Like other Lutheran pietists, he was both critical of conditions within the established church and loyal to it, and he called others to repentance and amendment of life. His message was carried in his preaching and his newspaper as well as by Lina Sandell-Berg's lovely hymns. In contrast to Hauge's, this was a less solemn piety, characterized by some of the joyousness of the Moravians.

Overall, the movement Rosenius led was, on one hand, nonseparatist, that is, willing to operate within the church, and on the other, nonsectarian, that is, open to cooperation with those outside it. That is not to suggest, however, that all Swedes agreed with this position. In the mid-1840s perfectionist Erik Jansson gathered a more radical, separatist group. They signaled their rejection of the state church by regularly holding their own services at conflicting times and more dramatically by burning copies of Luther's writings and other books favored by the readers. Beginning in 1846, Jansson and hundreds of his followers immigrated to Illinois, where they set up Bishop Hill, a communal theocracy. Jansson was assassinated in 1850, and the colony declined thereafter. The same year, adherents of the Church of Jesus Christ of the Latter-Day Saints launched a Scandinavian mission. From its base in Copenhagen, the mission was most successful among Danes, but more so among Swedes than Norwegians. By 1910 as many as 20,000 Swedish Mormons lived in Utah. Baptist and Methodist influence was also imported to Sweden, usually by Swedes who were converted in those churches while in the United States; thus, the development of these two groups among Swedes in both countries was closely linked. Controversy over Paul Peter Walderström's views of the atonement stimulated organization of the

Swedish Mission Covenant in 1878, giving the pietist movement a more visible manifestation while still maintaining contact with the state church.

All the groups represented in Sweden flourished in the United States as well. The Methodists and Baptists formed Swedish-speaking congregations and conferences and were able to draw upon the strength of those denominations in this country. In contrast, the Church of Sweden was largely uninterested in providing spiritual care for its former members in North America. Consequently, the Swedes who remained Lutheran, many influenced by Rosenius, made early alliances with other Scandinavians, the older Lutheran synods, and even with the Congregational American Board of Home Missions. When Lars Paul Esbjorn arrived in 1849, he began to gather Swedes into Lutheran congregations. Two years later they joined with moderate Norwegians and some English-speaking congregations to form the Synod of Northern Illinois, affiliated with the General Synod. This partnership was short-lived; the Scandinavians withdrew in 1860 and organized their own body. When the Norwegians and Swedes parted a decade later, the Swedes kept the name Augustana Synod. Among the Swedes there were disagreements about the nature of the church as a mixed body of saints and sinners or a gathering of believers and about Walderström's views of the atonement. These differences first prompted the organization of the Swedish Evangelical Mission Covenant and then its movement away from a Lutheran confession, leaving the Augustana Synod as the single Swedish Lutheran body in the United States.

The name Augustana Synod referred to the body's confessional standard: the Augsburg Confession. Unlike the Missouri Synod, which required subscription to the entire Book of Concord, the Swedish Lutherans were more willing to temper their confessional stance with cooperation. Their early associations with the Lutheran bodies of the East foreshadowed continued collaborations. Rather like the Ohio Synod, though not always in agreement with it, the Augustana Synod often stood on the border between the parties, and its concerns were indicative of the ongoing points of discussion. In 1867, when Ohio did not, Augustana did join the General Council, though the Swedes' position on three of the Four Points was more restrictive than the council's. Augustana was more strict about maintaining Lutheran pulpits and altar fellowship for Lutherans and less willing to grant exceptions, even if those were regarded as privilege rather than right, as the Akron Rule stated, and as the Galesburg Rule reaffirmed. Similarly, Augustana was uncompromising about membership in secret societies for any purpose. Though many Swedes were active in the temperance movement, this policy prevented members of Augustana congregations from participating in certain temperance groups that were organized as lodges.

OTHER GROUPS

Throughout the late nineteenth and into the twentieth centuries Lutheran emigrants from other European nations continued to arrive in the United States and to organize themselves into congregations and synods. Notable among them were Slovaks, Icelanders, and Finns. The Finns, like the groups considered earlier, divided themselves into church bodies reflective of the variety within the Church of Finland and its own pietistic awakenings. As the end of the century neared, the Finns were also divided by the stirring of the organized labor movement. Though antagonists to the churches existed in other initially Lutheran groups, among the Finns this antagonism coalesced with the labor movement in a particularly dramatic way.

The Finns located in the mining and timbering regions around the Great Lakes, particularly in Michigan and Minnesota, and formed congregations served by Finnish pastors, when they were available. When none were available, the people made do. In one local congregation, a German pastor learned to read the Finnish service, though he understood nothing of the language. These congregations were later gathered into several synods distinguished by attitudes about piety and church government. Organized in 1890, the Suomi Synod was the largest and the most comprehensive. Like the Church of Finland, it aspired to provide room for all sorts of Finns. The Suomi Synod did not regard itself as a gathering of the pure believers, but it did give much authority to its leaders, including its patriarch, Juho Kustaa Nikader.

The other two church groups differed on these points. Lars Laestadius, a pastor to Finns and Laplanders in northern Sweden, provided one party with a more revivalist view of the church and greater regard for lay preaching. The first congregation of this sort was founded in the 1870s, but the national body, the Finnish Apostolic Lutheran Church, was not organized until over fifty years later. A third body, the Finnish-American National Evangelical Lutheran Church, also preferred a more revival style of preaching, greater lay leadership, and a more democratic polity. Its concern for uniformity of doctrine would eventually provide a bridge into the Lutheran Church Missouri Synod.

Conditions in Finland nurtured the emerging labor movement, which also was growing in the United States. By the turn of the century newly arriving Finns were less likely to automatically join a congregation; more were associating themselves with unions. Thus, a distinction arose between the white church Finns and the red labor Finns. The differences between the two groups were often hostile rather than cordial, and on occasion there was violence, as on Christmas Eve 1913 in Calumet, Michigan. A labor, nonreligious Christmas party was crashed by a vigilante management group. Among those killed in the frenzy were fifty children. Although the panic was not caused by church folk, on the management side stood many Suomi Synod members who opposed socialism. As among the Danes, but in a more visible way, ethnicity was but one factor in Finnish adjustments to the American context; and for the Finns religion—or nonreligion—was an axis of even deeper conflict than it was for the Danes.

The plates of former and new national identity and those of religious belief and practices shifted and scraped together when these newcomers crossed the Atlantic and as they crossed the North American continent. The tectonics of personal identity and group formation were volatile, but in the movement there were discernible patterns. When the constraints and resources of state support were removed, differences of all sorts were subject to magnification and institutionalization. Similarities of practice or piety could bridge differences of emphasis in doctrine or language. Regroupings spanned new organizations—congregations and synods—surrounded by a growing set of related institutions—schools, publications, and social service establishments.

NEW ACTIVITIES

Certainly, there were aspects of church life in which all these newcomers had to play catch-up, developing through stages and attending to tasks that their Muhlenberg cousins had already gone through and accomplished. Nonetheless, most Lutherans in the United States in the late nineteenth and early twentieth centuries also expanded their activities into relatively new areas of education, social ministry, and evangelization. William Passavant's leadership in these fields, for example, his efforts to found a seminary in Chicago for training pastors for English-, Swedish-, and German-speaking congregations, often brought him into contact with immigrant Lutherans in the Midwest and made him a point of connection between them and the older, eastern groups. Although the Missouri Synod was reluctant, at best, to join forces with any group without complete agreement on matters of belief and practice, others were more willing to do so, as Augustana's membership in the General Council demonstrated. Even when joint projects were not undertaken, similar efforts were made by various sorts of Lutherans simultaneously. In addition to the arrival of immigrant groups and the beginning of new projects, this era was marked by the expansion of Lutheran women's responsibilities both within women's organizations and, for a smaller number, through the deaconess communities.

EDUCATION

Lutheran involvement in education began with the Reformation, so their involvement in the United States was no innovation. The difference was in the variety of types of education they were involved with and the sorts of support that they gave. In Europe responsibility for education was often lodged with the church, but the church was officially part of the state. Separation of church and state in the United States shifted responsibility for schools either to the state or to the church. Given this arrangement Lutherans selected both options, making use of publicly supported schools for some purposes and establishing their own for others. Schools for children ranged from the Missouri Synod's extensive system of parochial schools, to the Scandinavians' annual summer sessions, to weekly Sunday school on the Anglo-American model. Each synod supported its own secondary schools and seminary. These served the practical purpose of training lay and clerical leaders and the symbolic one of nurturing a sense of collective identity focused on "our school." Though little attention was given to adult education, the meetings of the newly formed women's organizations often included information about the church's mission work or a Bible reading, which provided one foundation for later adult education programs.

From earliest days, American Lutherans found an affinity between the offices of pastor and teacher. Some Germans in the colonial period advocated German schools as the best means of preserving both ethnic and religious identity. Henry M. Muhlenberg urged congregations to support schools, and he himself taught in them. Paul Henkel was sent to a German school, and the early output of his family's press made a major contribution to German instruction. Nonetheless, in eastern Lutheranism the end of speaking German seemed to be in sight until the arrival of a new wave of immigrants revived the language. These Germans reintroduced their language into churches across the nation. The Missouri Synod's commitment to pure doctrine and concern to preserve German culture reinforced each other and provided strong support for alternatives to the public schools.[3] These continued to be operated well into the twentieth century. By 1929 schools operated by a third of the congregations enrolled not quite half of the Missouri Synod's children.[4] During the world wars, their use of German provoked patriotic opposition from outside the church and fostered pragmatic alliances with Roman Catholics in defense of parochial schools.

The Norwegian debate about the value of such an alternative system peaked in 1869 at a meeting in Madison, Wisconsin. After that, Norwegian congregations followed the pattern common in the Swedish Augustana Synod and each year for several weeks held daylong sessions of summer school for preconfirmation-age children. These classes supplemented public education with Bible history, Lutheran teaching, and church music as well as instruction in the language and culture of the nation from which the students or their parents had come. The teachers were either local teachers who took on the extra session, students from the synod's college or seminary, or teachers specially trained for the task. Normal schools run by Lutherans, such as the one in Madison, Minnesota, had programs designed to prepare teachers for just this setting. The textbooks, published by the church presses, included Luther's Small Catechism, a Bible history, and ABC and grammar books in the language of the synod. The Augustana Book Concern also put out *Barnens andra bok* with articles on everything from Swedish history, to Abraham Lincoln, to electricity and Yellowstone Park.[5] Summer school provided students with a basic knowledge of Lutheran Christianity, which was reinforced and expanded when they received confirmation instruction from their pastor in their early teens. As the everyday use of Swedish or Norwegian declined, the task of these schools became more difficult. Rather than building upon what students learned at home, they had to teach a foreign language. More than one student simply memorized lessons in an incomprehensible language. By the 1920s the difficulty of the task and lack of interest in doing it reduced the number of such schools. In more and more congregations the sessions were shortened, the language of instruction shifted to English, and the curriculum narrowed to only religious topics.

Sunday school for children had been encouraged by John George Schmucker early in the 1800s. Likewise, his son Samuel was an advocate of these weekly lessons and participated in the American Sunday School Union. The General Council produced its own series of lessons rather than relying upon those produced by that non-Lutheran body. Missouri Synod leaders would have regarded this sort of education as too little; nonetheless, weekly Sunday morning classes and the Sunday school papers provided many young Lutherans with instruction in the basics of Christianity. On weekdays they went to public school, but on Sunday they were nourished in their baptismal covenant. By the mid-twentieth century Sunday schools were a usual and expected feature of Lutheran congregations.

Although public elementary schools were common in the late nineteenth century, high schools were less so. The Lutheran churches responded by founding boarding academies, which then provided the institutional basis for colleges.[6] These colleges, unlike those founded to provide preparatory work for future seminarians, were coeducational from the outset. Their purposes extended to the training of good citizens, well equipped to fulfill their vocation in many occupations. Among the immigrant groups these schools also provided a mediated contact with mainstream American culture, a way for young people to gain access to that culture without forgetting where they came from. Observers of Scandinavian Lutherans commented on their commitment to education. For example, one expressed amazement that a Norwegian family still living in a sod dugout would send its children off to attend Concordia College in Moorhead, Minnesota. These colleges reinforced the religious and ethnic identity of most of their students through required course work, the general social and religious atmosphere, and the formation of lifelong relationships. All the colleges sent men off to the seminaries as well as into classrooms and businesses. A few women used their training to do remarkable things as teachers, nurses, or missionaries, but many took their enlarged worldview back home to their families and local congregations. In addition there were a few schools for women, such as the Lutheran Ladies Seminary in Red Wing, Minnesota, and other female seminaries in Hagerstown and Lutherville, Maryland, as well as in Staunton, Virginia.[7]

Each synod had a college or more. Gettysburg belonged to the General Synod; Capital to Ohio; Newberry to the Synod of South Carolina and Adjacent States. The Augustana Synod had Gustavus Adolphus and Augustana (Rock Island), the Norwegian Synod had Luther, the United Church had Saint Olaf, the Lutheran Free Church had Augsburg, the Happy Danes had Grand View, and the Holy ones had Dana. Renewed ministry among African Americans included Alabama Lutheran Academy in Selma. Some colleges were founded by a group of lay and clerical leaders rather than by official synodical action. Early presidents and faculty members were also leaders in the synods and often busy with raising money to keep the ventures going. The support the synod and its members gave the college and the pragmatic and symbolic benefits the church derived from the college intertwined, strengthening both college and church. There also was a cross-fertilization between the colleges as graduates of one became faculty members or the president of another; usually, this movement was within the same group, but sometimes it crossed over and provided an early, personal basis for intersynodical cooperation. Indeed, the Association of Lutheran College Faculties was one of the first pansynodical organizations. Nonetheless, some have speculated that the large number of schools, each associated with a different synod, diverted Lutheran energies and resources from developing a major university.

The need to train pastors in the United States was a fundamental concern for each synod. The newly formed immigrant bodies included some pastors with degrees from European schools, but calls to the United States were not generally sought after by the best candidates. A call to the United States was regarded as an adventure analogous to a mission in India or China. As the newcomers settled into their lives here, and their children grew up with only secondhand memories of Europe, the need for locally trained clergy was more than a matter of numbers; it was also a matter of needing men who understood something of the American experience and situation. Although there were Lutheran seminaries already operating in Pennsylvania, South Carolina, and Ohio, and a few individuals attended them, most groups did not make use of those schools. There were some cooperative efforts such as the brief arrangement that allowed the Norwegian Synod to send students to the Missouri Synod seminary in St. Louis and the Synod of Northern Illinois' short-lived undertaking, which included Swedes and Norwegians as well as easterners. Passavant advocated establishment of a seminary in Chicago to serve the needs of several bodies; it opened in 1891 on the current site of Wrigley Field, and its cooperation was somewhat more successful than the others. The usual pattern, however, was for each Lutheran body to support its own seminary in order to train pastors whose doctrine, piety, and ethnic background matched those of most members.

HOME MISSIONS

In the late nineteenth century American Lutherans engaged in two sorts of domestic mission work that signaled their increasing maturity as a church. The first was directed primarily to their own kind, taking responsibility to provide the charitable institutions needed by members of their own synods and ethnic groups, though not limited to that audience. The second was evangelism, usually directed beyond those boundaries to persons without a prior family, ethnic, or religious connection to Lutheranism. While neither of these sorts of mission was unknown before the nineteenth century, they claimed more and more attention and energy as the century went on.

The realities of life in nineteenth-century America included the need for various sorts of social services that the state did not provide. These included medical care, orphanages, and old people's homes. A classic Lutheran confessional definition of the church had nothing to say about such charitable work; however, Luther's admonitions to be as a little Christ to one's neighbor and the example of Halle pietism pointed the way for Lutherans to engage in works of love as well as attending to the means of grace. Passavant's work founding hospitals and orphanages has already been mentioned. Similar institutions were organized and supported by Lutherans across the country. Often initiative to begin an institution was local, as was its support. Initially, many of these were intended to serve members of the church much as schools were for students who belonged to the congregation or synod that supported them. Despite the intention to respond to material needs, the workers found that their ministry sometimes moved from the physical into the spiritual. Similarly, the institutions did not limit their work only to people who were members of the associated church or ethnic group. Hospitals and schools were places where non-Lutherans came into contact with Lutheranism. Thus, these charitable institutions also could have evangelistic effects.

By 1913 Lutherans supported sixty-one orphanages, forty-two hospitals, thirty-six old people's homes, and five homes for the epileptic, crippled, and feebleminded.[8] The unique origin and history of each one of these charitable institutions cannot be reduced to an account of only one; however, here we will let the work of one man stand for many others. Eric Norelius was a pioneer pastor among the Swedish Lutherans in Minnesota. His leadership took several forms, including directing relief work and founding an orphanage. Though both activities were pressed upon him by circumstances, he was well prepared to respond. The 1862 Sioux uprising had devastating consequences for many Swedish Lutherans in southern Minnesota. Norelius, the pastor in Vasa, was well known and so received aid contributions from folks in several states and coordinated the work of the relief committee authorized by Augustana's Minnesota Conference. Three years later circumstances again pushed Norelius into action. He had been visited by Passavant and knew of his work as well as of the Augustana Synod's resolution to found a children's home in Illinois. But it was the death of recent immigrants leaving four children aged five to twelve orphaned that finally prompted him to begin the Vasa Children's Home. At first the home was merely a space in the church with Brita Nilson, a local widow, to look after the children. For over a decade the home was Norelius' own responsibility; then the Minnesota Conference took it on. The number of children increased so that in 1867 a nearby ten-acre site was purchased, and a dormitory built. This home was the model for other such institutions in the Augustana Synod. Eventually, it was incorporated into the larger structure of Lutheran Social Services of Minnesota.[9]

Unlike the advocates of the Social Gospel movement active in other Protestant churches in the same decades, the supporters of this ''inner mission'' work were seldom interested in social change. Their attitude and program were influenced by a combination of Lutheran teaching about the church's responsibility for the sacraments and preaching and by pietist concern for the spiritual well-being of the individual rather than by political or societal matters. In addition, the conditions in which they found themselves evoked immediate response to personal needs rather than efforts to change the whole of society or the structures that contributed to poverty and other ills. There were exceptions to general Lutheran disinterest in social and political issues. The temperance cause was supported by individuals and by a few synods. Several Lutherans were elected to local and state government offices. John Henry Wilburn Stuckenberg's sympathy with the Social Gospel view was unusual among Lutherans, as was his interest in sociology, as expressed in *Christian Sociology*, published in 1880. After a brief tenure at Wittenberg University, he lived in Europe. Distance did not diminish his interest in American Lutheranism, but it did reduce his real influence.

Instead of investing their efforts in social reform or even in political activity, the majority of Lutherans supported their churches' growing missionary ventures in the United States and abroad. These were part of a worldwide trend among Protestants, who in the early nineteenth century launched evangelism efforts around the world. The movement was fostered by the Second Great Awakening and encouraged by the same technological changes that supported increased immigration, in particular, the steam-powered ship and improved communications. These missionary ventures also coincided with political and commercial colonization efforts. Pietist Lutherans from Halle were among the earliest Protestant missionaries. They were sent to south India by the Danish Royal Mission in 1708. In the first half of the nineteenth century numerous European Lutheran societies were founded and sponsored missions around the globe. In some cases, such as Loehe's, the same impulse provided support for their coreligionists in the United States.

American Lutherans were relatively late in assuming responsibility for world mission work. In part this delay was due to their preoccupation with matters closer to home. This was especially so for the midwestern, immigrant groups that were busy making themselves at home. The task of home missions—locating, ministering to, and organizing Lutherans in the United States—occupied many of the Lutherans' resources. Their first efforts in foreign fields were in support of work initiated and carried out by European societies. By the end of the century the American synods and independent societies were assuming greater responsibility. Each one was associated with particular areas. The work and the workers were well known to members of the churches, who read about the missions in church papers and often met the missionaries while they were on furlough. Many congregations held annual mission festivals that combined preaching, fund-raising, and the pleasure of good food and company. Women and children were organized into societies devoted to support of ongoing work and recruitment of new workers.

The earliest mission society, organized by the Ministerium of Pennsylvania in 1836, was in support of both home and foreign work. Five years later it was reorganized by the General Synod and responded to an appeal from the Berlin Mission Society by sending Johann Christian Friedrich Heyer to India, where he served for a decade and a half. When transfer of the field to an English society appeared imminent, he volunteered to return and did so at age seventy-seven. This cemented the relationship between the General Council and Rajahmundry. The Lutheran Church Missouri Synod also established its work in India on the foundations built by a European mission. Augustana Synod activity in India resulted from the cooperation between that synod and the General Council in the United States. The first Augustana missionary sent to India was a graduate of Philadelphia Seminary.

Other bodies undertook work in Africa and additional Asian locations. These efforts were, of course, affected by organizational developments in the sending churches. The Chinese first received Thea Ronning, her brother Halvor N. Ronning, and his future wife, Hannah Rorem, from the independent Norwegian Lutheran Church Mission Society in 1890. That work was later transferred to the United Church and then combined with that initiated by the Hauge Synod. Similar shifts occurred in Madagascar and in Japan, although the particular church bodies and individuals were different.

The specific work done by Lutheran missionaries was similar to that undertaken by most missionaries in these decades of heightened activity and enthusiasm about evangelization around the globe. Linguistic training was an important step in missionary preparation. Missionaries set about learning the native language of their neighbors to use for teaching, preaching, and the tasks of daily life. For those who were immigrants to the United States this was the second new language in only a few years. Like their counterparts in other churches, Lutherans combined the work of education, health care, and social service with proclamation. Schools, hospitals, and orphanages were among their projects. For example, in China Thea Ronning's work included a school for about three dozen girls, translating for a medical doctor, and caring for the orphaned children of other missionaries. During her longer service in India, Anna Kugler concentrated on health care. Both men and women proclaimed the gospel in various settings from home visits, to Bible studies, to worship.

This global mission work was an indication that American Lutherans had moved from dependence on the older churches in Europe toward self-sufficiency, and beyond that they were assuming responsibility for others. This responsibility would grow in the 1900s, when wartime conditions cut some areas off from Europe and reduced the resources of European churches. Missionary efforts also provided a point of contact between American Lutheran groups, one distant from circumstances that highlighted their differences and disagreements.

WOMEN'S EXPANDING WORK

Though many women had been members of, and participants in, Lutheran congregations from the outset, and a smaller number had given leadership as teachers or in the quasi-official role of the pastor's wife, in the late nineteenth century new organizations and opportunities gave larger numbers of women a more active role in church life. Again, these developments within Lutheran churches parallel those in other American churches in which the burgeoning missionary movement stimulated growth of local women's missionary societies. So, too, larger social and educational trends encouraged the modern deaconess movement in several Protestant denominations and gave women new opportunities as teachers, nurses, and mission workers.

As the Second Great Awakening stirred religious enthusiasm, and the fledgling missionary movement began, American women in Protestant congregations began to meet together in support of the church's mission. Their organization paralleled the formation of women's societies devoted to abolition, temperance, suffrage, and other social reforms. Lutheran women, too, participated in specifically female groups whose stated purpose was to support their church's work through prayer and financial contributions. One of the earliest was formed in 1817 by women in Meadville, Pennsylvania; each woman contributed the value of a pound of butter each month in order to purchase a farm for the pastor's use. Precisely what factors brought the women of a specific congregation to the point of organizing were seldom recorded. Some may have observed their Methodist or Baptist neighbors and followed their lead; others may have known of similar efforts in Europe or have belonged to such a society in another Lutheran congregation. Once the movement was established, the federation urged congregations to form women's organizations. Often pastors' wives such as Emmy Evald and Lena Dahl provided the initiative for local groups and for the federations that linked them together around the turn of the century.

The purposes of the women's organizations were stated in their names: women's missionary society and ladies' aid were common. Both indicated that the members were women and that they were gathered to promote the church's work. The first was not always true, as men sometimes attended meetings and even served as officers. The second took on several forms. Women responded to specific needs, providing funds necessary if the churches were to be self-supporting. The women of Immanuel in Minneapolis organized themselves prior to the congregation in order to help young Danish men studying to be pastors. In congregations women raised the money for immediate projects such as a building, a teacher's salary, or an organ. They gave ongoing support to institutions such as children's homes, supplying items such as blankets and canned goods as well as cash. Foreign missions also received both tangible and spiritual support. Despite these commendable aims, women were opposed by some who regarded their meetings as potentially decisive and perhaps the first step toward a demand to preach.

There was no standard format for women's society meetings. Often they were held monthly at a member's home. The meeting could easily last all day, with refreshments provided by the hostess. A devotional program might be offered by the pastor or a member. This included a Bible reading, singing a hymn, prayers, and perhaps a selection from a missionary publication. The women brought along their handiwork, the sewing, knitting, or quilting they would later sell to raise money. Few rural women had ready access to cash, so they donated their labor. An annual auction was frequently held in conjunction with the fall mission festival. The benefits of these organizations to the church are obvious. Though the personal benefits to members were not named in purpose statements, those were also significant. Participating in these groups gave women an arena for interaction in which to develop their leadership skills. They learned about the church's work and about the world. The money they raised gave them some influence in churches that denied them a vote or leadership positions.

Early in the century Passavant brought deaconesses from Germany to staff his hospital. This reinvention of an ancient office gave women opportunities for full-time professional work in churches, even when the pastoral office was closed to them. It spread from Theodore Fliedner's German foundation to other nations and other churches. Among Lutherans several groups were organized both by the immigrant synods and by the older bodies, and deaconess institutions were established in Philadelphia, Milwaukee, Fort Wayne, Indiana, and Brush, Colorado. Women who became deaconesses generally received both occupational and spiritual training, though the length and quality of each varied from group to group and from time to time. There were obvious parallels with Roman Catholic women's orders: deaconesses often wore distinctive dress, were not married while in service, and received an allowance rather than a salary.

Their work ranged from nursing, to social services, to education, to missions in China, Alaska, and other places. Perhaps one of the best known of the deaconesses was Norwegian Elizabeth Fedde. She came to Brooklyn in the early 1880s in response to a request from a small group that included the pastor of the Seaman's Church and the wife of the Norwegian Counsel General. Her work teaching, visiting in homes, and giving medical care was supported by individuals and by a local women's society organized for that purpose. While in the United States she also helped to organize deaconess houses and hospitals in Chicago and Minneapolis.

Though the number of Lutheran deaconesses has never been large, early in the twentieth century they provided women with an important transitional step into more public ministry, and their ongoing work balances a traditional Lutheran emphasis upon word and sacrament ministry with attention to the works of love. For example, Pastor Charles Weltner and Augusta Weltner, herself a former deaconess, trained deaconesses in conjunction with their mission work in the mills of South Carolina. Their social ministry was carried on by Josephine Copeland, one of the few women who responded to their offer.[10] When the Lutheran Deaconess Association was founded in 1919, its Articles of Incorporation clearly stated its purpose and audience: "The object of this association shall be to educate and train Lutheran deaconesses for the care of the sick and poor in the congregations of the Evangelical Lutheran Synodical Conference and for the administering of charity and mercy in the charitable institutions and in home and foreign mission work of said Synodical Conference."[11] Despite support from specific church bodies, the sort of work deaconesses did often brought them into contact with nonmembers and perhaps altered their understanding of the church. Ingeborg Sponland, a colleague of Fedde, observed, "To us as deaconesses truth cries out that all human beings have soul which has been bought by the blood of Jesus Christ for the Kingdom of heaven. There can be no discrimination as to nationality or creed when it comes to serving our Master. . . . In modifying our methods so as to be able to serve people of various nationalities and creeds we gain a broader vision and a deeper sympathy and understanding—a compassion and love for souls that are without Christ."[12]

SUMMARY

As the nineteenth century turned into the twentieth, Lutherans in the United States were a more culturally, religiously, and geographically diverse group than a century earlier. The influx of European immigrant groups and some relatively small successes in evangelization contributed to the more visible presence of ethnic variety, often coincident with synodical organization. But those organizations were not formed solely on ethnic or racial bases. Concern for clarity of doctrinal stance and uniformity of practice was also significant. Although notable concentrations of Lutherans remained in Pennsylvania and the upper Midwest, Lutherans of all sorts moved across the whole of the continent along with other Americans. For example, in the 1860s Jacob M. Buehler of the Missouri Synod was busy ministering to church folk in San Francisco, and within a decade he was joined there by Christian M. Hvistendahl of the Norwegian Synod, who organized Our Saviors. In 1897 St. Paul's English Evangelical Lutheran Church was founded with seventeen members, ten of them sea captains.[13] In these many organizations and places, Lutherans had also become increasingly involved in work beyond preaching and administering the sacraments in Sunday morning worship. The means of grace were thus accompanied by works of love and embedded in a social community. In synods and in other associations Lutherans took up the local work of social welfare and education as well as contributing to the more distant work of foreign missions. All these were fruits of an increasingly mature tree.

NOTES

1. See, for example, Gottfried Duden, *Report on a Journey to the Western States of North America* (1829; modern ed., George H. Kellner, Adolph E. Schroeder, and Wayne Senner, eds. and trans., Columbia: State Historical Society of Missouri, 1980); Ole Rynning, *True Account of America for the Information and Help of Peasant and Commoner* (1838; modern ed., Theodore C. Blegen, ed. and trans., Northfield, MN: Norwegian American Historical Society, 1926).

2. Todd W. Nichol, *All These Lutherans: Three Paths to a New Lutheran Church* (Minneapolis: Augsburg Publishing House, 1986), p. 104 quotes the constitution.

3. Carol K. Coburn, *Life at Four Corners: Religion, Gender, and Education in a German-Lutheran Community, 1868–1945* (Lawrence: University of Kansas Press, 1992), Chapter 6, pp. 60–80, treats the school.

4. E. Clifford Nelson, ed., *Lutherans in North America* (Philadelphia: Fortress Press, 1975), p. 427.

5. Emory Johnson, "Swedish Elementary Schools in Minnesota Lutheran Congregations," *Swedish Pioneer Historical Quarterly* 30 (July 1979): 176–177.

6. For particular examples of this process see Richard W. Solberg, *Lutheran Higher Education in North America* (Minneapolis: Augsburg Publishing House, 1985), pp. 228–229.

7. Mary Elizabeth Markley, *Some Chapters on the History of Higher Education for Lutheran Women* (Philadelphia: Board of Education, United Lutheran Church in America, 1923), pp. 40–41; L. DeAne Lagerquist, " 'As Sister, Wife, and Mother': Education for Young Norwegian-American Lutheran Women," *Norwegian American Studies* 33 (1992): 111–118.

8. Christa R. Klein and Christian D. von Dehsen, *Politics and Policy: The Genesis and Theology of Social Statements in the Lutheran Church in America* (Minneapolis: Fortress Press, 1989), p. 10.

9. *The Journals of Eric Norelius: A Swedish Missionary on the American Frontier*, trans., ed., and intro. by G. Everett Arden (Philadelphia: Fortress Press, 1967), pp. 28–31.

10. Susan Wilds McArver, " 'A Spiritual Wayside Inn': Lutherans, the New South and Cultural Change in South Carolina, 1886–1918" (Ph.D. dissertation, Duke University, 1995), pp. 284–286, 302–306.

11. Cited by Wilma S. Kucharek, "A History of the Lutheran Deaconess Association," Valparaiso University, 1976 (Typescript).

12. L. DeAne Lagerquist, *From Our Mothers' Arms: A History of Women in the American Lutheran Church* (Minneapolis: Augsburg Publishing House, 1987), p. 70, n. 51; Ingeborg Sponland, *My Reasonable Service* (Minneapolis: Augsburg Publishing House, 1938), p. 69.

13. Eugene L. Fevold, *The Story of Home Missions in the Evangelical Lutheran Church* (St. Paul: n.p., 1962), p. 4.

6

THE NEXT STEP FOR AMERICAN LUTHERANISM

This chapter considers Lutheranism in the first half of the twentieth century, a time when the Lutheran Church was increasingly at home in its nation, self-sufficient, and able to take responsibility beyond itself. For Lutherans the beginning of the twentieth century is best indicated not by the year 1900 but by two other dates. The first is 1917, the quadricentennial anniversary of Luther's posting the Ninety-five Theses and thus symbolically the beginning of the Reformation. The tricentennial anniversary received small attention, but the quadricentennial was the occasion for larger celebrations, more publicity, and new cooperation among Lutherans. While 1917 is a Lutheran date, from the church's internal life, 1921 is a civic one. That was the year that the U.S. Congress passed the Johnson-Reed Act restricting immigration. Conditions in Europe may have slowed Lutheran immigration anyway, but this legislation ensured that henceforth Lutheran growth in the United States would come from natural increase or evangelism, not from the arrival of Lutherans from other lands. The shift intensified the need to develop into a church suitable for this place. The middle of the century (and the end of this chapter) is marked by two major realignments: the formation of the American Lutheran Church in 1960 and of the Lutheran Church in America in 1962.

The title of this chapter was used by Lars Boe for a brief essay he wrote in the 1930s.[1] There he argued that the next step for American Lutherans should be toward ever greater cooperation, and he outlined ways to take that step. This concern was dear to Boe and was characteristic of these decades. The century opened with dozens of Lutheran bodies in potential competition and conflict; by the midpoint of the 1960s there were three major synods. However, reshaping the large-scale structure was not the only sort of cooperation and change taking place. In addition to organic unions or mergers there were many common ventures such as celebrations, responses to war and other emergencies, preparation of worship materials, and congregational development. The internal life of the churches matured and became more complex. These changes can be seen in developments in the women's organizations, in various sorts of youth ministries, and in the management of the synods as well as in material changes such as improvements in buildings. By midcentury American Lutherans had assumed a significant leadership role in world Lutheranism. Some Lutherans were moving toward increased ecumenical cooperation as well.

THE SHAPE OF AMERICAN LUTHERANISM

Among Lutherans strong forces in the nineteenth century produced a large number of synodical bodies in varying degrees of fellowship with one another. In the context of American voluntarism, Lutheran growth in numbers afforded the possibility of such institutional variety and allowed differences to serve as the basis of noncooperation or even antagonism. In previous eras, when there were fewer Lutherans who were less well organized, cooperation between them was more vital. The ordination of Justus Falckner stands as a notable case in point. So, too, on the western frontier many Lutherans welcomed any Lutheran pastor who came their way rather than inquiring too closely about his synodical affiliations. In the final years of the colonial period, Henry M. Muhlenberg recognized the need for a more formal means of cooperation among Lutheran pastors and their congregations. Building upon common connections to the Halle institutions, the Ministerium of Pennsylvania was to serve this purpose. However, even then the differences between the Halle men and the more orthodox William Berkenmeyer made an organization that included all Lutherans in North America untenable.

In the following century and a half counterforces worked against a comprehensive organization of Lutherans despite efforts to establish one. These forces included the geographic, theological, and ethnic factors by which regional synods were defined. The General Synod was a second attempt to include all Lutherans in one body. Revival of confessional interest and a resurgence of immigration conspired against that goal. By the last quarter of the nineteenth century Lutherans were stratified into the Synodical Conference, the General Council, and the General Synod, with the United Synod of the South standing closest to the General Council. Cooperation among Lutherans tended to take place within these bodies rather than between them. They were distinguished by their willingness—or unwillingness—to have fellowship or share ministries with other Lutherans or other Christians. Thus, the General Synod was quite willing to cooperate with all who held basic teachings in common, but the Synodical Conference required complete, prior agreement on more points of theology and practice before it would take such a step. The Akron and Galesburg Rules expressed the General Council's more moderate position: Lutheran pulpits and altars were reserved for Lutherans, with exceptions allowed as a matter of privilege. Collaboration was somewhat easier when the joint project did not include preaching or the sacraments, those internal activities defined by the Augsburg Confession as constitutive of the church.

The formation of the United Norwegian Lutheran Church in America by three Norwegian synods in the 1890s signaled a new trend toward fewer, more comprehensive (and internally more diverse) organizations. The twentieth century would see several mergers, first reuniting groups with obvious doctrinal commonalities and shared ethnic origin and then bringing together synods that had no prior organic relationships. Alongside these organizational changes were new vehicles for cooperation even while maintaining separate church bodies. Early in the twentieth century intersynodical responses to the urgent situations caused by war and to the occasion of the quadricentennial were important steps in joining together.

As 1917 approached, Lutherans, as well as other Protestants, prepared to mark the anniversary of Luther's bold action launching the Reformation. In New York individuals from several synods, including the Norwegian and Missouri Synods as well as the expected eastern groups, formed the Reformation Quadricentennial Committee. Otto H. Pannkoke, something of a Missouri Synod maverick, provided important leadership. The committee encouraged popular and scholarly publication about Luther and Lutheranism. When the anniversary was past, the group transformed itself into the Lutheran Bureau in order to continue its public relations efforts. Pannkoke applied his considerable managerial skills to various fund-raising campaigns. He was willing to work for most Lutherans, though he wanted everyone to move beyond their old country ways and get on with being a great church. The Joint Lutheran Committee on the Celebration of the Quadricentennial was convened by the General Synod and brought together representatives of the eastern synods from the Muhlenberg branch. Like the New York committee it provided publicity and information to Lutheran and non-Lutheran audiences. A lecture series and a speakers bureau supported local celebrations. Worship services were held for all Lutherans, though not all Lutherans were willing to accept the invitation. But of more lasting significance than the celebration itself was the group's part in prompting the formation of the United Lutheran Church. Of course, not all the festivities were jointly sponsored. The Lutheran Church Missouri Synod was true to its reputation and constituted its own central committee, whose activities were similar, though directed only to its own members.

Cooperative projects such as these celebratory ones bridged organizational divisions, but mergers reshaped the landscape. Or, to return to a horticultural image, the cooperative projects provided cross-fertilization; mergers were new hybrids. In 1917 and 1918 two mergers took place, each one bringing together synods with common histories. The first was the formation of the Norwegian Lutheran Church of America. This was the culmination of several years of conversations between the various parties on disputed topics such as the proper role of laypeople, absolution, and the still troublesome issue of election. When the noted theologians were unable to resolve the latter conflict, parish pastors were given the task. Perhaps their practical experience with daily church life was the factor that equipped them to reach an agreement allowing variation in doctrine within an acceptable range. The new body included more than 90 percent of Norwegian American Lutherans. Like the Church of Norway it did so without imposing uniformity of worship style, doctrinal emphasis, or piety. Those who remained outside represented extreme positions. On the more low-church, pietist end were the Lutheran Brethren and the Lutheran Free Church; on the more orthodox end was the "little" Norwegian Synod organized in 1918 as an explicit protest to the formation of the Norwegian Lutheran Church of America.

The 1918 reunification of the Muhlenberg branch of American Lutheranism in the United Lutheran Church has already been mentioned. The United Synod, South, the General Council and the General Synod had been moving toward each other since the 1870s; when the opportunity presented itself, this final step was quickly taken. Work on the Common Service and an edition of the Small Catechism brought leaders into contact, and use of those resources provided common worship and educational experience among lay members. Late in the century official visitors began to attend each other's conventions. Women's, men's, and youth groups worked together across synodical lines. From the outset southern Lutherans and the General Council shared a confessional position more rigorous than the General Synod's. In response to the council's concerns, conveyed by its visitor to the synod's conventions in the early 1900s, the synod made more explicitly confessional statements in its constitution. This opened the way for the unification in 1918. The stated confessional position of the new body was more strictly defined than early nineteenth-century efforts, and its polity was more centralized than any previous synod's. As in the Norwegian merger, not everyone came along. Of the forty-three synods that made up the three merging bodies, forty-two joined. The Swedish Augustana Synod had stood to the conservative edge of the General Council, and at the last moment it withdrew.

The outbreak of war in Europe, followed by the United States' entry into the conflict on the side of the Allies, affected Lutherans as it did all Americans. In addition, the war forced Lutherans from the various synods to work together and created a dilemma for Lutherans whose ethnicity tied them to Germany. As American citizens they had a political loyalty to the United States, but, particularly for more recent immigrants and members of churches still using German, there was a continued emotional connection to Germany, now the enemy. This potential conflict was intensified by the response of non-German American citizens who were suspicious of their German-speaking neighbors. When suspicions became public action, Lutherans experienced the closest thing to persecution they ever encountered in the United States. Opposition came in incidents directed against individuals and congregations. Graffiti and vandalism expressed insulting opinions about Germans regardless of their religion or citizenship. Legislative efforts to restrict use of German in parochial schools were renewed.[2] The effect was to urge Lutherans to downplay, or to disassociate themselves from, their German ethnicity.

Despite such suspicions, Lutherans as a group responded to the war effort with vigorous loyalty. Women gave time and labor to the Red Cross, winding bandages and finding themselves in close and congenial contact with women from other churches. Many Lutherans served in the armed forces. Of course, their coreligionists wanted them to receive spiritual care from Lutheran chaplains. The national government was not impressed by the array of Lutheran groups willing to provide the pastors to do this; rather, it wanted to work with a single entity. Thus was born the National Lutheran Commission for Soldiers' and Sailors' Welfare. In the fall of 1917, this group brought together a dozen Lutheran bodies to respond to the immediate needs of Lutheran military personnel for physical and spiritual care. Despite initial interest, the Missouri Synod declined membership and conducted its own ministry. Frederick H. Knubel, later president of the United Lutheran Church, was the commission's president.

This cooperative work was expensive, and money, lots of money, was needed to support it. The money could not be taken out of existing synodical accounts, as the synods had only begun to develop annual budgets, and operating funds and their treasuries did not have adequate surpluses. The Lutheran Bureau was instrumental in raising the necessary cash as well as in-kind donations for relief work. A coordinated campaign was launched to raise $750,000 in one week's time. Volunteers were trained to make visits, and literature was printed. When the receipts were in, they showed that the ambitious goal had been far exceeded. The total was $1,350,000. This campaign was the first of a series of fund-raising efforts that financed special ministries and improvements in Lutheran institutions such as colleges. Their success was an indication of Lutherans' increased prosperity and of the continued growth of Lutheran churches and their work.

The purposes of the Commission for Soldiers' and Sailors' Welfare were clearly delineated, and much needed work fell outside those boundaries. Beginning with preliminary meetings in 1918, there was movement toward forming a cooperative organization with a more general mandate. That organization was the National Lutheran Council. Like the commission, it responded to the urgent needs of war, but the National Lutheran Council's work extended beyond military personnel to industrial workers in the United States and to relief efforts in Europe, particularly in France. Again Missouri declined membership. Hans Gerhard Stub of the Norwegian Lutheran Church served as the first president.

After the war, the National Lutheran Council continued as a cooperative agency whose activities reached beyond responding to emergency needs and included attention to social, economic, and social conditions. Its work gathering statistics and other information for the *Lutheran Almanac* and producing an encyclopedia of Lutheranism was noncontroversial. However, other projects pressed the limits of cooperation in external or practical matters only. The distinction between external and internal was meant to allow cooperation in activities unrelated to worship, preaching, and the sacraments, that is, those matters of practice that required agreement in doctrine. The council's provision of funding to European congregations for worship and educational materials, to pay pastors' salaries, and in a few cases to repair buildings had already pushed some members to question whether the council was overstepping its appropriate sphere. Was granting money, in effect, an endorsement of those churches like being in fellowship with them? The Iowa Synod thought so and withdrew from the council. Also during the war the council had sponsored ministry to American workers who left their homes for jobs in the war industries. The situation was not unlike the frontier missionary work of the previous century when scattered Lutherans were gathered together into congregations. Some of these wartime, emergency ministries also grew into congregations, and the issue of their synodical affiliation arose. The suggestion that the members of the council might divide the field and agree not to start congregations in competition with each other further blurred the distinction between internal and external matters. Finally, the issue was resolved by the formation of a slightly smaller agency composed of synods whose position on confessional subscription fell between the Missouri Synod's strict view and the United Lutheran Church's more lenient one. The American Lutheran Conference began its parallel operation in 1930 and continued until 1954. The National Lutheran Council also continued its work.

A third merger took place in 1930, when the American Lutheran Church was formed by joining the Iowa (which had earlier joined with Texas), Buffalo, and Ohio Synods and set up its offices in Columbus, Ohio. At the constituting convention the several groups' new unity, common heritage, and global connections were symbolized in the presiding officer's gavel, which was fashioned out of wood taken from historic American church buildings, from the chapel at Wartburg Castle, where Luther took refuge, and from both India and New Guinea. These groups shared a common German ethnic heritage and a moderately conservative confessional stance. The largest of them, the Ohio Synod, was also the oldest. It was organized by Lutherans who had moved west from the areas of colonial concentration. From early on, Lutheranism in Ohio included both an impulse toward adaptation to modernizing America and another toward a more conserving interpretation of the tradition. Leadership from theologians at Capital Seminary cultivated the latter position. Despite participation in the early stages of organization, the Ohio Synod did not join the General Council. Rather, it stayed in conversation with the Missouri Synod and the Norwegian Synod in the Synodical Conference. During the election controversy it withdrew from the Synodical Conference. Through the early years of the twentieth century the Ohio Synod continued to be in conversation with the more conservative groups.

Realignments in the first quarter of the century cleared the way for a Joint Merger Commission to begin work in 1925. Those deliberations were slowed by the need to reconsider a basic Lutheran teaching that only recently had become a point of contention. The sixteenth-century assertion of the centrality of scripture, *sola scriptura*, was not in question, but in the context of the debates about modernism and fundamentalism in many American churches the meaning of the declaration required attention.[3] When a constitution was proposed with the assertion that the Bible is "the inspired and inerrant Word of God," Johann Michael Reu argued that such a statement went beyond what the Bible claims for itself. After years of debate the original proposition was adopted. This satisfied many in Ohio but widened the gap between the new American Lutheran Church and the United Lutheran Church without convincing the Missouri Synod that the new body was entirely committed to this position.

Lutheran response to World War II followed the patterns developed in response to World War I. The habit of cooperation was more firmly established, and mechanisms were in place. American Lutherans were ready to provide services to American Lutheran military personnel and to industrial defense workers, to attend to needs of European victims of the war both in their homelands and as refugees, and to assume responsibility for mission work previously staffed by European churches or societies no longer able to do so. The National Lutheran Council was an important vehicle for getting this work done. Though steps had been taken toward international Lutheran cooperation in the years since World War I, this new battle rendered the Lutheran World Convention ineffective. Rather, the American Section acted in its stead. This organization was separate from the National Lutheran Council but interlocking in membership. Lutheran World Relief and Lutheran World Action also operated with overlapping constituencies and goals.[4] The American Lutherans would emerge from the war years as important leaders in the development of world Lutheranism.

In the two decades after the war multiple negotiations moved toward more profound cooperation between a larger number of American Lutheran bodies. The middle groups, namely, Augustana and the American Lutheran Church, worked to bring the extremes of the United Lutheran Church and the Missouri Synod together—whether for altar and pulpit fellowship or into a federation or with an organic merger. The Evangelical Lutheran Church tended to place itself between the American Lutheran Church and Missouri, though individuals were closer to Augustana. The smaller synods, such as those with Danish origins, played important, but quieter, roles. When the to-ing and fro-ing of conferences, declarations, and agreements stopped, the large-scale organization of American Lutheranism had two large new organizations, formed by mergers that transcended ethnic communities in favor of religious commonalities, and a third, the Missouri Synod, with a sprinkling of smaller groups. The big three encompassed about 90 percent of all Lutherans in their membership.

The popular view characterized the Lutheran Church in America as urban, eastern, and liberal; the American Lutheran Church as rural, midwestern, and pious; and the Missouri Synod as orthodox and self-contained. While there was a grain of truth in these sweeping generalizations, each church encompassed wide variety. Pious people were members of Lutheran Church in America congregations, Missouri congregations flourished on both coasts, and the American

Lutheran Church had its share of urban members and orthodoxy. Within the synods that existed before the 1960s the internal variety had increased in previous decades. Lutherans, like many Americans, moved around the nation in the postwar years. In a new location they often joined the convenient congregation even if it belonged to a different synod from the one their congregation back home was part of. Since the early 1900s, Lutheran campus ministries on state college campuses provided the meeting place for couples whose marriages were intersynodical. Thus, the in-law factor personalized relationships between church bodies as well as blurring distinctions. The easy distinctions of a tripartite scheme of neo-Lutheran, moderate, and old Lutheran could not be neatly lined up with the three bodies. As the next decades would show, differences in matters such as theological emphasis, styles of piety, and views of cooperation cut through the churches.

The American Lutheran Church merger in 1960 united three groups—the Evangelical Lutheran Church, the "old" American Lutheran Church, and the United Evangelical Lutheran Church. The constituting convention, held in Minneapolis, concluded with the premier performance of a new cantata written by Paul Christiansen for the occasion. Thus, the church was brought into being both by voting and by singing together. The national offices were set up in Minneapolis. Three years later the Lutheran Free Church also joined. The American Lutheran Church brought together synods whose ethnic origins were Danish, German, and Norwegian; whose membership included persons from those and other ethnic groups; and whose historic positions on issues such as congregational autonomy and the role of the laity were quite divergent. However, their theological positions generally tended toward a stricter confessionalism. The new body's attitude toward further cooperation or merger favored cooperation when necessary or when it was a useful strategy rather than regarding union as a primary goal. The legacy of congenial conversations between the old American Lutheran Church and the Missouri Synod kept alive the hope of continued and expanded good relationship in that direction.

In 1962 the Lutheran Church in America was formed by the United Lutheran Church, the Finnish Suomi Synod, the Danish American Evangelical Lutheran Church, and the Swedish Augustana Synod. Since its founding the United Lutheran Church had been joined by the Slovak Zion Synod and the Icelandic Synod. Thus, to an even greater extent than the American Lutheran Church, the Lutheran Church in America gathered in Lutherans from many backgrounds, including those descended from the African Virgin Islanders who had become Lutheran more than a century earlier and Spanish-speaking Lutherans in other parts of the Caribbean. At the Detroit convention a massed choir, robed in four colors, recalled the immigrant origins of the churches. The blending of their voices and the sight of their multicolored robes were one image of unity; the four triangular candles brought together to form a large, new one with a single flame was another. From the outset, the Lutheran Church in America regarded itself as one step in fulfilling the United Lutheran Church's constitutional commitment to ever greater cooperation, and many of its leaders looked immediately toward the next step. As he accepted the presidency, Franklin Clark Fry asked, "Pray for me and with me for the unity for which this church was founded and let us do it with abandon and devotion."[5] Somewhat ironically, this church committed to unity had offices in both New York and Philadelphia.

INTERNAL LIFE

In these decades when the organizational forms of Lutheranism changed a great deal, there were also changes within the churches. In local congregations, in the specialized work of women's and youth groups, and in the ways members participated in the larger society there were indications that Lutherans were maturing as a church and increasingly at home in the United States. From the perspective of half a century the extremes of social, political, and economic life in these decades are still visible but subdued. In these years the automobile and telephone changed transportation and communication in dramatic ways, making both tasks quicker and more individualized. The deep economic depression of the 1930s was followed by prosperity that appeared limitless. Ever larger numbers of people received ever more education. People who were shut out from all this expansion began to ask why and then to demand to be let in. Women gained the political right to vote, moved into the wartime workplace, and then were urged by government and private propaganda to redirect their talents and energies to home and family. African Americans returned from World War II with a new, critical perspective on the irony of segregation in the midst of American democracy. All of these developments touched Lutherans.

The ideal of assimilation was strong in the first half of the century. The immigrants who arrived before the 1920s were expected to become Americans, to meld together into an alloy that left ethnic peculiarities behind. Public schools trained children, and popular magazines gave women the recipes they needed to prepare American meals. Scandinavians with their Nordic appearance and pietist morality had long been regarded by many as excellent candidates for assimilation. German fondness for beer was a bit of a problem, but the nativism that surfaced during both world wars encouraged Germans to loosen their connections to the fatherland. Lutherans' growing sense of their political and social identity as primarily American rather than ethnic was expressed by the declining use of languages other than English and by the elimination of an ethnic designator in synod names in the 1940s.

The transition from other languages to English had been going on since colonial days. In the nineteenth century new immigration had abruptly reversed the process, which then began again. When looked at on the largest scale, the change was gradual and inevitable. On the small scale the shift was sometimes painful and often conflicted. The need to address younger members and potential members in English had to be balanced by recognition of the needs of older members. Though many congregations were founded with English-speaking,

-singing, and -praying as a defining feature, many others had to pass through this change, and each story was distinct. Perhaps English was first heard among the youth and then at an evening service; later, Danish was used only for one service a month and by the old women in Danish Aid. When Fredrik Schiotz was pastor of Trinity Lutheran in Brooklyn in 1940s, it functioned as two parallel congregations, with the Norwegian-speaking group holding worship upstairs in the main sanctuary and the larger, growing English one below in the smaller chapel. When the time came to reverse the spaces, the switch was put to the Norwegian group for a vote. After the proposal passed, Schiotz reported meeting a weeping, elderly woman who said, "I didn't want to [vote for it], I didn't want to; but I had to, I had to."[6] Certainly, there were others who did resist, but this woman spoke for more than herself. If Lutheranism in the United States was to flourish in the early twentieth century, it needed to speak English. The change came last in the groups most recently arrived and in least contact with others.

The shift to English in church reflected the same shift in language usage in other arenas of members' lives. Similarly, as their financial situation changed, and their livelihood was more secure, members could give more to their churches. Easier access to cash reduced the practice of in-kind donations. Introduction of the duplex envelope system regularized giving. In the United Synod, South the Lutheran Layman's Missionary Movement, founded in 1907, encouraged lay businessmen to take a more active role in the church and to apply their business acumen to its work both locally and abroad. Its members urged combining educational efforts with more efficient and systematic financial practice; the results included major increases in giving.[7] These financial changes had tangible results in improvements in church facilities. In the 1920s many rural, midwestern congregations dug basements under their buildings and equipped them with a kitchen and fellowship space. These facilities were no match for the impressive plants built by large urban congregations on the institutional church model, but they did provide the congregation with a place to gather for meetings and social occasions. Upstairs, electricity was added, along with a new organ and fresh paint. The days of meeting out-of-doors, in a barn, or in a log building were long gone.

By the 1940s there was a renewed era of expansion in the activity of founding congregations where none had been before. A century earlier this sort of home mission work was done by a pastor traveling thousands of miles on horseback as he searched out the Lutherans sprinkled across the frontier and plains. In the post–World War II period home missions were a carefully planned operation focused on areas of demographic growth, namely, the suburbs. Though mission congregations were developed across the nation, California was a particularly fertile field where Lutherans had been at work since the mid-nineteenth century. Between 1943 and 1954 the California Synod of the United Lutheran Church added fifty-seven missions and 9,000 members.

As had been the case in other regions, there were Lutherans in California before Lutheran congregations were organized and ministry was authorized by existing synods. Missouri Synod work began in the 1860s in response to an appeal sent to *Der Lutheraner* pleading for attention to the needs of German Lutherans in San Francisco. This anonymously submitted letter was written by Elizabeth Shreiber, who had moved west from Rochester, New York. When Jacob Buehler arrived in response to her appeal, her son gave him lodging. Buehler soon married Louise Wyneken and carried on in the tradition of his father-in-law, the famous home missionary. His ministry was largely to German-speaking Lutherans, whom he gathered into congregations, including St. Marks (1866) and St. Paulus (1867). The arrival of Louis Wagner as his associate allowed the two men to travel and organize congregations in other northern California towns. They cooperated with Norwegians who had been trained at the Missouri Synod's seminary in St. Louis. English work among Norwegians was also prompted by lay appeal, this from Mrs. Alethe Nelson to Ulrich Koren on behalf of her English-speaking grandchild. Work in the Los Angeles area began with spontaneous missions. F. W. Seeger (Buehler's brother-in-law), like many other "easterners," traveled from Ohio to Monrovia for his health in the 1890s; there he gathered a group for worship without support from any synod or agency. By the 1890s official work was undertaken; both the Augustana Synod and the General Synod had formed district synods in California.

For several decades Lutherans in California continued to focus their attention on collecting those who were already Lutheran into the fold and ministering to them there. However, in the 1940s the Pacific District of the United Evangelical Lutheran Church launched a mission among the Nisei and staffed it with missionaries recently returned from Japan. The work was interrupted by American internment of Japanese during World War II. By the mid-1950s two dozen Japanese American families were involved, and the question about whether to organize a separate congregation arose.[8] This endeavor did not have dramatic results, nor is there evidence that Lutherans involved in it made any distinctive response to the internment of Japanese during World War II. Also in the 1950s work among Los Angeles Japanese was undertaken by a former missionary and pastor Paul Nakamura. These small efforts to extend the boundaries of Lutheranism beyond those whose membership was "natural" were significant, both as early contacts with Asians and for its pointing toward the future. This work expanded more rapidly after the late 1970s, when Lutheran Immigration and Refugee Services facilitated resettlement of Southeast Asians. Eventually, Lutheran worship was conducted in Chinese, Vietnamese, Lao, and Korean on both coasts and in between.

As long as Lutherans were content to remain the descendants of Lutheran immigrants from Germany and Scandinavia, albeit Americanized ones, they would not come to terms with the relationship between ethnic culture and religious identity. This issue would become increasingly critical in the latter half of the century, and Lutherans from California would experience it with particular intensity. However, southern California home mission work was initially directed in the conventional way, toward those who were already Lutheran. In 1941 the California Synod of the Lutheran Church in America marked its fiftieth anniversary with a celebratory publication. The author enumerated characteristics of the state that retarded church work in California: the lure of varied scenic attractions, prevalence of many religious fads, the perishability of Lutheran loyalty, undue concern for big things, and an inadequate supply of leaders. He continued more hopefully and noted, "The missionaries began to discover that by means of adult instruction and confirmation non-Lutherans and wholly unchurched people could be turned into good Lutherans."[9] Leadership from energetic young pastors such as R. Dale Lechleitner of the American Lutheran Church and Philip S. Dybvig of the Norwegian Lutheran Church in America in the 1930s prepared the way for the postwar boom, which coincided with the state's growth, and they helped to develop the package mission approach used by the American Lutheran Church after 1951. Lechleitner observed that in California Lutherans were viewed as a rather exotic group because of their liturgical worship and as esoteric due to the requirement that adults joining their congregations receive catechetical instruction. The need for such instruction indicates that he and some other pastors defined their field broadly as "every resident of the community that was not an active vital member of another Lutheran church."[10] The "Preaching—Teaching—Reaching" mission approach was supported by the larger synod. An upfront subsidy for a building and equipment allowed congregations to get an early good start without worrying about paying for the electricity and other bills. It also paid for solid leadership and the additional work associated with expanding the scope beyond gathering mobile Lutherans. The goal was for rapid progress toward self-sufficiency and return of the money to be lent to yet another mission. With minor variations the method was used across the nation and by several synods.

The worship practices that made Lutherans seem peculiar in southern California were also undergoing changes. At the end of the nineteenth century the Common Service was widely used, not only in the three sponsoring bodies that became the United Lutheran Church in America but also in other groups. However, a great deal of variety still existed in the ways Lutherans in the United States conducted their corporate worship. Even those using the Common Service did so with their own musical settings, hymnals, and occasional services, such as weddings and funerals. Continued use of languages other than English was an obvious difference. Pietism's ongoing influence could be discerned in the very simple order of worship, consisting primarily of prayers, hymns, and sermon used in some Scandinavian congregations, in sharp contrast to the more complex orders used by others. Among the several factors that moved Lutherans toward more cohesive patterns by midcentury were the increased use of English, the example of other Protestant groups, and the liturgical renewal movement that flourished in the decades after World War II.

In the 1940s collaborative work was begun toward an order of service and hymnal that would be used by a larger portion of American Lutherans. Characteristically, the invitation to take up the project jointly was issued by the United Lutheran Church in America. Edward T. Horn III described the first meeting of the Commission on the Hymnal as like "twenty strange dogs released on the same block! There was much sniffing, and no one was quite sure of anyone else."[11] Decades of cooperative work had not erased some suspicion about members of other Lutheran groups. Worship was definitely an internal matter about which many Lutherans held strong opinions and had profound feelings. Horn and Luther Reed were among those who also served on the companion Commission on a Common Liturgy. That group based its work on the Common Service, with additional attention to the practices of the early church, the services of the larger Christian church, and contemporary practice. The result of this work was the 1958 publication of the *Service Book and Hymnal*, the so-called Red Book widely used by those groups that formed the American Lutheran Church and Lutheran Church in America only a few years later.

Certainly, the words, music, and rubrics printed in a book do give some indication of the worship life of a congregation; however, many other tangible and intangible factors shape the experience of those who gather. By midcentury pastors' Sunday morning vestments commonly were those described by one pastor as "churchly, colorful, simple, neat, economical and practical"[12]: a black cossack, a white surplus, and a stole of the color appropriate for the season of the church year. The Norwegian ruff and German tabs were stored away in the back of the closet behind the new choir robes. The trend toward celebrating the Lord's Supper more often was under way; nonetheless, Lutheran Church in America statistics make plain that seasonal or quarterly communion was still the norm.[13] More than two-thirds of Lutheran Church in America congregations reported using some sort of individual cups rather than a common chalice. In the early 1960s both the American Lutheran Church and the Lutheran Church in America published resources designed to introduce the Lutheran liturgy to general readers and to enhance worshipers' participation in worship. A similar concern for greater knowledge about worship was evidenced by the commencement of an annual Liturgical Institute at Valparaiso University in 1957.

Throughout the first half of the century, locally and churchwide, there were developments in ministry to and by special groups such as women and youth. To a great degree these mirrored changes in the church at large. By the early twentieth century the women's societies in most of the synods had moved to federate the local groups and to establish an organization that paralleled their respective synod's polity. Leadership both for forming federations and for their ongoing operation often came from the wives or daughters of pastors, women such as Lena Dahl of the United Church, Emmy Evald of the Augustana Synod, and Katherine Lehmann of the Ohio Synod. The women's federations continued the earlier emphasis on supporting the mission of the church both at home and abroad. Fund-raising and the publicity associated with that task were major activities in every case. Much of the money came from women in small donations, often made into special containers designed for thank offerings. Together these mites supported impressive programs that included direct salary support for overseas missions, gifts of buildings to colleges in the United States and to orphanages and hospitals abroad, and publication of magazines and other materials.

Gradually, the women's federations became more complex, and their organizations moved out of shoe boxes and into offices equipped with up-to-date machinery. In most synods elected officers functioned as executive staff without salary into the middle of the century. The Ohio Synod (later, the American Lutheran Church) Women's Missionary Society was an exception; Katherine Lehmann received a salary, perhaps because, unlike many of her counterparts, she was unmarried. By relying on volunteers the women kept their overhead low and were able to make their money go a long way. However, they were not always successful in determining how it would be used. Various arrangements tied the federations to their synods. Even when the women's group was separately incorporated, as was the Augustana Women's Missionary Federation, the overlapping connections of kinship and friendship held them together but did not prevent tensions. In the early 1920s the Augustana group, led by Emmy Evald, responded to a request that it support a new dormitory for women at Augustana College in Rock Island by raising $121,000.[14] Then a dispute erupted about where the building should be located. The Women's Missionary Federation officers wanted a prominent spot; seminary faculty and students had another place in mind; local women appealed to the synod, over the heads of college, seminary, and Women's Missionary Federation leaders. The dormitory was built on a less desirable lot, and no representative of the Women's Missionary Federation attended its dedication. The Lutheran Church in America women had a similar dispute about their desire to hire a staff person. Nonetheless, most of the time the women's organizations were stalwart supporters of their churches' programs, and the dirty laundry of conflict was kept in the closet.

As the federations grew, local women's organizations matured. By the middle third of the century more attention was paid to the needs of the members than had been the case before. In congregations with a large enough membership the group was organized by factors other than geography. Where there once was a north aid and a south aid, now there was a business women's group meeting in the evenings, a young mothers' group, a missionary society, and a Danish aid for the older women. The federations published materials to be used for Bible study and educational programs and to train officers to run business meetings. Many local activities such as the cradle roll and church suppers did not distinguish Lutheran women from their Protestant neighbors. Even the national publications used material borrowed from the publications of other churches in addition to articles by and about Lutherans. Nonetheless, these materials and these groups guided Lutheran women in religious practices such as the thank offering and provided them with theological interpretation for their lives.[15]

Like women's organizations, youth groups had their beginnings late in the previous century, though the origins of local groups were seldom recorded.

Some began as children's auxiliaries to the women's missionary societies; others were initially young women's groups. Their activities combined education, fundraising, and recreation. As the local groups joined together in synodical organizations, most were called Luther Leagues, but the Missouri Synod's youth distinguished themselves with the name Walther League. This group began as a young men's society formed in mid-nineteenth-century St. Louis, when a few men gathered themselves in support of a needy seminary student. In 1856 C.F.W. Walther promoted such groups in *Der Lutheraner*. Even with the support of such a venerable leader, the young men's societies were opposed by some who worried that they would become a divisive force within congregations and that they were not really Lutheran, or perhaps even Christian. To the contrary, one local society had "the goal to build and enlarge God's Kingdom as much as possible, to strive to support academic vocations, and to cultivate entertainment and edification in Christian spirit and mind."[16]

Local groups were linked together into the Walther League through the efforts of the members at First Trinity in Buffalo, New York. Their campaign for a national organization began in the 1880s and was fulfilled in 1893. By the turn of the century there were fifty Walther Leagues spread from New York to California. In 1901 the Pasadena chapter sponsored a Schiller Evening, at which members recited their favorite works by the poet. Other groups reported playing parlor games, going on picnics, conducting debates, and hearing lectures. These usual activities were quite like those going on in the dormitories and literary societies of Lutheran colleges in the same years. The Walther Leaguers were generally of an age with college students; teenagers were members of the Junior Society. Annual conventions brought members into contact with one another and provided them with practice in several areas of church life. By early in the twentieth century the league was no longer a men's organization; even at the national conventions women spoke in debate and voted, though their mothers did not vote in congregations or conventions of the Missouri Synod. In 1905 the Walther League launched its most enduring project, support of a tuberculosis sanatorium in Wheat Ridge, Colorado. The 1920s were a time of growth. Membership grew four times over, the synod gave official recognition, and the league hired its first full-time staff person. When O. P. Kretzmann became executive director in the 1930s, the league was thriving.

The Walther League and the Luther Leagues of the various synods gave young people a way to participate in their churches that recognized their stage of life and that would direct them into the church as they matured. Although confirmation once marked a Lutheran's entry into adult membership in the church, by the early twentieth century there was likely to be a lag between confirmation in the early teens and a person's full adult participation in the life of the congregation. The youth groups encouraged those young people to continue their connection with the church by giving them a vehicle for supporting the church's work, by cultivating their spiritual life, and by providing opportunities for them to form attachments to one another in the context of the church.

Young people gave financial support to local church projects as well as to mission in other locations, and they learned about that work. Monthly programs, summer Bible camps, the Pocket Testament League, and national conventions all contributed to development of spiritual disciplines, a moral life, and leadership skills. Of course, local youth group gatherings and annual conventions also provided a chance to have fun together and sometimes to test the expected standards of behavior.[17]

As the decades passed, youth were offered other programs as well. Bible camps, such as the Walther League's Camp Acadia and others run by a single congregation or as a joint effort by several congregations, combined outdoor activities with daily Bible study and worship. Though not all Bible camp music met standards for Sunday morning use in congregations, often the whole experience enlivened campers' Sunday school and confirmation class knowledge in ways that would have pleased their pietist ancestors. Friendships made at camp gave youth a sense of the Lutheran Church as bigger than their own congregation and family. Campus ministries and the Lutheran Student Movement provided college students with another opportunity to enhance their faith and participate in the larger church.

Ministry to students on Lutheran college campuses was assumed to be a natural part of college life. Pastors were present as members of the faculty and often as the college president. Courses in religion were required. Students belonged to numerous groups devoted to religious ends. Participation in weekday chapel and Sunday worship was often required. A charming, double-length postcard from early in the century shows students from the Lutheran Ladies' Seminary in Red Wing, Minnesota, making their way down the hill to services at a local congregation. On non-Lutheran campuses, where an ever-growing number of Lutherans were students, the arrangements were different. By the 1890s in Philadelphia and Ithaca, New York, there was local concern to attend to the religious life of Lutheran students. In State College, Pennsylvania, Iowa City, and Madison, Wisconsin, this concern led to founding of congregations with special responsibility for university students in addition to their local members.

When the United Lutheran Church formed, it expanded the active student program it inherited from the General Council. The dual purpose was to conserve and develop the faith of Lutheran students and to recruit church workers. After 1919 the staff included Mary E. Markley, formerly a faculty member of Agnes Scott College and recently part of the Commission for Soldiers and Sailors Welfare. With money from the Women's Missionary Federation, the United Lutheran Church was the first denomination in the United States to employ a woman as part of the student work staff.[18] The paid secretaries visited campuses to meet with students and encourage local workers. The United Lutheran Church was definite in its view that students should be integrated into normal church life and that campus ministry should include word and sacrament. On-campus programs often also included meetings that combined supper and a program as well as other social occasions. In some places a congregation provided the setting, and in others a house was purchased as a Lutheran student center. Because students came to non-Lutheran campuses from all the synods, student work was a logical arena for cooperative work. Approval for early cooperation was not always official, but cooperation was encouraged by agreements between officials.

The Lutheran Student Movement emerged from campus ministry in the 1920s. The first effort to organize Lutheran students on several campuses and from several synods was in Philadelphia in 1921. More than three dozen students from sixteen schools met on the Lutheran seminary campus. Their weekend conference was open to individuals as well as to representatives of specific programs and included students from both Lutheran and non-Lutheran campuses. The goal was to encourage students to develop their Christian character both in terms of their personal life and with regard to their activities on campus and in church. The next year a more national organization was launched, and its first convention was held in 1923 at Augustana College in Rock Island, Illinois. There Fredrik A. Schiotz, then a student at St. Olaf College, was elected president. Later he would be a leader in cooperative Lutheranism and be elected the first president of the American Lutheran Church. Though Schiotz's whole career cannot be attributed only to the Lutheran Student Movement, his work does suggest something of the success of the Lutheran Student Movement and campus ministry in developing a new cadre of leaders for the church, leaders whose friendships crossed synodical lines.

Important leadership came also from the laity, both in the church and beyond it in various activities from social services to politics. Although this work linked members of congregations and extended the church into the world, it is precisely that extension that makes it difficult to trace. The fraternal associations, Aid Association for Lutherans, and Lutheran Brotherhood, were one arena for this sort of lay leadership. Lutheran Brotherhood was founded through the initiative of two laymen, J.A.O. Preus and Herman Ekern. Both men had experience in state politics (Preus would later serve two terms as governor of Minnesota) and with the insurance industry as well as sufficient knowledge of the church to anticipate the objections that would be made to their proposal at the 1917 convention founding the Norwegian Lutheran Church in America. They were well prepared to answer the charge that buying insurance was a sign that the purchaser no longer relied on God to protect and provide. They laid the groundwork for Lutheran Brotherhood (LB) as a fraternal company committed to benefiting the whole Lutheran Church, not only its individual members or only the Norwegian Lutheran Church in America. Nearly from the outset, loans were made for congregational expansion; later, college students were given grants; a major Reformation library was established; and a multitude of other projects was made possible with "LB" moneys. Organization of members into branches, first related to congregations and by midcentury by geography, encouraged cooperation between them as well as supported service projects. The board membership and delegates to the governing meetings included Lutherans involved in many sorts of occupations from business, to industry, to politics, to congregations. A similar array would be found on the boards of other agencies and institutions, colleges, and hospitals. It was an indication of the variety of places in which Lutherans lived out their vocation.[19]

In the new century Lutheran attitudes about social ministry began to shift, and their involvement became slightly more active. Unlike those churches whose Social Gospel optimism had been dampened by World War I, Lutheran's views were changed more by their own growing security and in response to developments in the United States. The experience of giving relief aid to European war victims stimulated Lutheran willingness to do such work and to do it together rather than through each synod's independent program. Formation of the National Lutheran Council provided mechanisms for such cooperation. In the early 1930s its Committee on Social Trends conducted studies of topics related to family life, recreation, and political and economic systems. The Department of Welfare coordinated the work of social ministries related to the council's member bodies, represented Lutherans to governmental agencies, and established standards for training and service. These agencies and institutions—450 by the 1950s—continued to be operated by a variety of governing arrangements, not as branches of a central program.

Lutherans' response to the social issues that prompted amendments to the federal constitution in these years was mixed. Individuals could be found supporting nearly every position. Emmy Evald, president of the Augustana Women's Missionary Society, was an active supporter of woman's suffrage. Others, including some of the leadership of the Norwegian synods, regarded the notion as a big step in the wrong direction toward undoing the relations between men and women established by God. Temperance also had both supporters and opponents within Lutheran churches. The issue elicited official statements of support from some synods and moved Lutherans further into public debates about matters not strictly related to salvation. The General Synod passed its first resolution in support of limiting sale of liquor on the Sabbath in 1868. Before the century was out, the synod organized an ad hoc committee on temperance and in 1915 appointed a secretary to promote the cause in churches and Sunday schools. Among Scandinavians there was a history of temperance advocacy going back to Europe. Despite concerns that some temperance societies bordered on being lodges, many Scandinavian Lutherans were active members. In the first decade of the twentieth century the Augustana Synod adopted resolutions in support of the Anti-Saloon League and in favor of abstinence. Other bodies, notably, those with German heritage, were more moderate in their approach.[20] Of course, drinking could be construed as a matter of personal morality and thus within the usual purview of Lutheran concern. Nonetheless, the fact that two large general bodies responded corporately to an issue that also had political ramifications was significant.

The circumstances of refugees after World War II, known at the time as displaced persons, stimulated generous hospitality from Lutherans across the

United States. Their success in resettling thousands of people is one of the finest achievements of American Lutheranism and the basis of an impressive, ongoing ministry. Once again the coordinating agencies provided the mechanisms for this work. Through the National Lutheran Council 36,000 people were relocated and given a new start.[21] Much of the groundwork for this massive task was done in Europe by a cadre of young people who would emerge as leaders in the next decades. In the United States Cordelia Cox, formerly a professor of social work, directed resettlement services. Congregations acting as sponsors prepared housing and helped with finding employment. During the 1940s and 1950s most of the people whose journey the National Lutheran Council arranged and congregations welcomed had something in common with their hosts. If they weren't Lutheran, they were likely to be Christian. Though there was culture shock involved in moving from Estonia to Iowa, for example, there were also similarities and continuities. In a sense this work began as an extension of the nineteenth-century inner mission response to the needs of one's own kind. However, as the world situation changed, those needing help would be less like those who offered it.

During the second quarter of the century Lutheran thinking about social issues was also changing. The first obvious change was that more thinking about social issues was being done by the churches' theologians and leaders. While this burst of attention to social issues was not distributed evenly through the several synods, increased contact between leaders of the synods ensured that what went on in one would also influence the others. That influence would be extended into the future by the continued leadership of an emerging generation of theologians and churchmen. The new attention to social thought was part of a larger trend in American Protestantism as well as a response to Lutheran contact with social issues that called for a theological response. Practical experience in refugee service and with organizations such as the Young Men's Christian Association (YMCA) informed the subsequent ethical thought of people such as William Lazareth. Influential teachers also directed the thinking of a generation of scholars and pastors. At Lutheran institutions Alvin Daniel Mattson at the Augustana Seminary in Rock Island, Bertha Paulssen at Gettysburg, and both Martin Heinecken and Theodore Tappert at Philadelphia contributed to these developments. At Union Seminary in New York Reinhold Niebuhr, Paul Tillich, and Wilhelm Pauck, each in uneasy relationship with the Lutheran theological heritage, were important for a smaller group of Lutheran students. Along with these personal and educational experiences, many of these theologians took part in sustained conversations of ethical topics that were separate from official, church-sponsored projects. These meetings in New York, Valparaiso, Indiana, and Racine, Wisconsin, provided the participants with opportunities to think about, and discuss, social issues and Lutheran theology in one another's company and thus to develop relationships as well as ideas.[22] Among the participants in the DeKoven group was Joseph Sittler, who later recalled, "We met as people concerned about how resources of the Christian faith and particularly the Lutheran families

of it might better address the realities of the rapidly changing life of all our people.
. . . We simply eroded suspicious, prejudices, distances between people."[23]

Even as American Lutherans expanded their thinking and activities relative
to social issues, they were moving toward one another and Christians in other
churches as well. In the twentieth century they took on new roles among world
Lutheranism. Their missionary work allowed them to serve newly founded Lutheran churches as they had themselves been served by Europeans in early decades. Lutheran churches and people provided leadership, material resources,
and spiritual support to their religious relatives in places such as India, Madagascar, New Guinea, and Japan. Their experience of working together to meet
the needs of American military personnel during World War I and to give aid
to both the European churches and the "orphaned" missions expanded American Lutherans' view of their own role in the larger Lutheran context. Participation in their activities and with other groups led to increased contacts outside
Lutheran circles as well.

The proposal to explore an ongoing organization for Lutheran churches in
North America and Europe grew directly out of the American experiences during
and after World War I. It was presented to the National Lutheran Council by
John A. Morehead in 1919. The council adopted Morehead's suggestion and
issued an invitation to the European churches. Clearly, the American Lutherans
were no longer the dependent branches of the plant. Rather, they took the lead
and pointed in new directions. The first meeting of the Lutheran World Convention was held in Eisenach, Germany, in the summer of 1923. The delegates, just
over 150 from twenty-one nations, asserted their common faith in a statement
that named both the Bible and the Confessions, more particularly, the Augsburg
Confession. Three areas of cooperation were identified: relief work, Lutheran
unity, and the larger ecumenical task. To carry on this work, two committees
were formed with Morehead as the chair of the executive group. For the next
dozen years the Lutheran World Convention continued as a free assembly of
Lutheran churches without power to bind its members. World War II canceled
the 1940 meeting scheduled in Philadelphia and prevented joint action as well
as the normal functioning of the conference. By and large its work was carried
on by the American Section.

Following the war's end, the Lutheran World Convention convened in Lund,
Sweden, in 1947 with delegates from two dozen nations. Among them were
persons whose nations had been at war with one another not long before but
whose common confession of Christ drew them together. Forty-four delegates
came from American churches along with visitors from the Lutheran Church
Missouri Synod. There the older organization was transformed into the Lutheran
World Federation with Swedish bishop Anders Nygren as president and American Sylvester C. Michelfelder as executive secretary. The new federation, like
its predecessor, was concerned about various sorts of practical work such as war
relief, internal Lutheran relations, and the larger ecumenical movement. Federation offices were located in Geneva on the campus of the World Council of

Churches. Initially, this proximity allowed Michelfelder to carry on his work with the World Council's relief efforts and in the long run provided easy exchange between the two groups. Well into the middle of the century, when Franklin Clark Fry was elected president at the Minneapolis Assembly, Americans continued to offer significant leadership to the federation. At the same assembly in 1957 the federation voted to expand the scope of its conversations and cooperation by establishing a commission on interconfessional research.

Lutherans extended their involvement in the larger ecumenical movement by membership in international and national bodies and through bilateral dialogues. Differing views of the basis of, and need for, contacts beyond Lutheranism dictated that not all churches participated with the same enthusiasm or by the same means. Consistent with its careful stance toward inter-Lutheran cooperation, the Lutheran Church Missouri Synod was primarily an observer; by contrast, the Lutheran Church in America's ecumenical activities appeared aggressive, with the American Lutheran Church taking the middle ground. Franklin Clark Fry of the United Lutheran Church in America gave early and formative leadership to the World Council of Churches and served on its Central Committee. Five of the American Lutheran churches joined the council immediately upon its formation in 1948; the Missouri Synod declined; and the Evangelical Lutheran Church delayed for nearly a decade. In the meantime, Lutherans contributed to the council's work in various ways. Of particular note was Joseph Sittler's address to the New Delhi assembly in 1961. His remarks, "Called to Unity: Redemption within Creation," set the ecumenical agenda within the context of environmental concerns just beginning to be articulated. As in the world arena, so, too, in the national one, Lutherans responded variously to opportunities for contacts beyond their own confessional family. Once again Fry was a key figure in the National Council of Churches. Generally, those Lutheran bodies active in the World Council also joined the National Council. Although neither the Missouri Synod nor the American Lutheran Church (1960) ventured full membership, they did participate selectively.

The work of these two councils was wide-ranging, encompassing Faith and Order as well as Life and Work, and their membership stretched to include as many types of Christians as possible. Bilateral dialogues were more limited in both their participants and their agenda. These conversations among official representatives of churches from two distinct traditions began with discussion of key theological topics, often topics about which the two groups had disagreed in the past. Lutherans first engaged in dialogue with the Reformed tradition, beginning in 1962. Three years later a team of Lutherans began a round of dialogue with Roman Catholics. In the next three decades other dialogues, both national and international, would be held with Baptists, Methodists, Orthodox, and others. The exercise not only served to develop relationships between the two traditions involved in a particular dialogue but also fostered conversation among Lutherans of various sorts. As these official activities extended Lutheran contacts beyond their own boundaries, local groups and individuals were also making ecumenical contacts. By the 1906s, the next steps that Lars Boe had called for in the 1930s were being taken and perhaps some he had not imagined as well.

NOTES

1. Lars Boe, "The Next Step in American Lutheranism," *Lutheran Herald*, April 10, 1934.

2. Carol K. Coburn, *Life at Four Corners: Religion, Gender and Education in a German-Lutheran Community, 1868–1945* (Lawrence: University Press of Kansas, 1992), p. 146 notes that in 1919 laws in twenty-one states required that English be the only language used in both private and public schools.

3. For a very useful discussion of the larger Lutheran and American context of this dispute see Todd Nichol, " 'Timely Warnings': Notes on Inerrancy and Inerrant," *dialog* 24 (Winter 1985): 52–60.

4. The development of Lutheran World Relief from its initial concern with European postwar relief to its current involvement in development around the globe is traced in John W. Bachman, *Together in Hope: 50 Years of Lutheran World Relief* (New York: Lutheran World Relief, 1995).

5. Quoted in W. Kent Gilbert, *Commitment to Unity: A History of the Lutheran Church in America* (Philadelphia: Fortress Press, 1988), p. 129.

6. Fredrick Axel Schiotz, *One Man's Story* (Minneapolis: Augsburg Publishing House, 1980), p. 67.

7. Susan Wilds McArver, " 'A Spiritual Wayside Inn': Lutherans, the New South and Cultural Change in South Carolina, 1886–1918." (Durham, N.C.: Duke, 1995), pp. 244–255 traces the foundation of this movement, noting the role of gender in its motivations and rhetoric. By 1909 the average per capita giving in the United Synod in the South, $2.29, was nearly double that of the next highest, the General Synod, whose average was $1.41 (pp. 253–254).

8. Andrew Juhl, ed., *A History of the Pacific District of the UELC (1930–55)* (Blair, NE: Lutheran Publishing House, 1955), p. 25.

9. John Edward Hoick, *The Fruitage of Fifty Years in California* (Evangelical Lutheran Synod of California, 1941), n.p.

10. Interview of R. Dale Lechleitner by Ray F. Kibler III, 1981, Archive of Cooperative Lutheranism, Lutheran Council in the United States, held by Archives of the Evangelical Lutheran Church in America.

11. Inter-Lutheran Consultation on Worship, "Preparation of the Service Book and Hymnal," *Liturgical Reconnaissance* (Philadelphia: Fortress, 1968), p. 91.

12. J.A.O. Stub, *Vestments and Liturgies*, p. 15 (privately published, perhaps 1929), found in Stub's biographical file at Evangelical Lutheran Church in American Region III archives, St. Paul, MN.

13. Gilbert, *Commitment to Unity*, p. 50.

14. Jane Telleen, " 'Yours in the Master's Service': Emmy Evald and the Women's Missionary Society of the Augustana Lutheran Church, 1892–1942," *Swedish Pioneer Historical Quarterly* 30 (July 1979): 191.

15. For a detailed study of these materials, see Betty DeBerg, "The Spirituality of Lutheran Women's Missionary Societies, 1880–1930," in "Missionary to America: The

History of Lutheran Outreach to Americans,'' ed. Marvin Huggins, *Essays and Reports 1992* 15 (St. Louis: Lutheran Historical Conference, 1994), pp. 142–160.

16. Jon Pahl, *Hopes and Dreams of All: The International Walther League and Lutheran Youth in American Culture, 1893–1993* (Chicago: Wheat Ridge, 1993), p. 17, n. 35.

17. Clarence Peters, ''Developments of the Youth Programs of the Lutheran Churches in America'' (Th.D. dissertation, Concordia Seminary, 1951), p. 185.

18. Mary E. Markley, *The Lutheran Church and Its Students* (Philadelphia: Muhlenberg Press, 1948), p. 31.

19. Hakala Associates, *A Common Bond: The Story of Lutheran Brotherhood* (Minneapolis: Lutheran Brotherhood, 1989), pp. 13–17.

20. Christa R. Klein and Christian D. von Dehsen, *Politics and Policy: The Genesis and Theology of Social Statement in the Lutheran Church in America* (Philadelphia: Fortress Press, 1989), pp. 13–14.

21. Abdel Ross Wentz, *A Basic History of Lutheranism in America* (Philadelphia: Muhlenberg Press, 1955), p. 335.

22. Klein and von Dehsen, *Politics and Policy*, Chapter 2.

23. Interview of Joseph A. Sittler by Robert H. Fischer, 1978, Archive of Cooperative Lutheranism, Lutheran Council in the United States. Held by Archives of the Evangelical Lutheran Church in America, pp. 40, 42.

7

AN AMERICAN
REFORMATION?

For Lutherans whose forebears at the Diet of Augsburg in 1530 were the original Protestants, the word ''Reformation'' has particular resonance. Reformation Sunday is observed in many congregations with a celebration and is understood as not unlike a religious parallel to Independence Day. The Reformation is sometimes limited to its specific historical referent. Like the American Revolution celebrated on July 4, it is a past event. So think some; others might argue that as the Revolution must continue, so, too, must the Reformation. The motto *''Ecclesia reformata et semper reformanda''* (the church, reformed and always reforming) is quoted. Historian Jaroslav Pelikan has suggested that Lutheranism's development in the United States has followed a pattern the reverse of that in Europe. Here the earliest adherents were pietists; in the nineteenth century an era of orthodoxy set in; and ''it is only in the twentieth century that American Lutheranism, in its piety, ethics, and theology, began to come to terms with Martin Luther himself.''[1] Perhaps the dynamism of Luther, made available in the scholarly revival of interest in Luther, then infuses the church with a like vigor and yields new life. In general use, the term ''reformation'' may point toward a new shape or toward renewal. The question then comes, Have Lutherans in the United States in the last half of the twentieth century participated in either sort of reformation?

In the first half of the twentieth century American Lutherans came a long way toward settling themselves in their nation. Though they had not achieved the goal of having all Lutherans living in one house, the generational pace of mergers and experiences with collaborative projects and in cooperative agencies brought them much closer. By the mid-1960s, to say that all Lutherans belonged to one of three bodies was an exaggeration, but it was close enough to true to be said with some regularity. If reformation is a synonym for making a new shape, there seemed little of that work left to be done. Nonetheless, this chapter treats two more episodes of realignment: first, the painful division of the long-stable Lutheran Church Missouri Synod; then the formation of the Evangelical Lutheran Church in America from the minority and the other two large groups.

What of the second meaning for reformation? There were points of dynamism and renewal in Lutheranism in these decades. Lutherans became much more engaged in social issues than they had been in the previous centuries. As individuals and as churches they, like members of other churches, responded to the Civil Rights movement, to women's liberation, to war and antiwar. Statements, policies, and actions signaled Lutherans' efforts to come to terms with the specific conditions in which they and their neighbors lived, efforts that went beyond concern for personal salvation and doing works of love. This shift had its opponents, whose dismay seemed to grow with the passage of years and the adoption of more and more social statements. A second point of engagement was with other Christians in various sorts of ecumenical forums. Lutherans who long had been characterized as unwilling to cooperate with one another, much less with other Christians, joined in and were lively participants in bilateral dialogues as well as in larger efforts and grassroots experiments that echoed the union congregations of the colonial era. The internal life of congregations also showed signs of change prompted both by initiatives from the larger church and by societal trends. Several programs of adult Bible study were launched. Sacramental practices were altered dramatically when the link between the rite of confirmation and first communion was dropped and the frequency of communion was increased. A new emphasis on baptismal piety emerged. Laypeople—both men and women—took more visible roles in leading worship. By the twenty-fifth anniversary of women's ordination in 1995, one woman had been elected a bishop. Were these signs of renewal and reformation? Perhaps they were. But after a peak in the 1970s membership declined in the next two decades, so even an affirmative reply leads to other questions about how to define and measure renewal and how renewal or reformation is related to quantifiable success.

REFORMATION AND RENEWAL?

Was the second half of the twentieth century a time of renewal and reformation for Lutherans in the United States? Did they grasp something of the sixteenth-century reformer's evangelical dynamism? Or did they merely replicate the contentiousness of those years without the breakthroughs in theological insight or the benefits for the life of faith? Likely, the 1990s are still too soon to give a final answer to these questions. Some of the discussions are still in process, and the staying power of the innovations is not yet well tested. Nonetheless, something can be said about the evidences of liveliness in these decades in the realm of social policy, in the sphere of women's activities, in ecumenical relationships, and in worship and other activities of the congregational life.

In the 1960s the whole nation seemed caught up in energetic reevaluation of former assumptions about how life—individual and corporate—is best to be lived. While radicals called for revolutions of various sorts, other citizens made more moderate, but still noticeable, changes in their lives. People who belonged to Lutheran churches were affected by, and took part in, every aspect of these social changes. Those changes that did not come directly into their lives they experienced indirectly when watching the evening news, vicariously through the experiences of friends or family, or didactically via the churches' publications and programs. The expansion of interest in social policy and ethical thought that began in the 1940s and 1950s came into fuller expression in the next decades. All three major church bodies—each following its own process and sometimes jointly—sponsored studies and issued statements on pressing issues of the day. Their policies on such things as allocation of money for new congregations were influenced by contemporary events such as the Civil Rights movement. Leaders and members came to participate in nonchurch-sponsored organizations and activities such as the antiwar group, Clergy and Laity Concerned, or the anti-abortion group, Lutherans for Life. Congregations also adapted to new trends in varying degrees with even so simple a change as listing female members' first names in their publications and records or taking part in a community-sponsored Thanksgiving eve service.

From their first encounter with North America, Lutherans experienced the doubleness of identity defined by religion and ethnicity, usually a minority ethnicity. Even before the first congregation was organized, Lutherans were a multicultural community. Language was always an issue, if not always with the same intensity in every congregation or synod. The first Lutheran worship in New Jersey was held in the home and at the invitation of an African. A growing majority of Lutherans in the Virgin Islands were African American. Evangelizing Native Americans was part of Johan Campanius' charge in colonial New Sweden and a primary task for Loehe's missionaries in Michigan in the nineteenth century. Contacts with Hispanic people in Puerto Rico were initiated in the 1890s by a Swiss seminarian associated with the Augustana Synod. Asian ministries were begun in the mid-1900s. Despite this litany of activity, by mid-century American Lutheranism was still largely made up of descendants of German and Scandinavian immigrants and the occasional convert from some other European ethnic group. When race emerged as a major national concern, Lutherans, as a group, had relatively little practical experience to bring to bear on the issue, and surprisingly little constructive attention was paid to what could be learned from their own history.

The churches' official response came through social statements and actions addressed both to their own internal life and to the larger context of American government and society. The last, giving direction to members about how to act as citizens and to the government itself, was a relatively new response for American Lutherans, who were more inclined to providing information and guidance. Fredrik Schiotz's comment about the California grape boycott is typical of the earlier stance: "The church should sift facts, make them available to its people, and leave it to the conscience of its people to do what each may judge right."[2]

Nonetheless, the urgency of the situation was such that in 1961 the American Lutheran Church council adopted "A Christian Affirmation on Human Relations," and in 1964 the Lutheran Church in America convention passed a statement simply titled "Race Relations." People involved in drafting the Lutheran Church in America statement had participated in the informal discussions of the previous years and contributed to the foundational work, *Christian Social Responsibility*, published in 1957.[3] The Lutheran Church in America statement introduced two innovations: "corporate church involvement in social action and moral justification for civil disobedience to unjust laws."[4] It was unique in its explicit appeal to the Prayer of the Church for its format, some of its language, and its claim upon church members. The statement asserted: "Unless we mean what we say, and live as men who intend to do what we mean, the holy gravity of our prayer condemns us." With similar seriousness, the subsequent 1974 American Lutheran Church statement identified racism with sin and asserted that the time for study and statements was past—action was needed.

There were, of course, more statements, but attention should also be given to action by Lutheran bodies and by individual Lutherans. As part of a general restructuring of the Lutheran Church in America, a Consultation on Minority Group Interest and a staff team were devised. The consultation included representatives of the black, Hispanic, Asian, Native American, and Caucasian communities and thereby gave those representatives a channel into the church's governing structure. The "Goals and Plans for Minority Ministry, 1978–1984" called for very specific and measurable changes such as an increase of 15,000 members per year until racial makeup of the Lutheran Church in America matched that of the nation.[5] The board of American Lutheran Church Women took a decisive step in 1983, when it set aside its constitution and appointed three women of color to its elected body. Its next General Convention affirmed the innovation and made this strategy for ensuring leadership by women of color an ongoing policy.[6] The churches designated scholarship money for students of color. Between 1970 and 1980 the American Lutheran Church, for example, gave more than 1 million to 1,764 students.[7] Bringing a few students onto campuses populated primarily by white students, many of whom knew only others who shared their racial and ethnic identity, was not without difficulty, but it also fostered some relationships, expanded some understanding, and gave some people opportunities they would not otherwise have had. The Lutheran Church Missouri Synod inherited the "Colored Missions" of the Synodical Conference; in 1947 it moved to integrate this work into the synodical structures. The mixed responses to this move included the suggestion that the concerns of African American members would be diluted, and isolation might follow. The Lutheran Church Missouri Synod continued to operate Concordia Junior College in Selma, where early in the century Rosa Young had been an influential teacher for many African American students and a leader in the church.[8]

In addition to official church statements and actions, Lutherans expressed their concerns and commitments about racial matters through ad hoc groups and para-church organizations. Some, like the Lutheran Human Relations Association and the Conference on Inner-City Ministries, had racially mixed memberships. This was less the case in others such as the Association of Black Lutherans and the Association of Black Lutheran Clergymen, the majority of whose members were African American. These sorts of groups worked both to make changes they deemed necessary within the churches and to address their own needs. They also provided opportunities for their members to exercise leadership. "A Hispanic Lutheran Declaration" presented to the 1972 Lutheran Church in America convention by the National Lutheran Hispanic Caucus articulated needs that would have been familiar to pioneer pastors like Muhlenberg and Henkel: trained leaders, educational and worship materials in their own language, and adequate buildings.[9]

By the 1970s Lutherans were challenged by growing Native American activism. In response to demands made to their 1970 convention by the American Indian Movement (AIM), the Lutheran Church in America supported the establishment of an office for Indian Ministry in the Lutheran Council in the USA. Eugene Crawford became the director of the National Indian Lutheran Board, an agency related to Lutheran Council in the USA. The first Native American to hold such an office, Crawford had both Sisseton Sioux and English heritage. At the outset this agency used much of its budget to fund community development projects and advocacy efforts on behalf of Native American sovereignty and treaty rights. By the early 1980s interest revived in a more conventional Lutheran approach, the ministry of word and sacraments. When AIM occupied Wounded Knee, South Dakota, in 1973 Pastor Paul Boe, executive director of the American Lutheran Church's Division for Social Service, was invited to be with them. His relationship with AIM went back to the late 1960s. Though his presence at Wounded Knee exaggerated Lutheran involvement with Native American causes, it was notable. It demonstrated that he was regarded as trustworthy by AIM leaders, and it showed that in the right circumstances some Lutherans were willing to act on the moral justification for civil disobedience that the Lutheran Church in America's 1964 statement of race relations identified. When he refused to identify those who had guns during the occupation, Boe was charged with contempt of court. His appeal, claiming the privilege of clergy confidentiality, was supported by all three major Lutheran churches and others; however, the original charge was dismissed on a technicality.

During the next decade individual pastors and some congregations were vigorously engaged in social and political struggles, both with the support of the larger church and in opposition to it. Alzona Lutheran in Phoenix, Arizona, defied federal immigration laws to shelter refugees from Central America in the 1980s; they responded to Immigration and Naturalization Service infiltration of their congregation and of three Presbyterian congregations with a civil suit charging that their First and Fourth Amendment constitutional rights had been violated. In 1990 the U.S. Federal Court found in the churches' favor and limited the range of government activities in such situations, although it did not require agents to secure a warrant.[10] In the same years two Pennsylvania pastors were involved with Denominational Strategy Ministries and its efforts to respond to the unemployment in the Pittsburgh area. In contrast to the Arizona congregation, which received legal and financial support from the American Lutheran Church, both men were removed from the clergy roster by the Western Pennsylvania-West Virginia Synod of the Lutheran Church in America.

These were decades in which a second wave of feminism swept over the nation. In the nineteenth century woman's rights advocates drew inspiration and skills from Christianity in various forms. In the midst of revivals women's voices were heard. The missionary movement was supported by women's organizations, and many woman were sent out to do its work. Moral reform efforts such as antiprostitution and temperance drew support from churchwomen. Though some women already regarded the church as part of the problem, and some churchmen regarded such women as a threat, Christianity made a contribution. In the mid-twentieth century the influence was often in the opposite direction, from the secular women's movement into the church. Young activists in the Civil Rights and antiwar movements and discontented middle-class women found common cause in women's liberation. The accusation that the Christian church was one of women's most powerful captors was more forcefully made than in the past, and at the outset few feminists argued that Christianity could serve as the basis of liberation. This would change by the 1980s, when an array of strong proposals for feminist Christianity was articulated. But in the meantime even those who prefaced their statements with the phrase, "I'm not a feminist" began to ask that women participate more fully in the life of the church, as they were beginning to do in the larger society.

This call for women's full participation took various forms. In congregations it meant that women were elected to church councils and offices and that as lay leadership in worship was expanded, women read lessons, distributed the communion elements, and served as assisting minister. In larger arenas such as regional synods and districts, committees were formed to study women's roles and to suggest actions such as increasing the number of women delegates to church conventions. A group of Lutheran Church Missouri Synod women involved in civil rights work organized themselves into the Lutheran Women's Caucus. The caucus soon had members from other Lutheran bodies as well. These women published a newsletter and held meetings to educate themselves and others in the hope of combating sexism in the church. Connie Parvey, a campus minister from the Boston area, directed "Toward a Community of Women and Men," a World Council of Churches project. Of course, some churchwomen regarded all this as unnecessary or even against the Bible's teaching; and some thought that the church was beyond repair. The American Lutheran Church and Lutheran Church in America women's organizations were led by women whose public stance was progressive but moderately stated. American Lutheran Church Women director Margaret Wold was a pastor's wife who had founded a preschool at their mission congregation in North Hollywood. In her book *The Shalom Woman*, she based her call for a mild feminism upon a rereading of traditional Christian sources.

When the first Ladies' Aids were formed, detractors regarded the groups as a dangerous step toward women's demanding to be pastors. At the time women's organization leaders denied any such intentions. By the 1960s, however, the request was being made by women in several denominations, and women's organization leaders gave their support. Though women were already being ordained in some European Lutheran churches and other American Protestant churches, they were not in any American Lutheran ones. Women answered their callings to public ministry by becoming deaconesses, teachers, or administrators or serving as lay workers in campus ministry. The question of women's ordination arose and required a response.[11] The response was made deliberately with much study. The Lutheran Council in the USA sponsored a study, as did both American Lutheran Church and Lutheran Church in America. As part of the Lutheran Church in America process, Margaret Sittler Ermath, a history professor at Wittenberg University, wrote *Adam's Fractured Rib*, a short volume that relied heavily on contemporary secular materials. Margaret Wold and Evelyn Streng, a professor at Texas Lutheran, served on the American Lutheran Church study group. Seminary faculties debated the issue with regard to the Bible, the Confessions, and the present context. Though by no means everyone was convinced, no compelling reasons were advanced to prevent women from being ordained. Already a handful of women was enrolled in master of divinity programs. Finally, at their 1970 conventions both Lutheran Church in America and American Lutheran Church voted to extended ordination to women. Within the year Elizabeth Platz (LCA) and Barbara Andrews (ALC) were ordained, each was the first female pastor in her church.[12] Both had previous experience in campus ministry, which Platz continued. Andrews took a parish call. The Lutheran Church Missouri Synod did not make a similar decision and regarded the American Lutheran Church's move as evidence of its flawed reading of the Bible and a barrier to its continued fellowship.

In the first years the numbers of women who went to seminary and sought ordination continued to be small. Slowly, the numbers grew so that in 1988 there were 1,068 ordained women in the newly formed Evangelical Lutheran Church in America.[13] The presence of women in seminaries drew attention to other related issues. Discussions of inclusive language, of women's absence from the theological canon, and of the image of God went on alongside practical concerns such as the difficulty women had receiving calls and finding appropriate garb that fitted well. Even more slowly than women moved into parish calls, they assumed other leadership roles as seminary teachers and in the ecclesial structure. In the 1910s Jennie Bloom Summers taught nontheological topics at Pacific Theological Seminary in Portland, Oregon; and Bertha Paulssen was an influential teacher of sociology at Gettysburg Seminary from 1945 to 1963. However, the first ordained Lutheran woman to teach one of the Lutheran seminaries with full faculty status was Margaret Krych, who went to Philadelphia in 1977.[14] Barbara Lundblad of New York was one of the four final candidates for election as presiding bishop when the Evangelical Lutheran Church in America was formed; however, none of the sixty-nine regional bishops was a woman until April Ulring Larson was elected in the LaCrosse area synod of the Evangelical Lutheran Church in America in 1992.

The 1960s were a decade of heightened ecumenical interest in many Christian churches and of expanding ecumenical contacts by Lutherans. Although the three large Lutheran bodies all belonged to the Lutheran Council in the USA, their participation in other sorts of conversations and cooperative ventures varied according to expected patterns. The Lutheran Church in America was a member of the Lutheran World Federation as well as both the World and the National Council of Churches; the American Lutheran Church was a member of the Federation and the World Council; and the Lutheran Church Missouri Synod was a member of none. These memberships provided the structures for ongoing contacts and development of new relationships, both between churches and between leaders. Roman Catholic willingness to engage in conversations not directed toward conversion of its partners to Catholicism increased dramatically after Vatican II and contributed to the use of bilateral dialogues as a strategy for ecumenicism.

These dialogues resembled the free conferences Lutheran groups held in the previous century as an early step toward greater cooperation. Although the participants sometimes took up topics that had been the basis of disagreements between the partners, the goal was to move toward deeper mutual understanding and perhaps even toward closer fellowship. Individuals from Lutheran churches or another church or family of churches would meet over a period of years to discuss matters of mutual concern, usually theology rather than practice, and then issue a report or reports. The precise standing the individuals held within their own churches varied, as did the representativeness of their views. In early dialogue rounds the Lutheran delegation was sponsored by the USA National Committee of the Lutheran World Federation; later, the Lutheran Council in the USA assumed that responsibility and included members from each of its member churches. Disagreements were articulated within Lutheran delegations as well as between them and their dialogue partners. These dialogues took place both nationally and worldwide. The first set in the United States was initiated from the Reformed side and began in 1962. Dialogues with Roman Catholics, Episcopalians, Methodists, Baptists, Conservative Evangelicals, and Orthodox followed and were carried on simultaneously by separate Lutheran delegations. The most influential were the Reformed and the Episcopalians, with whom American Lutherans had some old history of cooperation, and with the Roman Catholics, with whom their relationship had been less cordial.[15] By its 1997 assembly, the Evangelical Lutheran Church in America was on the threshold of significantly closer, though distinct, relationships with all three groups.

While dialogues were conducted by highly trained theologians, at the local

level grassroots experiments in ecumenism were also taking place.[16] A conflu-
ence of practical and theological concerns stimulated interest in space-sharing
arrangements that recalled the union congregations of the colonial era. In Madison, Wisconsin, Advent Lutherans built and shared a facility with Community
of Hope, United Church of Christ. After Trinity Congregation in Minneapolis
lost its large building to freeway construction, the members tried out various
neighborhood locations for worship, including a theater and a coffeehouse; they
then moved in with Our Lady of Perpetual Help, sharing with the Roman Catholics both the former rectory converted to office space and the parish church
building with multiple altars, an infant of Prague, and the stations of the cross.
Such arrangements encouraged social contact between members and could give
rise to shared activities from a joint quilting group, to common Thanksgiving
services, to members participating in one another's ordinary worship. Even when
space was not shared, by the last quarter of the century Lutherans were increasingly willing to take part in community-wide ecumenical activities such as special worship services or the local ministerium.

The Service Book and Hymnal of 1958 had continued—and some say had
been the culmination of—the concerns that produced the Common Service in
1888. When the American Lutheran Church and Lutheran Church in America
were formed, large numbers of the involved congregations were already using
"the red book." Of course, the hundreds of hymns and two settings of the
liturgy combined with other variations in local customs to ensure that common
practice would not be totally uniform. The next step toward common practice
was taken with the hope of including an even larger majority of Lutherans. In
the mid-1960s the impetus to form the Inter-Lutheran Commission on Worship
came from the Lutheran Church Missouri Synod. That such a project was undertaken jointly signaled remarkable optimism and a new openness from the
Lutheran Church Missouri Synod. The goal of producing a common book for
groups with various prior practice assumed that everyone would have to make
some changes; however, there were revisions that not everyone could accept.
The final result was two very similar books—the Lutheran Church Missouri
Synod's *Lutheran Worship* (1982) and the *Lutheran Book of Worship* (1978),
used by the other churches.

Along the way several paperback editions of provisional services were tested
in congregations. Printing technology had advanced a long way from the handwritten copies of Muhlenberg's agenda that were distributed among the colonial
clergy. The final versions of the books were issued just in time to have responded to the call for modern diction and gender-inclusive language. While
some early reviews were quite positive about the way these concerns were addressed, reaction to the language from the church members who sang the hymns
week after week were mixed. Although the language of old and familiar hymns
was updated, the book came too early to include many of the modern hymns
that responded to these concerns with new texts. Efforts to eliminate linguistic
sexism addressed references only to people, not to God. Thus, while some wor-

shipers were annoyed by any changes, others were irritated that not enough had been done. There was also mixed response to changes made in hymn tunes and to the three settings for the liturgy. The collection contained a small number of hymns from sources other than the usual European and American ones. But here, too, this early effort was soon surpassed by hymnals produced by other churches and, for all its makers' good intentions, regarded as inadequate by proponents of greater inclusiveness.

This book moved Lutherans further along in an ecumenical direction in their worship practice.[17] It included a three-year series of Bible readings used by Roman Catholics, Episcopalians, and other churches. Beyond providing a eucharistic prayer before the words of Jesus instituting the Lord's Supper, it made this the preferred option while allowing for variations in local customs. Baptism was given a greater emphasis throughout the liturgy, and parents were urged to have their children baptized in the company of the gathered congregation during the Sunday service, rather than at a private one. The people's participation in worship as an encounter with one another and with God was highlighted.[18] When this book was used in congregations that responded to liturgical renewal by moving their altar away from the wall, buying their pastor an off-white alb to replace the black cassock and white surplice, and relocating their baptismal font front-and-center, then the visual, physical, and auditory experience of worship was dramatically changed. Sharing the peace of the Lord required worshipers to turn and touch their neighbors. The final words of the liturgy, "Go in peace, serve the Lord," propelled them out into the world.

The liturgical emphasis upon baptism extended into other aspects of the church as well. Theologian Eugene Brand asserted its centrality for understanding the life of faith. "Baptism, then, cannot be viewed individualistically; it is at the center of the life of the *community*. Nor can baptism be viewed simply as one step in a biographical sequence. It is paradigmatic for the person and for the community because it implants us into a community which lives from the future—from the resurrection life we grasp even now by faith."[19] Parents of an infant were given a candle and urged to burn it on the anniversary of the child's baptism. Other ways of celebrating and recalling that event were suggested. At national youth gatherings young people were invited to remember their baptismal identity, which extends into their daily lives, by regarding themselves as always wet with the waters of baptism, thus "walking wet." This emphasis upon a baptismal spirituality was reminiscent of Luther's exhortation to daily die to sin and arise anew each day to live in God's grace.

Although Luther demoted the rite of confirmation from its sacramental status, confirmation instruction has long followed baptism as a part of Lutheran educational practice. Indeed, its importance in Scandinavian countries in the last century may have contributed to the relatively high rates of literacy among immigrants from that area. In preindustrial societies the rite of confirmation functioned to mark entry into adulthood at an age that twentieth-century Americans judge children hardly ready to be left home alone. In the United States confirmation instruction, or reading for the minister, continued to be the primary means of transmitting the content of Lutheran teaching to the churches' youth. Even when summer schools and Sunday schools were held, some special instruction by the pastor—likely involving memorization of Luther's Small Catechism—was required for all boys and girls. In some nineteenth-century congregations Sunday services included a period of catechization during which members were quizzed on their knowledge. The rite of confirmation remained a festive and solemn entry into mature membership. Many church basement walls are galleries of photographs of young people scrubbed and dressed in new clothing for the solemn occasion. Though the methods may seem primitive by contemporary standards, the hoped-for result was a basic theological education for all members.

By the mid-twentieth century both the role of the rite of confirmation and the instruction leading up to it were being reconsidered. Though junior high-age students spent Wednesday afternoons being instructed in the catechism, church history, and the Bible, questions were raised about the appropriateness of casting these pearls of religious knowledge before a herd of adolescents, only some of them attentive. When occasionally an honest student took the rite seriously and declared herself or himself unwilling to go through with it, the tangled intertwining of familial expectations and religious meaning was laid bare. Others merely regarded the rite as their right and, once it was over, disappeared from the congregation. The 1970 report of the Joint Commission on the Theology and Practice of Confirmation urged separating the rite of confirmation from first communion. The subsequent lowering of the age of first communion removed the basis of the popular view that the rite of confirmation was the gateway to the communion table. But it did not solve the problem of what, how, and when to teach young people the basic content of the Lutheran theological tradition. Various experiments using such innovations as individualized instruction or replacing weekly classes with less frequent retreats were carried out with more or less success.

Along with the separation of first communion from confirmation, there were other changes in communion practices and thinking about those practices. The *Lutheran Book of Worship* provided eucharistic prayers as the preferred option. Increasingly, terminology shifted from the Lord's Supper to the Great Thanksgiving or the Eucharist. A more joyful mood of response to God's promise of grace replaced the somberness and self-examination formerly associated with participation. Members of congregations began to use ordinary home-baked bread and to bring both bread and wine forward as part of the offertory. Some congregations returned to the common cup. The invitation to receive was often broadened, no longer limited to members of the local congregation. The sacrament was celebrated more frequently. By 1990 *The Lutheran* reported that 1,690 Evangelical Lutheran Church in America congregations—about 15 percent—celebrated communion weekly.[20]

Luther received the theological insight that God's reconciling love comes by grace through faith as he studied the Bible and when he was a teacher of Bible. Again and again, in the history of Christianity such clarity has come in an encounter with the living Word of God in the written text. Bible reading was a definitive activity for European pietists such as Spener. Lutherans have continued to read, sing, and pray the Bible, and in the middle decades of the century they renewed their study of it. Women's organizations long sponsored regular, usually monthly Bible study by publishing materials for use in local circles. Young people were taught the content of the Bible in Sunday school, vacation Bible school and confirmation classes. In the early 1960s Bethel Lutherans Church in Madison, Wisconsin, developed a multiyear Bible curriculum for adults. Using didactic pictures and memory work, the Bethel Series engaged thousands of Lutheran adults in sustained study of the Bible. Both the Lutheran Church in America and the American Lutheran Church later produced their own programs. Word and Witness and SEARCH each combined materials written by biblical scholars with local leadership and small group work. While there can be no doubt that individuals increased their knowledge of the Bible and that relationships within congregations were encouraged by these programs, there is little evidence that these programs fostered any truly radical reforms.

RE-FORMATION = NEW SHAPE

If reformation is understood as a change in external forms or as taking on a new shape, American Lutheranism went through a two-part reformation in the last half of the century. The first painful step was the splitting apart of the Lutheran Church Missouri Synod, which took place throughout the 1970s. The debate can be traced in convention actions and published statements concerning proper interpretation of Scripture and the nature of the church, but these sorts of documents are inadequate to convey the conflict's traumatic aftermath for at least a generation of church members. The organization of the Association of Evangelical Lutheran Churches (AELC) in 1976 was contrary to the trend toward fewer church bodies; however, the second step in the re-formation continued that trend. In 1988 the Association of Evangelical Lutheran Churches joined with the far larger and relatively older American Lutheran Church and Lutheran Church in America to form the Evangelical Lutheran Church in America. Though this step was more pleasant, it was not without difficulty or detractors.

Since its inception in the mid-nineteenth century the Lutheran Church Missouri Synod had been committed to preserving doctrinal purity and had been attentive to proper understanding of the nature of the church. C.F.W. Walther rose to leadership, in part on the strength of his theses in support of the group's status as truly church even after they deposed their first leader, Martin Stephan. The synod's early polity responded to that crisis by affirming the congregation's authority and providing the synod itself with an advisory role. Similar issues came under debate again in the 1970s with dramatic consequences. The complex series of events that culminated in the formation of the Association of Evangelical Lutheran Churches had two primary subplots and an overlapping cast of characters. One plot was played out in relation to Concordia Seminary in St. Louis; the other in relation to the synod's mission work. Both concerned the degree of doctrinal uniformity judged essential within the synod and the means to ensure such uniformity.

By midcentury the Missouri Synod's cohesiveness could not be taken as total uniformity of views, if it ever could. Already in the 1930s, just after the first American Lutheran Church merger process included debates about the Bible, synod leaders engaged in public disagreements about how the authority of the Bible was to be grounded. Former synod president Franz Pieper issued a statement asserting that the Bible was verbally inspired and inerrant in all matters. Walter Maier, popular preacher on the radio *Lutheran Hour*, suggested a less doctrinaire position. In the mid-1940s a group of forty-four moderate pastors and professors made their own statement, calling for greater attention to the church's mission and less to debate about ambiguous aspects of theology. On the basis of its openness to ecumenical contacts, a subsequent convention demanded that the statement be withdrawn. If members of congregations were not preoccupied by these debates, they could not help noticing the synod's more lenient attitude toward activities such as buying life insurance, Scouting, dancing, and birth control.[21] While some laypeople took advantage of the new latitude, others wondered what had happened to the old certainties.

At the 1965 convention in Detroit the synod adopted a set of Mission Affirmations that represented a moderate, open attitude toward other churches and concern for ministry to the whole person. Their supporters were not radicals or even theological liberals. Rather, their regard for the Lutheran Confessions was tempered by their concern for the gospel, and they considered the Confessions more as a bridge connecting them to other Christians rather than as a fortress keeping out the less orthodox. The same convention moved the synod toward cooperation with the two other large Lutheran bodies through membership in the Lutheran Council in the USA. Over the next few years, however, this attitude of engagement and openness eroded, and a more conservative group won leadership positions and stimulated distrust among members. Actions taken four years later at the convention in Denver demonstrate both impulses. The convention both authorized closer fellowship with the American Lutheran Church and elected conservative J.A.O. Preus as president.

From his new office Preus led the effort to return the synod to a more uniform and conservative doctrinal position. The mission work of the synod was reconsidered. The Mission Affirmations of the mid-1960s were viewed by the conservatives as inadequately concerned with preservation of pure doctrine, and those who followed them were considered too willing to work with others whose confession was suspect. Martin Kretzman, their author, was removed from his post with the Board for Missions. At the same time the faculty and president of Concordia Seminary in St. Louis came under scrutiny individually and as a group. That President John Tietjen had worked for Lutheran Council in the USA was indicative of his positive interest in greater cooperation with other Lutheran churches, an interest regarded as wrongheaded by conservatives. The faculty published a "Call for Openness and Trust," in which they declared their resistance to "the temptation in our own church body which would hold men to complete agreement in formal and informal doctrinal propositions or would make doctrines rather than God himself the object of faith."[22] This statement expressed precisely what Preus and his allies found objectionable about the faculty: their tolerance for doctrinal variety and their willingness to use historical-critical methods of biblical study. Nonetheless, the first investigation found that the faculty was not teaching false doctrine. Preus made his own views clear in his "Statement of Scriptural and Confessional Principles."

Convention action in 1971 moved toward greater centralization of authority in the synod, the lines of disagreement were drawn ever more clearly, and the stage was set for a confrontation at the New Orleans convention in 1973. In New Orleans Preus' allies were given positions on key committees, and the rules of procedure were used to direct the outcome. This is not to say that the outcome was determined ahead of time. Floor debate about the situation at Concordia Seminary consumed hours, and business scheduled for late in the meeting had to be postponed. The drama of the event was high. When Preus' statement was transformed from a personal declaration into a synodical standard by convention vote, its opponents came forward singing "The Church's One Foundation" to record their disapproval. The convention also slowed the process of establishing fellowship with the American Lutheran Church and focused further attention on Concordia's president, John Tietjen.

Despite the drama and the clarity of the conflict in New Orleans, the break in the Missouri Synod was not complete for another three years. During those years the official *Lutheran Witness* and the unofficial *Christian News* kept congregational members up-to-date. Of course, both publications also suggested how events and persons should be understood, with the *Christian News* sounding an alarmist, conservative message. The tensions extended into every part of the synod, affecting congregations, colleges, agencies, and individuals. Soon after the New Orleans convention, Evangelical Lutherans in Mission (ELIM) was formed with leadership from John Tietjen and Pastor F. Dean Lueking of Grace, a large congregation near Chicago. Evangelical Lutherans in Mission provided the moderates with a formal identity and a channel for contact and action. In the winter of 1974 the situation at Concordia blew up. The synod continued efforts to remove Tietjen from his office and pressured other faculty members. The majority of students organized support for the majority of their teachers. Finally in February the faculty majority and their students walked out and established a seminary in exile, Seminex. The need to secure parish calls for Seminex graduates stimulated the next crisis. Eight district presidents authorized ordinations for Seminex graduates who were not approved by the remaining Concordia faculty. When four of the presidents were removed from office, the break was made, and moderates took the final step to form the Association of Evangelical Lutheran Churches.

The Constituting Convention in December 1976 was attended by 172 delegates representing 150 congregations. The numbers of sympathetic people—both lay and clergy—who remained members of the Lutheran Church Missouri Synod or who transferred into the American Lutheran Church or Lutheran Church in America are more difficult to determine. Like many of the nineteenth-century synods the Association of Evangelical Lutheran Churches was based in a theological position that called for greater latitude and tolerance for variety among those who shared basic Confessional commitments. The Association of Evangelical Lutheran Churches immediately acted on this position by moving to establish fellowship with the American Lutheran Church, the Lutheran Church in America, and Lutheran Church Missouri Synod, as well as membership in Lutheran Council in the USA and Lutheran World Federation, and by investigating membership in National Council of Churches and World Council of Churches. The association's embrace of tolerance was demonstrated by the way women's ordination was handled. Unlike the Lutheran Church Missouri Synod, it asserted that neither the Bible nor the Lutheran Confessions provide a decisive word on this topic; but the next step was not to require all synods and congregations to endorse women's ordination. Rather, the Pacific Synod was allowed to move ahead, and the Board of Directors of the association was instructed to assist congregations in their response. In 1984 the Association of Evangelical Lutheran Churches elected Pastor Will Herzfeld as bishop. He was the first African American to serve in such an office in an American Lutheran church body. Thus, the ALEC demonstrated commitment to another sort of inclusiveness as well.

From the outset, the Association of Evangelical Lutheran Churches had understood itself as a temporary organization. Its stated commitment to Lutheran cooperation pointed toward the possibility of joining with other bodies to form a single church. Although it was the smallest and the youngest group involved, the Association of Evangelical Lutheran Churches, played a critical role in pushing for the formation of the Evangelical Lutheran Church in America. When the Evangelical Lutheran Church in America came into existence in 1988, American Lutherans were gathered into two major bodies, though a minority belonged to the remaining small synods such as the Wisconsin Synod, the Lutheran Brethren, and the American Association of Lutheran Churches. The founders of the latter declined to join the new church for reasons that the nineteenth-century founders of the Tennessee Synod might have approved: its view of biblical interpretation was too weak, and its polity was too centralized. The formation of the Evangelical Lutheran Church in America could be represented by several images: as the reunion of a family, as a merger of corporate bodies, or as replanting three trees in a new orchard. However it is characterized, this second part of the late-twentieth-century reforming of American Lutheranism was very likely the last such development in American Lutheranism for a long time.

Though in one sense the Evangelical Lutheran Church in America was the culmination of a process that had been going on since the 1890s, the actual deliberations began in 1980, when both the American Lutheran Church and the

Lutheran Church in America conventions approved moving forward in response to the Association of Evangelical Lutheran Churches' call for merger. Certainly, the momentum in American Lutheranism was pushing this merger along. Some members passively regarded it as inevitable; others championed it as a good thing in itself or as a step that would allow Lutherans to combine their energies and resources and to make a more effective combined witness; nonetheless, some vocal leaders had reservations. David Preus, then president of the American Lutheran Church, stated publicly his view that in the absence of "scandalous division" the altar and pulpit fellowship and a common confession that already existed were sufficient unity. He suggested that evangelism should be the church's first priority, with strengthening congregational life, doing justice, supporting higher education, and participating in the larger ecumenical movement all as more urgent priority, merger of three Lutheran bodies.[23] But Preus agreed to abide by, and support, the decision of his church.

Unlike the mergers that coincided with the quadricentennial of Luther's Ninety-five Theses early in the century, the formation of the Evangelical Lutheran Church in America took place over an extended period, and the process was visible to anyone who cared to watch. Once the Lutheran Church in America and American Lutheran Church responded positively to the Association of Evangelical Lutheran Churches' invitation to consider joining together, a task force was carefully selected to consider what sort of church this new body would be. Known colloquially as the Seventy, the Commission for a New Lutheran Church was composed of that number of people. In previous merger negotiations care had been taken that representatives of each merging body were part of the decision making. That concern was present here as well, so there were thirty-one members each from the American Lutheran Church and the Lutheran Church in America and eight from the smaller Association of Evangelical Lutheran Churches. In addition, new criteria were introduced ensuring that the commission would be reflective of the actual membership of the churches. Gender, lay or clergy status, and racial and linguistic identity were also taken into account. (That racial and linguistic identity often would have been implicit in earlier synodical membership was seldom articulated in justifications for this practice.) Thus, the commission's composition included thirty-three pastors and thirty-seven laypeople; forty-two men and twenty-eight women; fourteen persons of color or whose primary language was other than English. The group assembled in 1982 to hold the first of their meetings. Over the next five years they traveled across the nation conducting much of their business in sessions open to all observers. Their ongoing work was widely reported both in the churches' periodicals and in special bulletins. Responses from church members were sought on an array of issues, including the basic structure of the organization.

The commission's practice of holding open meetings and regularly reporting its discussion as well as its actions highlighted the sometimes contentious task of designing a new church. Congregational members were made aware of the difficulty of resolving differences about matters both profound and trivial, and they frequently were caught up in the debate themselves. Among the issues that generated controversy were the name of the church, the location of its national offices, pension plans, congregational property rights, teaching and practice regarding the office of the ministry, and deliberate constitutional efforts to ensure participation by laity, women, people of color, and those whose primary language was other than English in the governance of the church. Negative response from local members and from leaders in the women's organizations to the original decision not to include a women's organization in the new church resulted in one being added. Other issues were postponed to be dealt with after the merger was complete. The complex theological and practical issues related to the ministerial office were delayed.

A structural innovation was the inclusion of two commissions in the national offices: the Commission for Women and the Commission for Multicultural Ministries. Unlike the more familiar units such as the Divisions for Global Mission or for Ministry, these two offices were the outgrowth of the growing social consciousness of some church leaders. The constitution gave both commissions the responsibility to "assist this church in addressing specific tasks of particular urgency." The Women of the Evangelical Lutheran Church in America had as its primary audience female members of the church; the Commission for Women's audience was the whole church, and among its specific tasks was the charge to help the church to "realize the full participation of women" and to promote justice for women both in the church and in the larger society. Similarly, the Commission for Multicultural Ministries was to enhance participation by African American, Asian, Native American, and Hispanic members and assist the whole church in becoming more multicultural. The existence of these commissions, combined with membership goals and stipulations about composition of committees, stimulated sharp exchanges. In editorials in church periodicals and in conversations in church basements the disagreement was cast in characteristically Lutheran terms: law and gospel. On one hand, some argued that such matters were in the purview of gospel freedom, not the law's regulation. On the other hand, some said that even forgiven sinners need some regulations to guide their behavior. The commissions and the representative principle stayed, but they continued to be the subject of debate and convention resolutions into the 1990s.

Once the general design of the structure was determined, and the date for actual merger came closer, dozens of committees went to work in the sixty-nine proposed regional synods to prepare for the transitions. Here, too, efforts were made to include as many people as possible in the work and to take account of various identity factors that might be significant to the outcome. Those persons who served on these committees, regionally or nationally, had the opportunity to experience the merger as it was taking place. Though not every moment in the process was exhilarating or even pleasant, many found that as they worked together, the stereotypes based on church affiliations dissolved into the actual personalities of their individual coworkers, with whom they had much in common.

When the Evangelical Lutheran Church began its legal existence in January 1988, its national staff had already been hard at work in its Chicago offices for some weeks, its congregations had been hearing the gospel and receiving the sacraments for decades, and the church itself had been constituted in Columbus, Ohio, the previous spring. Like previous events this one was marked by ceremonies both for bidding the old churches farewell and for welcoming the new one. At the opening worship David Preus, James Crumley Jr. and Will Herzfeld, the bishops of the three merging churches, each poured water into a single baptismal font; and at the closing eucharist, they did the same with the wine, mingling the three decanters into a single chalice and representing both the union of the churches and their unity in Christ. The principal business was adopting a constitution and electing officers. The constitution prepared by the commission and its work groups provided a statement of faith that identified the Evangelical Lutheran Church in America as centrally Lutheran by its vocabulary and its explicit acceptance of the Unaltered Augsburg Confession "as a true witness to the Gospel" and of the other writings in the Book of Concord as "further valid interpretations of the faith of the Church." The still troublesome issues about the Bible were addressed without use of the inflammatory language of inerrancy. Rather, the canonical Scriptures were described as "the inspired Word of God and the authoritative source and norm of [this church's] proclamation, faith, and life." Regulations about composition of committees and delegations to conventions made clear that this was a church that regarded the congregation and lay members as significant partners with the clergy. Herbert Chilstrom, a Lutheran Church in America bishop deeply connected to the rural Midwest, was elected presiding bishop. Christine Grumm, a health educator and active member of an Association of Evangelical Lutheran Churches congregation in San Francisco, was elected vice president, the highest lay office; her grandfather once held the same office in the Lutheran Church Missouri Synod.

Directions were set for the future by other convention actions. The ecumenical commitments of the church's predecessors were affirmed by the vote to consider membership in the World Council of Churches, and the National Council of Churches and to continue participation in bilateral dialogues. The Lutheran World Federation was represented by general secretary Gunnar Staalsett, who preached at the closing worship. Social issues were addressed in resolutions responding to the specific situation of South African apartheid and outlining a process for developing further social statements. The unsettled questions about ministry were passed on to be addressed in a six-year study. The newly formed Evangelical Lutheran Church in America had 5.36 million members, more than twice the number in the Lutheran Church Missouri Synod, and was the fourth largest Protestant church in the United States.

EPILOGUE

More than three and a half centuries since the first Lutherans arrived in North America, Lutherans on the cusp of the third millennium live in an American context much changed from one that greeted their religious forebears or that surrounded those who lived only 100 years ago. Society and nation have changed; so, too, have the churches. Just as the Lutherans of New Sweden lost control of their colony and with it their status as an established church, in a similar way all religious groups in the United States have been obliged to find their place as one organization among many. The legal disestablishment of churches in the post-Revolutionary era was followed by cultural disestablishment in which Christian churches lost first hegemony and then influence. Through these changes, Christians have developed that characteristically American form, the denomination that is neither a sect nor a church in the classic sense.

To assume that the denomination is, and has been, just one thing is, however, to be mistaken. As Russell Richey and Craig Dykstra have shown, the denomination has passed through several stages on its way to its current form.[24] Richey identifies five. The colonial stage of ethnic voluntarism gave way to purposive missionary associations, which were succeeded by ''churchly'' denominationalism and then by corporate organizations that mimicked the characteristics of American business. The fifth and current stage is the one Dykstra labels by analogy to government regulatory agencies; Richey suggests a more complex situation and names it postdenominational confessionalism. He goes on to ask if the denomination in this phase has a dynamic and adhesive principle. Without a clear purpose, a legitimate question arises about the viability of the denominations. This question is sharpened by the work of sociologists such as Robert Wuthow who document the groups' decreasing distinctiveness from one another. The success of the ecumenical movement, both at the grass roots and in official negotiations, also echoes the question, What is the value of denominations in the third millennium?

Another sociologist, Nancy Ammerman, suggests three aspects of denominational definition and along the way provides clues about the value of denominations in general and perhaps of Lutherans in particular. She identifies beliefs and practices, organizations and cultural identity as overlapping components of denominations. As in other denominations, Lutherans have organizations. Since late in the nineteenth century they have reorganized those organizations in nearly every generation. Finally, by the mid-1990s, 90 percent of Lutherans belonged to two major Lutheran bodies. This 100 years of realignments has absorbed enormous energies, rather like moving one's residence every year and each time incorporating new people in the household. Along with the managerial tasks, appropriate to this fourth phase of denominational development, these shifts have entailed cultural negotiations as the community of the church has become more various in its ethnicity and its affinities with American society, in its religious habits and practices, and in other cultural characteristics. This has not been merely the side effect of mergers; it is also the consequence of deliberate efforts to proclaim the gospel outside the boundaries of prior membership.

The reduced number of national organizations, now called churches rather than synods, ensures that debate about what constitutes authentic Lutheranism is within the churches as much or more than between them. Thus, Lutherans face the third millennium continuing their struggle to define themselves as authentically American and genuinely Lutheran. An easy equation of Lutheranism with a few ethnic groups is no longer descriptively valid, if it ever was, and cannot serve as the dynamic and adhesive principle Richey says is lacking in denominations. Like the state, or folk, churches from which so many immigrant Lutherans came, today's churches must contain within their fellowship a rich array of positions. They encompass those who lean far toward the pietist tradition and those committed to the concerns of orthodoxy as well as an equal range of positions on other axes, political, aesthetic, and social as well as theological. Like other American religious groups Lutherans are in the midst of what Richey calls "postdenominational confessionalism." In this era, Lutherans may be freed from prior cultures and organizations, but they continue to be in need of both culture and organization.

One hundred and twenty years ago, after fifty years of public engagement in the major theological and organizational controversies of his time, John G. Morris observed optimistically: "Lutheranism is a hardy plant. It thrives in all climates, and under all circumstances, and it is hard to exterminate."[25] In order for this plant to thrive and to bear fruit in this place in the next decades, Lutherans need to articulate their particular gospel insight and nurture it faithfully. That insight was re-discovered by Luther long before there was a Lutheran Church or movement and is not dependent on such a container, but without it the church lacks a dynamic force. The theological root must be cultivated with practices and structures that are suitable for this temporal and cultural context while also appropriate to the root stock. The challenge of American Lutheranism continues to be learning again and again the difficult task of being both/and.

NOTES

1. Jaroslav Pelikan, "Lutheran Heritage," *Encyclopedia of American Religious Experience*, 3 vols. (New York: Charles Scribner's Sons, 1988), vol. 1, pp. 419–430.

2. Byron Lee Schmid, *The American Lutheran Church and Public Policy* (Ann Arbor: University Microfilms, 1989, c. 1971), p. 187.

3. Harold C. Letts, ed., *Christian Social Responsibility: A Symposium in Three Volumes* (Philadelphia: Muhlenberg Press, 1957).

4. William Lazareth, quoted in Christa R. Klein and Christian D. von Dehsen, *Politics and Policy: The Genesis and Theology of Social Statements in the Lutheran Church in America* (Minneapolis: Fortress Press, 1989), p. 50.

5. W. Kent Gilbert, *Commitment to Unity: A History of the Lutheran Church in America* (Philadelphia: Fortress Press, 1988), p. 298.

6. L. DeAne Lagerquist, *From Our Mothers' Arms: A History of Women in the American Lutheran Church* (Minneapolis: Augsburg Publishing House, 1987), p. 175.

7. Richard W. Solberg, *Lutheran Higher Education in North America* (Minneapolis: Augsburg Publishing House, 1985), p. 326.

8. Jeff Johnson, *Black Christians: The Untold Lutheran Story* (St. Louis: Concordia Publishing House, 1991), pp. 166–170.

9. Gilbert, *Commitment to Unity*, pp. 210–212.

10. Charles P. Lutz, "Spying in the Churches: The State vs. the First Amendment," *The Christian Century* 108 (June 26–July 13, 1991), pp 650–652.

11. For more complete accounts of the process see Gracia Grindal, "Getting Women Ordained," in *Called and Ordained: Lutheran Perspectives on the Office of the Ministry*, ed. Todd Nichol and Marc Kolden (Minneapolis: Fortress Press, 1990), pp. 161–180; John H. P. Reumann, *Ministries Examined: Laity, Clergy, Women and Bishops in a Time of Change* (Minneapolis: Augsburg Publishing House, 1987), pp. 120–125.

12. See Elizabeth Platz, "My Story, Our Story" and Susan Thompson, "Barbara Andrews," in *Lutheran Women in Ordained Ministry, 1970–1995*, ed. Gloria E. Bengston (Minneapolis: Augsburg Fortress, 1995), pp. 45–51, and 52–58.

13. *Twenty-five Years after the Ordination of Women: Participation of Women in the Evangelical Lutheran Church in America* (Chicago: Evangelical Lutheran Church in America, 1995), p. 4.

14. Phyllis Anderson, "Lutheran Women in Theological Studies: Headway, Hard Work, Hurt and Hope," in Bengston, *Lutheran Women in Ordained Ministry*, p. 132.

15. Darlis Jean Swan, *The Impact of the Bilateral Dialogues on Selected Religious Education Materials Published by the Lutheran Church in America* (Washington, DC: Catholic University of America, 1988), Chapter 3, pp. 64–102 describes each dialogue in turn.

16. Darlis J. Swan and John T. Ford, eds., *Twelve Untold Tales: A Study Guide for Ecumenical Reception* (Grand Rapids: Eerdmans, 1993).

17. Eugene Brand, "The Lutheran Book of Worship: A Shaper of Lutheran Piety in North America," *Word and World* 9 (1989): 39.

18. Michael B. Aune, *Making Sense: An Exploration of Worship in Word and Sacrament*, Berkeley, CA, 1995 (Typescript), p. 94. Throughout Chapter 4, " 'The Liturgical Question': What Is and What Is Not Evangelical Worship," Aune draws attention to the continually unresolved debate among Lutherans about the relationship of doctrine to practice in worship that goes on alongside the more formal discussions of forms of worship.

19. Brand, "The Lutheran Book of Worship," p. 43.

20. This was out of a total of 11,067 congregations. *The Lutheran*, 17 October 1990.

21. Alan Graebner, "Birth Control and the Lutherans: The Missouri Synod as a Case Study," in *Women in American Religion*, ed. Janet Wilson James. (Philadelphia: University of Pennsylvania Press, 1980), pp. 229–252.

22. Quoted by Bryan V. Hillis, *Can Two Walk Together Unless They Be Agreed? American Religious Schisms in the 1970s* (Brooklyn: Carlson, 1991), p. 52.

23. *Lutheran Standard*, 25 November 1980, p. 29.

24. Russell E. Richey, "Denominations and Denominationalism: An American Morphology," ed. Richey and Robert Bruce Mullin in *Re-imagining Denominationalism: Interpretive Essays* (New York: Oxford University Press, 1994), pp. 74–98. Richey's

morphology provides a more nuanced set of five stages in contrast to Dykstra's still instructive three.

25. J. G. Morris, *Fifty Years in the Lutheran Ministry* (Baltimore: James Young, 1878), p. 558.

CHRONOLOGY

1517   Martin Luther posts the Ninety-five Theses in response to John Tetzel's intention to sell indulgences in Wittenberg.

1530   The Augsburg Confession, largely written by Philip Melanchthon and signed by princes and representatives of free cities, is presented to Emperor Charles as a statement of Protestant belief.

1555   The Treaty of Augsburg sets out the principle of religious territoriality by which the ruler of a region determines its religion.

1580   The Book of Concord, containing statements of the central teachings of the Lutherans, is published.

1619   Rasmus Jensen, a Danish Lutheran pastor, conducts worship for a group of sailors in North America.

1620   New Amsterdam, a Dutch colony with a Lutheran minority, is established.

1642   New Sweden is established with a mandate to provide spiritual services to both the Swedish settlers and the native people.

1648   The Treaty of Westphalia concludes the Thirty Years' War and reasserts the principle of territoriality, extending it to include Calvinists as well as Roman Catholics and Lutherans.

1666   In Charlotte Amalie, in the Danish colony in the West Indies, the second Lutheran congregation in the Western Hemisphere is founded.

1675   Philipp Jacob Spener's pietist classic *Pia Desideria* is first published as a Preface to Johann Arndt's *True Christianity*.

1703   German Justus Falckner is ordained by Swedish Lutherans to serve the congregation in New York.

1708/1709	Following an extraordinarily severe winter in Germany, the first group of Palatine immigrants arrives in North America/the Hudson River Valley/New York.
1734	A group of Salzburgers, who were evicted from their homeland three years earlier for religious reasons, arrive in Georgia to found a settlement.
1748	With leadership from Henry Melchior Muhlenberg, the Ministerium of Pennsylvania is organized in an effort to unite Lutherans in the colonies.
1759	Israel Acrelius' *A History of New Sweden*, based on his observations while a pastor in New Sweden, is published.
1762	The congregation in New York devises a constitution that will serve as the model for many others.
1780	Norwegian Hans Neilsen Hauge is converted while working in the fields and commences a ministry of lay preaching.
1790	The Ministerium of New York is founded with leadership from John Christopher Kunze.
1797	With funds provided by Johann Christopher Hartwick's estate, a program of theological training is launched.
1814	Frederik Henry Quitman's catechism is published by the Ministerium of New York.
1817	Formation of the Prussian Union uniting Lutheran and Reformed churches in Prussia.
1820	A second attempt to unite all Lutherans in the United States is attempted with the formation of the General Synod.
1826	The General Synod opens a seminary in Gettysburg, Pennsylvania, with Samuel Simon Schmucker as its professor.
1832	Pennsylvania College (now Gettysburg College) is begun in order to prepare students to attend Gettysburg Seminary.
1841	John Christian Frederik Heyer is sent to Guntur, India, by the General Synod.
1845	The Buffalo Synod is founded by a group of Germans who immigrated to New York in protest against the "unionism" prevalent in Germany.
1847	A group of Saxons arrives in Perry County, Missouri, having left Germany in reaction against "unionism." Later, this group founds the Lutheran Church Missouri Synod.
1849	William Passavant brings four deaconesses from Germany to staff his infirmary in Pittsburgh, the first Protestant hospital in the United States.
1851	The Henkel family's press in New Market, Virginia, brings out an English translation of the Book of Concord.

1855   *The Definite Synodical Platform* proposes alterations in the Augsburg Confession to bring it more in line with current Protestant views.

1861   The Norwegian Synod withdraws its ministerial students from Concordia Seminary in St. Louis and founds its own Luther College.

1863   The General Synod of the Evangelical Lutheran Church in the Confederate States of America is organized by those who have withdrawn from the General Synod.

1866   With leadership from William Passavant, Thiel College is founded with a coeducational program.

1867   The General Council is formed by regional synods with stricter confessional standards than obtain in the older General Synod.

1870   Swedish Lutherans organize the Augustana Synod.

1872   The Synodical Conference brings together regional and ethnic synods with the most stringent of Confessional standards.

1879   The Women's Federated Missionary Society of the General Synod is the first Lutheran group to bring together local women's organizations into a larger body.

1883   Deaconess Elizabeth Fedde arrives in Brooklyn to begin deaconess work among Norwegian Lutherans.

1887   The Common Service is adopted by the General Council, General Synod, and General Synod of the South.

1889   African American pastors organize the Alpha Synod of the Evangelical Lutheran Church of Freedmen in America.

1890   The three moderate Norwegian Lutheran bodies come together to form the United Norwegian Lutheran Church.

1895   The Luther League of America links local youth groups.

1917   The Norwegian Lutheran Church of America is founded with 90 percent of Norwegian Lutherans in its membership.

1917   In response to the needs of military personnel the National Lutheran Council organizes a cooperative agency, the Commission for Soldiers' and Sailors' Welfare.

1918   The United Lutheran Church in America reunites Lutherans from the colonial era, including the United Synod South.

1923   The first meeting of the Lutheran World Convention convenes in Eisenach, Germany.

1928   The Women's Missionary Conference of the Joint Synod of Ohio establishes a paid staff position assumed by Katherine Lehmann.

1930   The American Lutheran Church brings together the Iowa, Joint Ohio,
            Texas, and Buffalo Synods.

1945   The National Lutheran Council assumes ministry to college students begun
            by the United Lutheran Church in America.

1947   The first assembly of the Lutheran World Federation is held in Lund,
            Sweden.

1955   The publication of the American edition of *Luther's Works* commences.

1958   *The Service Book and Hymnal* is issued for use in congregations of most
            synods, excluding the Lutheran Church Missouri Synod.

1960   The American Lutheran Church is formed by the merger of the American
            Lutheran Church (1930), the Evangelical Lutheran Church, and the United
            Evangelical Lutheran Church.

1962   The Lutheran Church in America unites the United Lutheran Church in
            America, the Augustana Synod, the Suomi Synod, and the American
            Evangelical Lutheran Church.

1962   The first round of bilateral dialogues with Reformed theologians marks
            the beginning of a new era of ecumenical conversation.

1970   Both the American Lutheran Church and the Lutheran Church in America
            vote to ordain women for pastoral ministry.

1973   Evangelical Lutherans in Mission (ELIM) is organized by a group pro-
            testing conservative developments within the Lutheran Church Missouri
            Synod.

1978   The *Lutheran Book of Worship* is issued for use in American Lutheran
            Church and Lutheran Church in America congregations; the Lutheran
            Church Missouri Synod issues the nearly identical *Lutheran Worship* in
            1982.

1984   Will Herzfeld is elected bishop of the Association of Evangelical Lutheran
            Congregations, the first African American to head a national Lutheran
            body in North America.

1988   The Evangelical Lutheran Church in America forms from the American
            Lutheran Church, the Lutheran Church in America, and the Association
            of Evangelical Lutheran Congregations.

1992   The LaCrosse Area Synod of the Evangelical Lutheran Church elects April
            Ulrich Larson as its bishop, the first woman to serve as a regional bishop
            in a North American Lutheran church.

1997   Delegates to the Evangelical Lutheran Church in American church-wide
            assembly voted to approve the "Formula of Agreement" establishing full
            communion with the Presbyterian Church (U.S.A.), the Reformed Church
            in America, and the United Church of Christ. They defeated the "Con-
            cordat of Agreement" that would have done the same with the Episcopal
            Church.

BIBLIOGRAPHIC ESSAY

Historical study of American Lutheranism has been largely defined by concern for matters theological or by interest in organizations such as synods, institutions such as colleges, and groups such as ethnic groups. This definition has extended to both topic and approach. Often, historical work has been undertaken for practical and/or polemical reasons, for example, to provide guidance in the preparation of an order of worship or to demonstrate the validity of a particular doctrinal position. Only in the final third of the twentieth century has Lutheran historiography been significantly influenced by social and cultural history. Indeed, during the years that this volume was in process several notable studies of this newer sort have appeared, for example, Susan Wilds McArver, "Recent Trends in Denominational Historiography and Implications for American Lutheran Scholars," *Lutheran Historical Conference, 1996*, in press.

GENERAL HISTORIES

Those seeking an accessible and brief overview of Lutheran history in the United States are well served by Christa R. Klein's essay "Lutheranism," in Charles H. Lippy and Peter W. Williams, eds., *The Encyclopedia of American Religious Experience: Studies of Traditions and Movements*, 3 vols. (New York: Scribner, 1988), pp. 431–450. Her carefully drawn sketch introduces readers to the major themes, periods, and players as well as to the patterns of interpretation found in other works. Jaroslav Pelikan's companion essay, "Lutheran Heritage," pp. 419–430 in the same work, is equally useful for setting out the larger theological context of the movement extending back to the Reformation. For a more extensive treatment of this longer history Conrad Bergendoff's *The Church of the Lutheran Reformation: A Historical Survey of Lutheranism* (St. Louis: Concordia Publishing House, 1967) continues to be helpful. Eric W. Gritsch's more recent, briefer work, *Fortress Introduction to Lutheranism* (Minneapolis: Fortress, 1994), provides the basics, both historical and theological, along with a well-selected guide to further reading.

Since the late 1800s five major volumes have treated the whole sweep of American Lutheranism. Edmund Jacob Wolf of Gettysburg Seminary reveals his thesis in the title of his volume *The Lutherans in America: A Story of Struggle, Progress, Influence and Marvelous Growth* (New York: J. A. Hill, 1890). Despite its sermonic tone, the illustrated volume provides a detailed portrayal of the years prior to its publication. Similarly, Henry Eyster Jacobs, *A History of the Evangelical Lutheran Church in the United States* (New York: Charles Scribner's Sons, 1893), treats events up to the decade of its writing. Jacobs, a professor at the Philadelphia Seminary, was deeply involved in Lutheran affairs of his time; he was also a practitioner of the emerging scientific methods of historical study who served as president of the American Society of Church History. His general work contains an index, some notes, and a bibliography. Jacob's work is discussed further in L. DeAne Lagerquist, "Does It Take One to Know One?: Lutherans and the American Religious Historical Canon," *dialog* (1986): 201–206; Paul A. Baglyos, "Lutheran Stories and American Context: Three Histories of American Lutheranism from the Late Nineteenth Century," *Concordia Historical Institute Quarterly* 64 (Winter 1991): 154–175.

Abdel Ross Wentz of Gettysburg Seminary produced two general histories. In the first, *The Lutheran Church in American History* (Philadelphia: United Lutheran Publication House, 1933) he asserts, "The people in the Lutheran churches of the land are a constituent and typical element of the American nation" (Preface to revised edition, p. 3). This emphasis upon the continuities between the Lutheran Church and its American context is characteristic of Wentz's interpretation and no doubt was influenced by his membership in the older, Muhlenberg strand of the church. This early volume includes helpful comments about the book's predecessors. Wentz's *A Basic History of Lutheranism in America* (Philadelphia: Muhlenberg Press, 1955) served as the standard study for more than a quarter century. It, too, takes the American context as the frame for Lutheran history. Although without notes, it has both index and chapter-by-chapter bibliography.

Since 1975 *Lutherans in North America* (Philadelphia: Fortress Press) has served as the principal history. It was a joint effort by several noted historians (August R. Suelflow, Fred W. Meuser, R. George Anderson, and Theodore G. Tappert), each responsible for a chronological section. E. Clifford Nelson of St. Olaf College and Luther Seminary served as editor. Although additional projected volumes were abandoned, in this one efforts were made to include significant excerpts from primary sources (printed in bold) and to provide extensive citation to both primary and secondary sources in the form of marginal notes. The underlying theme of the volume is the movement of Lutheranism from manyness to unity as it adapts to the American setting. The authors' careful attention to detail and comprehensiveness make this an invaluable resource that the present volume does not try to duplicate or replace. A special section added behind the index carries the narrative through the Missouri Synod's turmoil in the late 1970s. Unfortunately, the volume gives little attention to women's history, nor does it often move beyond standard topics of institutions, clergymen, and theology.

In preparation for the formation of the Evangelical Lutheran Church in America Augsburg Press brought out Todd W. Nichol's *All These Lutherans: Three Paths toward a New Lutheran Church* (Minneapolis, 1986). This accessible book is aimed to introduce members of the merging bodies to the distinctive characteristics of these groups. It does this in readable fashion while emphasizing the richness of each.

REFERENCE WORKS AND PERIODICALS

In addition to these monographs several less extensive, but nonetheless instructive, treatments are readily accessible in reference works. For basic historical and statistical information about Lutheran churches around the globe the best source is E. Theodore and Mercia Brenne Bachmann's *Lutheran Churches of the World: A Handbook* (Minneapolis: Augsburg Publishing House, 1989). Robert C. Wiederanders and Walter G. Tillmans, *The Synods of American Lutheranism* (St. Louis: Lutheran Historical Conference, 1968) is more limited in geographic scope but equally valuable for its comprehensive attention to the many phases of synodical organization. A new edition appeared in 1998. The wide range of topics covered in the one volume of Erwin L. Lueker, ed., *Lutheran Cyclopedia* (St. Louis: Concordia Publishing House, 1975), necessarily limits each entry to the briefest treatment. More extensive articles are available in the larger Julius Bodensieck, ed., *The Encyclopedia of the Lutheran Church*, 3 vols. (Minneapolis: Augsburg Publishing House, 1965). Of course, the impossibility of including events, persons, and developments since its publication renders this work less useful for topics related to women, the laity, or groups not conventionally associated with Lutheranism.

Notable among periodicals that regularly include Lutheran history is *The Concordia Historical Institute Quarterly*. Although the institute is associated with the Lutheran Church Missouri Synod, the *Quarterly*'s scope encompasses Lutheranism of all varieties. The wide variety of methods and sorts of training represented by its authors results in articles of uneven quality. *Essays and Reports*, the Proceedings of the Lutheran Historical Conferences' biennial meeting, is more consistently scholarly in nature. The conference newsletter carries an annual bibliography of relevant materials from the previous year. This organization of archivists, librarians, and historians is the primary national group devoted to the study of Lutheran history; there also are active, unaffiliated regional associations.

Although not devoted exclusively to historical topics, other journals include useful articles. The several series of *The Lutheran Quarterly* are valuable both for interpretation and as a primary source. *Word and World, dialog, Currents in Theology and Mission*, and *Concordia Theological Monthly* all occasionally publish historically oriented materials.

SYNODICAL, REGIONAL, AND ETHNIC HISTORIES

At one time there were more than three score extralocal Lutheran bodies in the United States. When those that were formed and then went out of existence are added, the number grows even larger. Add to these the various ethnic groups associated with Lutheran churches, and the possible subjects increase even more. Not all these bodies have written histories, but many do. Their value to historians and general readers varies, as do their formats. Some are not much more than compilations of data about congregations and clergy. Others are instructive narratives that lead readers into the life of the church in particular times and places.

A sample of useful volumes each focused upon a particular synodical body, sometimes with an ethnic identity or defined by a region, includes Theodore E. Schmauk, *A History of the Lutheran Church in Pennsylvania, 1683–1820* (Philadelphia: General Council, 1903) and Harry J. Kreider, *History of the United Lutheran Synod of New York and New England, 1786–1860* (Philadelphia: Muhlenberg Press, 1954). Both are concerned with the early history of the most enduring beginnings of Lutheranism in the United States. Willard D. Allbeck, *A Century of Lutherans in Ohio* (Yellow Springs, OH: Antioch Press, 1966) considers several groups with varying theological positions, all with their geographic center in Ohio, an area of later expansion. Suzanne Geissler's *Lutheranism and Anglicanism in Colonial New Jersey: An Early Ecumenical Experiment in New Sweden*

(Lewiston, N.Y.: E. Mellon Press, 1988) looks beyond the Lutheran churches. In the most recent entry in this category, *Press toward the Mark: History of the United Lutheran Synod of New York and New England, 1830–1930* (Metuchen, NJ: ATLA and Scarecrow Press, 1995), Robert F. Scholz attends to the nature of the region and its geography as he examines "the history of a Christian denomination seeking its own confessional identity in a time of rapid change and increasing pluralism" (Scholz, *Lutheran Church*, p. 5).

Most of the synods formed by nineteenth-century immigrant groups have been the topic of at least one history. The Swedes are the subject of Gothard Everett Arden, *Augustana Heritage: A History of the Augustana Lutheran Church* (Rock Island, IL: Augustana Press, 1963). The range of Lutheran options within the Norwegian community (with the exception of the Lutheran Free Church) is covered by E. Clifford Nelson and Eugene L. Fevold, *The Lutheran Church among Norwegian-Americans*, 2 vols. (Minneapolis: Augsburg Publishing House, 1960). Both parties within the Danish group are included in Thorvald Hansen, *Church Divided: Lutheranism among the Danish Immigrants* (Des Moines, IA: Grand View College, 1992). The Lutheran Church Missouri Synod has regularly published histories to celebrate significant anniversaries, such as Augustus Lawrence Graebner, *Half a Century of Sound Lutheranism in America; A Brief Sketch of the History of the Missouri Synod* (St. Louis: Concordia Publishing House, 1897). Walter Otto Forester, *Zion on the Mississippi: The Settlement of the Saxon Lutherans in Missouri, 1839–1841* (St. Louis: Concordia Publishing House, 1953) is less grand in its intention but instructive nonetheless.

A more recent publication, coinciding with the formation of the Evangelical Lutheran Church in America, treats Lutherans in North Carolina, one of their strongest southern locations: Raymond M. Bost and Jeff L. Norris, *All One Body: The Story of the North Carolina Lutheran Synod* (Salisbury: North Carolina Synod, 1994). H. George Anderson's earlier work. *Lutheranism in the Southeastern States, 1860–1886* (The Hague: Mouton, 1969), considered a larger area and continues to be valuable. Susan Wilds McArver's dissertation, " 'A Spiritual Wayside Inn:' Lutherans, the New South and Cultural Change in South Carolina, 1886–1918" (Duke University, 1995), adds to the small corpus of scholarly studies of Lutheranism in the South.

Synods formed in this century have also found their historians. The body that merged in 1930 is studied in Fred W. Meuser, *Formation of the American Lutheran Church: A Case Study in Lutheran Unity* (Columbus, OH: Wartburg Press, 1958). Another volume includes Meuser's subject as one of the antecedents of the American Lutheran Church established in 1960; Charles P. Lutz, ed., *Church Roots: Stories of Nine Immigrant Groups That Became the American Lutheran Church in America* (Minneapolis: Augsburg Publishing House, 1985). Just as the Evangelical Lutheran Church in America formed, a history of one of its predecessors appeared: W. Kent Gilbert, *Commitment to Unity: A History of the Lutheran Church in America* (Philadelphia: Fortress Press, 1988). The most recent addition in this category is Edgar G. Trexler, *Anatomy of a Merger: People, Dynamics, and Decisions That Shaped the Evangelical Lutheran Church in America* (Minneapolis: Augsburg Publishing House, 1991).

The interaction of ethnic and religious identity among some groups of Lutherans makes it inevitable that an approach to Lutheran history can be made through ethnic studies. Each major group has its own resources, often including a periodical such as *Norwegian American Studies and Records* or the *Swedish-American Historical Quarterly* or the *Journal of German-American Studies*. These periodicals frequently publish articles on religious topics. In addition, there is a myriad of monographs that begin from ethnicity and illumine religion. Notable among these are Jon Gjerde, *From Protestant to Farmer: The Migration from Balestrand, Norway to the Upper Middle West* (Cambridge: Cambridge University Press, 1985); Carol Coburn, *Life at Four Corners: Religion, Gender and Education in a German-Lutheran Community, 1868–1995* (Lawrence: University Press of Kansas, 1992); and Robert C. Ostergren, *A Community Transplanted: The Trans-Atlantic Experience of a Swedish Immigrant Settlement in the Upper Middle West, 1835–1915* (Madison: University of Wisconsin Press, 1988).

Scholarly attention to Lutheranism among groups of other than Scandinavian or German origins is in the first stages. The fullest account of African American Lutherans is found in Jeff G. Johnson, *Black Christians: The Untold Lutheran Story* (St. Louis: Concordia Publishing House, 1991). Johnson includes all synods as well as the Virgin Islands, Surinam, and Guyana in his sociologically informed study. More popular and limited treatments of African American, Asian, Native American, and Hispanic Lutherans were published in an Evangelical Lutheran Church in America curriculum, *Living Water of Faith Series*, 9 vols. (Minneapolis: Publishing House of the Evangelical Lutheran Church in America, 1988).

TOPICS, ACTIVITIES, AND ORGANIZATIONS

Another set of studies approaches Lutheran history using other lenses, such as theological debate, education, and women's organizations. Indeed, treatments of Lutheran theological debate might be said to have their own history. Vergilius Anselm Ferm, *The Crisis in American Lutheran Theology: A Study of the Issue between American Lutheranism and Old Lutheranism* (New York: Century, 1927) was an early entry in the subgenre. Two more recent volumes continue it: David A. Gustafson, *Lutherans in Crisis: The Question of Identity in the American Republic* (Minneapolis: Fortress Press, 1993); Paul P. Kuenning, *The Rise and Fall of American Lutheran Pietism: The Rejection of an Activist Heritage* (Macon, GA: Mercer University Press, 1988). Most writing about the major battles that split the Missouri Synod in the 1970s has come from partisans. Bryan V. Hillis, *Can Two Walk Together Unless They Be Agreed?; American Religious Schisms in the 1970s* (Brooklyn: Carlson, 1991) is an early effort at a less passionate study that places the Lutheran controversy in a larger comparative context.

Rather than highlighting conflict, another group of studies focuses attention on cooperation among Lutherans and movement toward unity of various sorts. Richard C. Wolf, ed., *Documents of Lutheran Unity in America* (Philadelphia: Fortress Press, 1966) provides access to primary materials related to the full range of efforts from 1730 until 1965. Federick K. Wentz, *Lutherans in Concert: The Story of the National Lutheran Council, 1918–1966* (Minneapolis: Augsburg Publishing House, 1968) traces the work of this agency, which fostered cooperation between synods. E. Clifford Nelson, *Rise of World Lutheranism: An American Perspective* (Philadelphia: Fortress Press, 1982) recounts the history of the Lutheran World Federation.

Among the topics about which Lutherans have disagreed, worship and social or political activity rank high, and yet, in worship and in doing works of love they have also come together. Both are subjects of instructive studies. No comprehensive history of worship has been produced. Luther D. Reed, *The Lutheran Liturgy: A Study of the Common Service* (Philadelphia: Muhlenberg Press, 1947), though exhaustive in some regards, is limited in scope. With regard to political and social action the field is richer, including Christa R. Klein and Christian D. von Dehsen, *Politics and Policy: The Genesis and Theology of Social Statements in the Lutheran Church in America* (Minneapolis: Fortress Press, 1989). Klein and von Dehsen begin their investigation long before the actual formation of the Lutheran Church in America, making it more comprehensive than a literal reading of the title might suggest. The postwar work of relief and resettlement has two recent histories: Richard W. Solberg, *Open Doors: The Story of Lutherans Resettling Refuges* (St. Louis: Concordia Publishing House, 1992); John Bachman, *Together in Hope: 50 Years of the Lutheran World Relief* (New York: Lutheran World Relief, 1995). A more activist response to war is the subject of Steven Schroeder, *A Community and a Perspective: Lutheran Peace Fellowship* (Lanham, MD: University Press of America, 1993).

Lutheran involvement in education has been vigorous. Although usually officially associated with synods, colleges also have distinct histories, and many have anniversary volumes that tell the particular story of their own place and people. The whole group of colleges and universities, at least those still in operation, is considered extensively and together in Richard W. Solberg, *Lutheran Higher Education in North America* (Minneapolis: Augsburg Publishing House, 1985).

Within and between congregations many Lutherans have been active participants in official auxiliaries and parachurch enterprises. These, too, have received recent historical attention. Youth and women's organizations are treated in Jon Pahl, *The Hopes and Dreams of All: The International Walther League and Lutheran Youth in American Culture, 1893–1993* (Chicago: Wheat Ridge, 1993) and L. DeAne Lagerquist, *From Our Mothers' Arms: A History of Women in the American Lutheran Church* (Minneapolis: Augsburg Publishing House, 1988). Frederik S. Weiser, *Love's Response: A Story of Lutheran Deaconesses in America* (Philadelphia: Board of Publication, United Lutheran Church, 1962) provides a different angle on women's ministry by its account of deaconess work. The only sustained historical study of laity is Alan Graebner, *Uncertain Saints: The Laity in the Lutheran Church Missouri Synod* (Westport, CT: Greenwood Press, 1975).

INDEX